To Dad
Happy Birthday
May 11, 1985
Love, Donna

WITHDRAWN

A Guide to
European Painting

I **Johann Joseph Zoffany,** *The Tribune of the Uffizi in Florence* (detail) 1772–8, Windsor Castle

A Guide to
European Painting

Michael Jacobs

CHARTWELL BOOKS

Dedication   For Ben and Joe

Acknowledgements   I am grateful to the following for their generous contributions:

                                    David Exserdjan,
                                    Anthony Jaye,
                                    Mark James,
                                    and Malcolm Warner

                                    The captions are by Desmond Shawe-Taylor

                                    The book was co-ordinated by Jean Ellsmoor

British Library Cataloguing in Publication Data

Jacobs, Michael, b.1952
A guide to European painting
1. Painting, European
I. Title
759.94   ND450

ISBN 0–89009–381–4
LOC 80–68672

Published by Chartwell Books, a division of
Book Sales Inc. of Secaucus, N.J.

Printed in The Netherlands
by Royal Smeets Offset Weert

Contents

Introduction

The pleasure we derive from looking at a work of art is often entirely irrational and bears little relation to the quality of the work in question. External factors, such as the architecture, the lighting and even the smells of the building in which the work happens to be housed, all play a part in our appreciation of it. Moreover, even without such distractions, it is rarely possible to dissociate our reactions to a painting or a sculpture from purely personal areas of experience: thus, while looking at a landscape by Cézanne, our mind might easily wander to a holiday once spent in the south of France. Since the appreciation of art seems to have such an indeterminate and capricious basis, we might question if the enjoyment of a painting is in any way enhanced by reading about it. Generally speaking, it is not: art criticism invariably throws more light on the writer than on the art which he is meant to be discussing, and art history is more frequently a pedantic hindrance than a source of enlightenment. If the study of art has any value at all other than to a small circle of scholars, it is to make us aware of the context for which the work of art was originally created. Far too often we approach art from a limited 20th-century point of view in the mistaken belief that a painting or a sculpture is only an object intended for a museum; even the personality of the artist who created it is made to conform to present-day notions of genius. It should never be forgotten, however, that the character of a work of art has been largely determined by such factors as the patron who commissioned the work, the function which it originally served and the building for which it was intended; in addition, throughout much of history, the artist has not been the inspired creator so beloved today, but rather a craftsman or even a purveyor of luxury goods. Many artists from the Renaissance onwards have admittedly objected to such an apparently demeaning status, but the fact remains that the intellectual painter with a selfless devotion to art, or the lonely genius unable to conform to the generally banal demands of his society, has been a comparatively rare phenomenon until the Romantic era. To look at art with as much historical objectivity as possible is inevitably to adopt a pedestrian approach to the subject; but in so doing we are also freeing art from the mystique which constitutes the greatest barrier to a spontaneous enjoyment of it.

The way in which 20th-century attitudes distort our understanding of the art of the past is especially apparent when we look at art before the Renaissance. Thus today we appreciate prehistoric cave paintings (pl. 3) for purely aesthetic reasons, while tending to ignore their original social function. Similarly we now look at such expressive and naturalistic works as the Romanesque mural at Tahull (pl. 4) with eyes accustomed to the art of a Picasso, and fail fully to appreciate how and why the medieval artist came to achieve such stylization in the first place. This *Guide to European Painting* purposefully begins at a relatively late date (the 13th century), at a time when the disciplines of archaeology and art history become more clearly separated, when

2 Gustave Courbet
The Studio of the Painter (detail), 1855
Musée National du Louvre, Paris

This painting, which Courbet said summed up 'seven years of my artistic career', is an allegorical representation of his conception of the artist's role in society.

European art owes less of a debt to that of the East, when painting itself can more properly be studied independent of other arts such as manuscript illumination, enamelling and stained glass, and, most important of all, when distinctive artistic personalities come into being. To begin in the 13th century, with the discussion of the Florentine painters, Cimabue and Giotto, is also a tacit acknowledgement of the first major book of art history, Vasari's *Lives of the Artists*, which was first published in 1550.

In the opening lines to his *Life of Cimabue*, Vasari wrote: 'The flood of misfortunes which continuously swept over and submerged the unhappy country of Italy not only destroyed everything worthy to be called a building but also, and this was of far greater consequence, completely wiped out the artists who lived there. Eventually, however, by God's providence, Giovanni Cimabue, who was destined to take the first steps to restoring the art of painting to its earlier stature, was born in the city of Florence, in the year 1240.' Vasari discussed the history of painting in terms of a logical process of ever increasing refinement which led from the tentative works of Cimabue up to the perfect masterpieces of his own day. Although today we are reluctant to accept such qualitative judgements, we nonetheless continue to be attracted by Vasari's basic tenet that the European tradition in painting is fundamentally concerned with the realistic portrayal of the human figure, and moreover, that art develops in an entirely logical manner. Thus we see art progressing from the primitive shapes of cave painting through to the harmonious and sometimes very realistic representations of human form which were achieved by classical artists (pl. 5), and then regressing, throughout the Early Christian and Romanesque periods, to become increasingly stylized and hieratic. We interpret the

3 Prehistoric painting
Standing Bison (detail), Magdalenian, *c.* 13500 BC
The Great Hall, Province of Santander, Altamira (Spain)

In these cave paintings it was perhaps hoped that some of the strength of the animals might be transferred to the hunters by the very act of their portrayal.

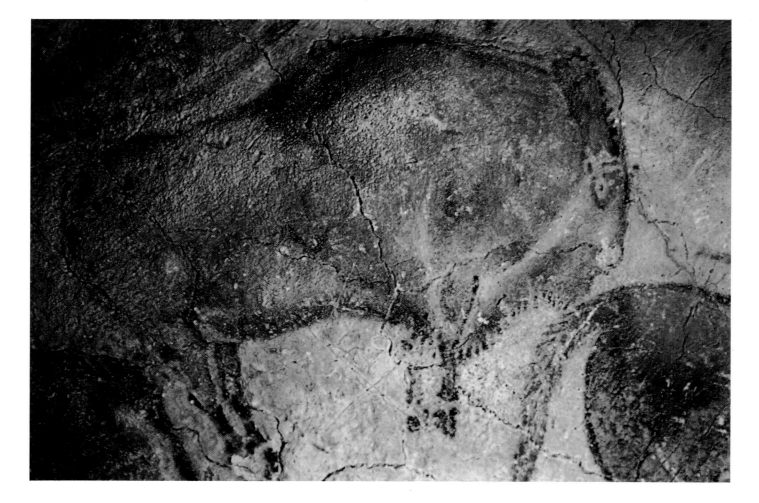

4 Master of Tahull
Christ Pantocrator (detail), 1123
Museo de Arte de Cataluña,
Barcelona

This primitive image of Christ as
the Creator of all things (Pantocrator)
was in a remote Romanesque village
church until transferred to the
Barcelona Museum.

Renaissance, intimations of which are felt in the works of Cimabue
and above all of Giotto, as a return to the standards set by classical
antiquity. These standards, although challenged during the periods of
Mannerism and Rococo, prevailed right into the 20th century, to the
time when Picasso reasserted the value of primitive modes of
representation, and when pure abstraction was finally evolved.

The fact that we are still prepared to accept Vasari's rather
simplisistic notions of artistic development, despite all evidence that
the history of art is an infinitely more complex affair and that we are
now in a period of intense stylistic confusion in which nothing is
certain, shows how our attitudes towards art are severely limited by
our constant need to explain baffling phenomena in purely logical
terms. Throughout history language has in fact been sadly inadequate
to describe visual experiences; and, worse still, the limitations of
critical terminology have invariably resulted in prejudices and narrow-

5 Roman painting
Primavera, 50–60 AD
Museo Archeologico Nazionale,
Naples

The Roman frescoes of Pompeii have
been preserved for us in this
miraculously fresh state by the ashes
of Vesuvius.

mindedness. If we ask ourselves such questions as why primitive art was not appreciated until the 20th century, or why Rococo painting was dismissed in the 19th, or why the 17th-century Bolognese artist Guido Reni could once be regarded as one of the greatest artists of all time and then be almost completely forgotten, we realize that the answer lies partly in the inability of language to come to terms with a particular phenomenon at a particular time. Although we are now better informed about the history of painting than at any other time in the past, it would be arrogant to claim that we are in any way more enlightened or unprejudiced in our approach towards art. For instance, we might find today that the Renaissance division of painting into the essential components of *disegno* and *colore* (draughtsmanship and colour), and the subsequent discussion as to which of these was the most important, as rather absurd; but any glance at a recent book on art history or criticism will reveal a wealth of jargon which is equally meaningless. The seriousness with which art is now taken is indication of an even greater weakness in our approach and one which dates back to the 19th century, to a time when art was made to seem synonomous with morality, and to be regarded almost as an alternative religion. There is really no reason at all why art should constitute a 'life-enhancing' area of human experience, or why that art which is straightforwardly entertaining should be any less valid than that which is more serious in intention. While it is unforeseeable that art criticism will ever be truly objective, it is to be hoped that the dropping of this particular prejudice will at least clear the air of the staleness which surrounds so much present-day discussion of art.

Painting in Central Italy from Giotto to Pisanello

In the early 14th century the poet Dante longed for Italy to be united by the Holy Roman Emperor Henry VII; but his dreams were not to be realized until 500 years later. For much of its history, Italy was a patchwork of autonomous city states, whose allegiance to begin with was divided between the Holy Roman Emperor and the Pope; to add to the confusion, the Papacy was in exile in the French city of Avignon between 1309 and 1377.

The Italian 14th century (or Trecento) saw the beginnings of the great social and cultural revival known as the Renaissance. The resurgence of artistic activity during this period can partly be related to the prosperity brought about by the country's exceptionally advanced economic systems. The character of each of the states varied enormously; and the most remarkable were those which were ruled by prosperous mercantile families rather than by a court. The wealthiest and most advanced of these democracies were Florence and Siena, which were also the liveliest centres of artistic activity during this period. The new intellectual movement which accompanied the Renaissance was Humanism, which advocated an empirical observation of natural phenomena and, above all, a renewed interest in classical civilization; the effects of this movement on the visual arts, however, were not to be properly felt until the 15th century.

'Cimabue thought he was first among painters, but now the cry is for Giotto and Cimabue's fame has been dimmed.' Dante's words from his epic poem, the *Purgatorio*, point to the great differences of style between the two major Florentine artists at the beginning of the 14th century. These differences are brought out in a detailed comparison between Cimabue's altarpiece for the Florentine church of Santa Trinità (pl. 6) and Giotto's for the church of the Ognissanti in the same city (pl. 8). The subject-matter of both works is the Madonna enthroned, surrounded by worshipping angels and prophets.

Cimabue depicts the heavenly company in a way that had been the norm for centuries; Vasari described the style as Greek, though in fact today we would term it Byzantine. In common with the Byzantines, Cimabue shows no concern with exact representation of natural appearances: Mary's throne is not structurally plausible, there is no attempt to render the angels in perspective, and the prophets are on a smaller scale than the other figures, although they are nearer to us. One only has to look at the way he paints the angels' wings to recognize that he is more concerned with surface pattern than with their chances of flying. The treatment of the Virgin's drapery in terms of a network of gold lines is ultimately derived from sophisticated classical attempts to analyze the fall of clothing; but it is now the intricacy of the surface design that matters most. What started as an experiment has ended as a convention.

In contrast to Cimabue, Giotto has avoided an excessive use of gold, as this would have detracted from his principal aim – the definition of volume. The Virgin is a more solid and a less idealized figure than

6 Cimabue
Madonna Enthroned, c. 1280
Galleria degli Uffizi, Florence

Commissioned by monks of
Vallombrosa, a village near Florence,
the four figures under the throne are
from left to right: Jeremiah,
Abraham, David and Isaiah.

7 Giotto di Bondone
The Kiss of Judas (detail), 1304–6
Cappella dell'Arena, Padua

Giotto here flaunts convention by making the incident of St. Peter cutting off the soldier's ear take place behind an insignificant figure with his back to us.

Cimabue's; moreover, she actually appears to sit in her Gothic tabernacle, and to give more convincing support to her child. The new depth and realism is also achieved through Giotto's treatment of the flanking angels: instead of being decorative cut-outs with faces which stare impassively outwards as in Cimabue's work, they are now conceived in terms of a group of figures standing one behind the other, and who, in common with the neighbouring prophets and saints, all turn towards the Madonna. The sense of emotional involvement in a drama is entirely novel.

The quasi-narrative presentation of a visionary subject, as in the Ognissanti altarpiece, hints at Giotto's brilliance as a story teller. His major surviving work is a fresco cycle in the Arena Chapel in Padua: in a series of scenes painted all over the walls Giotto illustrated scenes from the lives of the Virgin and of Christ, as well as the Last Judgement. The originality of these frescoes is exemplified in the *Kiss of Judas* (pl. 7). By placing spears and torches in a criss-cross pattern

8 Giotto di Bondone
Madonna di Ognissanti, 1310–15
Galleria degli Uffizi, Florence

This work is generally assumed to be by Giotto because of its stylistic similarity to the frescoes at Padua.

against the sky, Giotto evokes all the chaos of a crowd scene in a way that had never been attempted before. But underlying all the turmoil and wealth of incident portrayed in the fresco is a remarkable economy of expression: everything leads to the figure of Christ whose intense stare and impassive stance act as powerful stabilizing elements amidst all the surrounding confusion.

Giotto's last extant frescoes, which decorate two chapels in Santa Croce in his native Florence, include a scene of the death and ascension of St. Francis. In these, a mere century after the Saint's death, his life was already seen as resembling that of Christ. The legend of a sceptic who plunges his hand into the sacred wound in St. Francis's side is clearly derived from the story of Doubting Thomas, and the fresco bears a clear compositional resemblance to Giotto's earlier *Lament over the Dead Christ* in Padua. These frescoes mark the emergence of a new development in Giotto's style. A comparison with his Paduan work shows that the relative restraint of the later frescoes can only partly be attributed to the difference in subject-matter. Realism is deliberately played down in favour of an elegance in the representation of the figures who kiss the sacred wounds which would never have been contemplated by the Giotto of the Arena Chapel. It was this manner and not his earlier one that was to be followed by Giotto's Florentine successors, such as Orcagna and Taddeo Gaddi. No Italian artist before Masaccio was indeed to capture again that blend of realism and monumentality that had characterized Giotto's frescoes in Padua.

After Florence, the nearby city of Siena was the most important centre of early Renaissance art. The commanding achievement of Giotto has overshadowed the art of his Sienese contemporary, Duccio di Buoninsegna, who in certain respects was a comparable innovator, although his style departed less from that of the existing Byzantine tradition. Duccio's greatest work, the *Maestà*, was painted for the High Altar of Siena Cathedral; the front of the altarpiece, depicting the Virgin in Majesty flanked by the patron saint of Siena, adheres to the time-honoured tradition of the hieratic Byzantine Madonnas in Glory (pl. 9). In contrast, the back of the panel, illustrating scenes from Christ's Passion, shows a considerable understanding of the new-found principles of spatial illusionism. Moreover, genre-like details are used to make the narrative more vivid: in the *Flight into Egypt*, for instance, the ageing Saint Joseph is poignantly depicted walking out into the wilderness with his possessions tied up at the end of a stick. The art of Duccio's younger Sienese contemporary, Simone Martini, shares many of the progressive elements of his work; but these are combined with an even greater refinement and elegance (pl. 10). This more sophisticated manner of painting was later adopted by the Papal Court at Avignon, where Martini went to work for several years, and formed the basis for what has been subsequently termed the International Gothic style.

Most of the paintings that survived the Italian Trecento are of religious as opposed to secular subjects: churches were less frequently sacked than castles or palaces, and whereas religious paintings gained a greater sanctity with age, secular works seemed old-fashioned to later generations and were often destroyed. The frescoes in the town Hall in

9 Duccio di Buoninsegna,
The Virgin in Majesty (front of the Maestà Altarpiece), 1308–11
Museo dell'Opera del Duomo, Siena

At a time when pious instruction was the sole aim of art it was necessary to identify all the saints in writing.

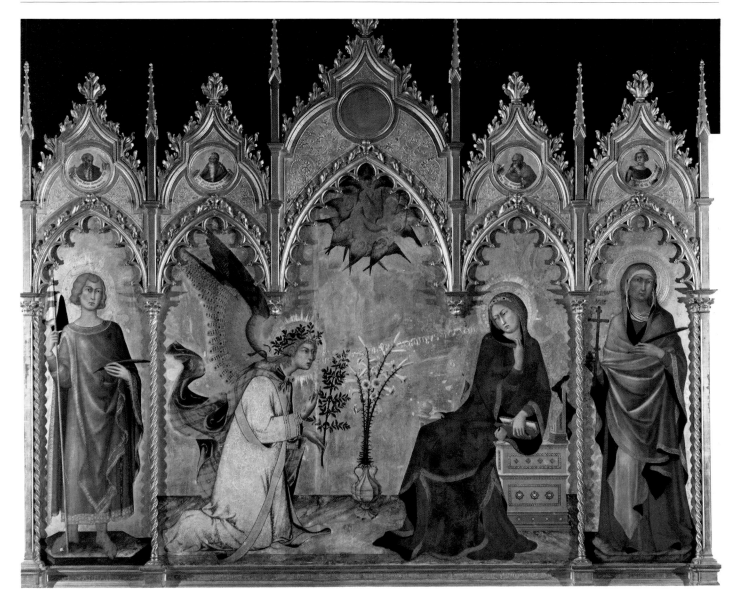

10 Simone Martini and **Lippo Memmi**
The Annunciation and the Saints Ansanus and Julitta, 1333
Galleria degli Uffizi, Florence

Simone Martini can explain figures either by florid linear design, as with the Virgin, or by an extremely subtle transition from light to dark, as with St. Ansanus.

Siena by Ambrogio Lorenzetti, a Sienese contemporary of Martini, are exceptional examples of secular art from this period, and show great advances in naturalism. The *Effects of Good Government* (pl. 11) contains in fact an unprecedently realistic depiction of town and country, and incorporates such recognizable landmarks of Siena as the towers of the Cathedral and of the Town Hall. Moreover it is filled with lively anecdotal detail: for instance, labourers are shown working on scaffolding, a scholar lecturing to an attentive audience, and a shepherd driving a flock of sheep across the main square of the town.

In 1348 Italy was swept by the Black Death. Ambrogio Lorenzetti is thought to have died of it, and one only has to read Boccaccio's chilling account of its horrors to understand what a destructive effect it had on Sienese, and to a lesser extent, Florentine art. Barna was the only great Sienese painter to survive and the cruelty and directness of his work is strangely shocking after that of his predecessors. In the late 14th century Sienese art has often a delicate colourful charm, but neither in quality nor in historical importance can it be compared to the golden age that preceded it.

It is perhaps symptomatic of the change in the relative importance of the two cities that the first major 15th-century painter from either place was a Sienese artist who went to work in Florence. Lorenzo Monaco was another exponent of the so-called International Gothic,

11 Ambrogio Lorenzetti
The Effects of Good Government on the Town (detail), 1338–9
Palazzo Pubblico, Sala della Pace, Siena

Good Government brings prosperity and scholarship, shown in realistic vignettes, but above all harmony, shown by the time-honoured symbol of the dance.

the style which was stimulated by the work of the Italian artists in Avignon, and further developed at the Courts of the Dukes of Burgundy and that of Paris. The influence of northern art helped to accentuate the realistic elements that belied the style of courtly elegance. Lorenzo's *Adoration of the Magi* combined a cavalcade of colourful and exotic figures with witty and sometimes coarse details such as a servant restraining an excited dog. An artist who worked in a similar vein to Lorenzo Monaco was Gentile da Fabriano. Gentile can in fact be more accurately described as an International Gothic painter, because he worked in such centres as Venice, Bergamo and Rome, which had very close contacts with the courts of France and elsewhere.

The last great exponent of the International Gothic was Pisanello, who worked in various parts of Italy, and ended his career, in 1455–6 at Naples, which was then the only remaining Italian court to favour this style. But Pisanello's elegant manner incorporates a detailed study of natural phenomena that makes even the realistic elements in Lorenzo's and Gentile's art seem naive. His drawings of animals, or even his portrayal of a butterfly in his portrait of an Este princess (pl. 12) display a scientific curiosity. Not surprisingly, such empiricism was admired by the humanists who indeed found it more readily comprehensible than the revolutionary works of an artist who is generally but mistakenly associated with humanism, Masaccio.

12 Pisanello
Portrait of a Princess (Ginevra d'Este), *c.* 1433
Musée National du Louvre, Paris

Ginevra d'Este, who can be securely identified by
the emblems on her sleeve, was later poisoned
by her husband Sigismondo Malatesta.

Renaissance Painting
in Central Italy

The 15th century is famous for its revival of interest in antiquity, an interest mirrored both in the forms of religious art and also in the emergence of a new category of painting – mythologies. Neoplatonism, the most important philosophical movement of the time, attempted a reconciliation between the pagan world of antiquity and Christianity. Towards the end of the century, however, the conflict between these two worlds became more marked and a fanatical Dominican preacher called Savonarola launched a violent attack on what he considered to be the excessive secularization of his age.

By far the most influential and original centre of painting in 15th-century Italy was Florence, and the first great innovator was the Florentine artist Masaccio. Within a very short life-span (1401–28) he developed a truly original style of painting that owed more to Giotto than to any contemporary artist; moreover, he was possessed of an emotional power and depth of characterization that no other Florentine artist, save for the sculptor Donatello, was ever to recapture. But Masaccio was no intransigent modernist, unwilling to adjust his style to meet the requirements of a particular commission, as is shown by a comparison of his Pisa *Crucifixion* (pl. 13) and his fresco of the *Holy Trinity*. The startling stylistic difference between the two works, painted only one year apart, are explained by the different contexts for which they were intended; the first, in which painful suffering is expressed in the melodramatic colouring and pose of the Magdelene, was originally the top of a Gothic altarpiece to be seen from below, while the second, a meditation on the mystery of death and transfiguration, was placed above a tomb slab at floor level. In the *Trinity* a complex theological idea was expressed and Masaccio invented a new form of composition to accommodate it. The architectural framework is accurately classical, and serves to emphasize the balanced disposition of the figures in the shape of a triangle receding in space. The threshold between our reality, represented by the kneeling donors, and that of the sacred personages is scarcely accentuated and, most originally of all, while the figures are represented on the same scale, a trick of perspective makes God the Father seem to tower above all of them.

The most extensive body of work in Masaccio's short career is the fresco cycle in the Brancacci chapel in the church of the Carmine in Florence. This depicts both the Fall of Man and scenes from the life of St. Peter, a subject for which there was little pictorial precedent and which thus presented a considerable challenge to an artist's imagination. The *Tribute Money* (pl. 14) shows the moment when Peter asked Christ if it was fair to pay taxes to the Roman Emperor Caesar, to which Christ made the famous reply: 'Render unto Caesar that which is Caesar's and unto God that which is God's'. The naturalistic scale of the buildings and the way in which the landscape is portrayed in acute perspectival foreshortening, indicate Masaccio's concern to create a plausible setting for the story. But it is the figures who interest him above all: with their cast shadows and strong realistic modelling they

13 Masaccio
The Crucifixion (detail of the central panel of the polyptych of Pisa), 1426
Museo e Gallerie Nazionali di Capodimonte, Naples

One feels that Masaccio's strongly modelled figures would exist more comfortably in space than fitted into this flat background.

give an impression of solidity that had never been attained by earlier painters. In addition Masaccio reveals such subtlety of characterization that each gesture and expression, however slight, is a telling one. Much more dramatic, and supremely economical, is the depiction on a thin band of wall of the *Expulsion of Adam and Eve* (pl. 15), where tragedy is expressed in every detail: the look of pity and not of anger on the face of the Angel, the leaden tread of the protagonists, Adam's hiding of his head, and the way in which Eve screws up her eyes to beg for pity. The naked bodies are rendered with tremendous conviction, and though the darkened condition of the Brancacci chapel is misleadingly sombre, the scenes must always have possessed a severity closer in spirit to Roman art. The pose of Eve is in fact derived from classical statues of Venus just as some of the heads of the apostles in the *Tribute Money* are based on Roman portrait heads.

Florentine painting in the generation immediately following Masaccio was dominated by three artists, none of whom were fully able or willing to assimilate his radical style of painting. Least affected by his innovations was Fra Angelico, a Dominican monk whose devout lifestyle was matched by a sentimental piety as an artist. Fra Angelico's *Annunciation* (pl. 16) in his own monastery of San Marco, was probably based on a lost work by Masaccio which likewise showed an annunciation taking place behind columns; it is hard to imagine,

14 Masaccio
The Tribute Money, c. 1425
S. Maria del Carmine, Cappella
Brancacci, Florence

Michelangelo, in a drawing after this
figure, shows his admiration for the
way in which mass gives emphasis to
the gesture of Peter on the right.

however, that Masaccio would ever have given such a vapid humility
to these figures or would have made them seem so much like
cardboard cut-outs. Fra Angelico had a slightly greater awareness of
the severe realism of Masaccio in later life when he was called to Rome
to fresco a series of scenes of the early history of the church for the
chapel of Pope Nicholas V in the Vatican. In his *St. Laurence Receiving
the Gifts of the Church* (pl. 17) he has tried to create a setting appropriate
to the story by incorporating architectural features derived from early
Christian buildings; he has even attempted, if rather crudely, to
express emotions.

The art of Fra Filippo Lippi – who was likewise a monk but later
married a nun – developed in a different way to Fra Angelico's:
whereas his early works showed remarkably close borrowings from
Masaccio, his later ones became increasingly decorative and prettified.
The style which he evolved in later years was in fact typical of much
15th-century Florentine art. A lingering trace of Masaccio's style is
evident in the heavy and rather muscular baby in the *Madonna and
Child* of *c.* 1465 (pl. 18). The painting as a whole, however, reveals the
artist's greater interest in the rendering of minute naturalistic details
such as the intricate lace veil or the string of pearls across the
Madonna's head; moreover the composition tells of a greater love for
delicate surface patterns than for realistic three-dimensional forms.

Paolo Uccello is the most unusual Florentine painter of this period,
and his strange style led to anecdotes about the eccentricity of his
personality. His particular passion was for perspective; Vasari relates
how he would stay up all night labouring over some problem
connected with this and taking no heed of his poor wife's pleas for him
to come to bed. *The Flood* (pl. 19), perhaps his most bizarre work, is
more an exercise in complex perspectival arrangement than in clear
and logical story-telling. The *Rout of St. Romano* (pl. 20), one of a
series of battle scenes painted for the Medici, is unprecedented in some
of its perspective effects such as the foreshortening of the dead man
lying on the ground. It also reveals the contradictory nature of
Uccello's art: for in spite of his scientific approach to the problems of
rendering pictorial space, his compositional style remained a purely
decorative one.

Florence dictated the artistic fashions of Northern Italy in the mid-

15 Masaccio
The Expulsion of Adam and Eve,
1424–5
S. Maria del Carmine, Cappella
Brancacci, Florence

One sees in the exaggerated
roundness of Adam's back the way in
which Masaccio would use outline to
express modelling.

15th century. No matter where an artist originally came from, it was definitely advantageous for his career if he went to study in Florence; and similarly, Florentine artists such as Lippi and Uccello were often employed in other North Italian towns in preference to local talents.

Domenico Veneziano (whose name literally translated means Dominic of Venice) was typical of many Italian painters of this period who were attracted to Florence from afar and fell heavily under the influence of Florentine art. Although little is known about his life, an early painting in Berlin portraying the Adoration of the Magi reveals that he began his career under the shadow of artists such as Gentile da Fabriano and Pisanello whose work was exceptionally popular in his native Venice. Probably arriving in Florence in the middle of the 1430s, he soon appears to have abandoned the old-fashioned manner of his youth in favour of a more radical one that was in keeping with his new artistic environment. His major surviving work, the *St. Lucy Altarpiece* (pl. 21) is a strange fusion of different Florentine influences. The Masaccio-like clarity of the composition accentuates a decorative richness that owes much to more recent Florentine artists such as Lippi; meanwhile the architectural setting and the finely-graded recession of the floor displays a mastery of complex perspective that is worthy of Uccello. Domenico, however, departed from Florentine precedents in his subtle use of light and colour to accentuate the sense of spatial depth.

An equally individual genius was Domenico's pupil, Piero della Francesca, who was born and worked for much of his life in the small Tuscan town of Borgo San Sepolcro near Arezzo. He seems to have

16 Fra Angelico
The Annunciation, 1438–43
Convent of S. Marco, Florence

Once established, the pictorial device of having the Virgin decorously separated from the angel by a column and yet sharing the same space became canonical.

17 Fra Angelico
St. Lawrence receiving the Gifts of the Church, 1447–50
Musei Vaticani, Cappella Niccolina, Vatican

Ordered by the Roman Prefect to surrender the treasures of the Church, St. Lawrence presented the Prefect with the city's poor saying, 'This is our treasure'.

18 Fra Filippo Lippi
Madonna and Child, c. 1465
Galleria degli Uffizi, Florence

This impish angel is the type of detail
which led the Victorian poet
Browning to envisage Filippo Lippi
as a man enamoured of all life.

been a man of private means, and one of the first European artists to
regard painting as an art and not merely as a trade: not only did he take
a great interest in the intellectual problems concerning painting but he
also exasperated his patrons by working on a picture for years on end
in an attempt to reach perfection. The *Baptism of Christ* (pl. 22),
painted for a church in his home town, was executed shortly after
completing his training in Florence under Domenico; its serene
luminosity and the measured simplicity of its composition reveal an
obvious debt to his master. Another, and less apparent, influence is
that of Sienese painting. One must remember that the major work of
art which Piero would have known in his native town was an
altarpiece by the Sienese master Sassetta in the church of San
Francesco; although Piero would have found the composition of this
work naive and old-fashioned, he seems to have been attracted by its
Sienese charm and richness of colour. It is however a self-defeating
exercise to discuss Piero's art purely in terms of the painters who
influenced it; for it was essentially an isolated phenomenon. When
Piero died in 1492 he was almost entirely forgotten by his contem-

19 Paolo Uccello
The Flood, 1446–8
S. Maria Novella, Chiostro Verde,
Florence

This panel, showing Noah wisely
retiring with the ark, was painted
under the arch of a cloister above a
scene showing the flood subsiding.

20 Paolo Uccello
The Rout of St. Romano, c. 1456
National Gallery, London

The story of the Florentines routing
their local rivals, the Sienese, is told
in three parts; here the Florentine
attack is launched.

poraries (he received only the briefest of mentions in Vasari's *Lives*),
and he was largely considered a provincial curiosity until the late 19th
century when he was suddenly discovered to be one of the most
original artists of the Italian Quattrocento. The most important
commission in Piero's career was the decoration of the choir of San
Francesco in Arezzo. The subject-matter of these frescoes, *The Legend
of the True Cross* (pl. 23), was most unusual and, as with Masaccio in
his scenes of *The Life of St. Peter*, the artist could rely on little pictorial
precedent. This apocryphal tale, concerning the discovery of a
fragment of the Cross and the subsequent fate of this relic, was
recorded in a hagiographical compilation called the Golden Legend;
the actual story provided Piero only with a point of departure for a
highly original series of scenes which disregarded continuity of
narrative and fidelity to the text in favour of an overall formal
harmony. The experimental quality of these works is illustrated above
all in the *Dream of Constantine* which shows the as yet unconverted

21 Domenico Veneziano
Madonna and Saints (St. Lucy Altarpiece) 1442–8 (formerly in the Church of S. Lucia dei Magnoli) Galleria degli Uffizi, Florence

This is one of the earliest examples of a type of picture known as a *Sacra Conversazione*; this recently-coined term is used in reference to paintings in which the Madonna occupies the same space as the saints who surround her.

Roman Emperor being visited in his sleep by an angel who tells him that he will triumph through the sign of the Cross. Although scenes of the Nativity were occasionally given a night-time setting by Quattrocento artists, this was the first time that a painter had tried to give an illusion of night on such a large scale. Moreover, the brilliance of the light emanating from the swooping angel in Piero's fresco has a visionary intensity which looks ahead to Raphael's *Liberation of St. Peter* (pl. 67) and also to the work of Caravaggio and his followers in the 17th century.

Although, after his training under Domenico Veneziano, Piero worked largely in a provincial environment, he continued to frequent extremely sophisticated cultural and intellectual circles. The most important of his patrons was Federigo da Montefeltro, Duke of Urbino. Federigo combined a life of cultural and intellectual pursuits with one of action, was a commander of the papal army, and lost his right eye and the top of his nose in a jousting accident. In Piero's portrait of him (pl. 24) with his wife Battista Sforza, he appears in convenient profile. The work is in fact a curious mixture of realistic and idealized elements. The portrayal of the Duke's warts and the

22 Piero della Francesca
The Baptism of Christ, c. 1460
National Gallery, London

Piero has made no attempt to give us
any more than a symbolic suggestion
of the river, although the reflection of
the sky behind Christ's feet is a
beautiful naturalistic touch.

meticulous rendering of the Duchess's pearls and brocades reflect Federigo's love of Flemish art; but the actual composition is probably derived from classical portrait medallions. Federigo reappears clad in armour in Piero's *Madonna and Saints*, a picture which was probably painted as a thanksgiving for a military victory. The subject-matter of this altarpiece is essentially the Madonna enthroned in glory and surrounded by Saints, yet symbolical and not easily unexplained details, such as the hanging egg, point to hidden complexities. The work's sophistication is also expressed in the architectural setting,

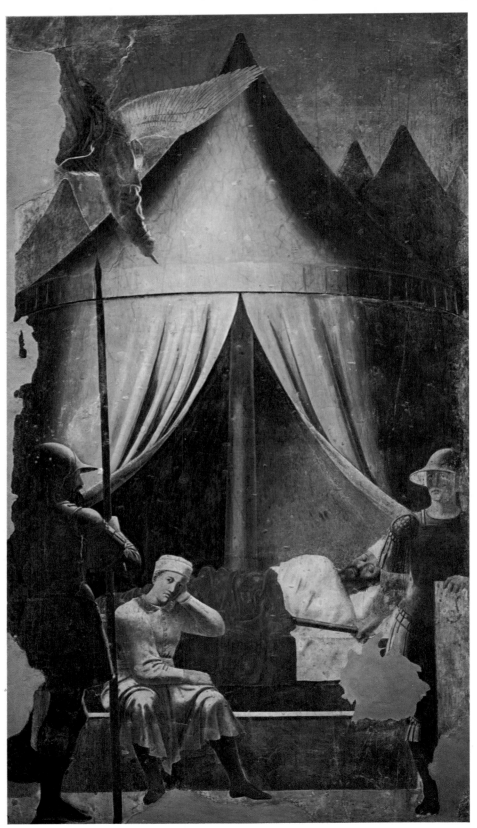

23 Piero della Francesca
The Dream of Constantine (detail from the *Legend of the True Cross*), 1452–9 S. Francesco, Arezzo

Piero places this scene to the right of a window so that the angel seems to emanate from its light.

24 Piero della Francesca
Federigo da Montefeltro and his Wife Battista Sforza (front panels of a diptych), *c.* 1465
Galleria degli Uffizi, Florence

On the reverse of each of the two panels is an allegory depicting the triumph of the sitters.

which reveals Piero's detailed knowledge of perspective, a subject to which he in fact later devoted a detailed and very learned treatise. In comparison with the colourful loggia with slightly pointed arches in Domenico Veneziano's *St. Lucy Altarpiece*, Piero's setting is one of great restraint and incorporates the most refined and archaeologically correct classical detailing.

Although Piero had little interest in the rendering of emotions, his art, in its measured stateliness, represented in many ways the closest approximation to that of Masaccio. It certainly had a seriousness which was largely lacking in the work of his Florentine contemporaries. Medici patronage of the arts in this city, in the second half of the 15th century, fostered in fact few religious paintings of note; symptomatic of the tastes of this family were the frescoes they commissioned from Benozzo Gozzoli for their palace chapel. The *Journey of the Magi* (pl. 25), a work in which the colourful tapestry-like composition seems closest stylistically to Florentine art before the time of Masaccio, shows a rather light-hearted treatment of a religious subject, and incorporates portraits of the Medici family and of their friends. In view of the not altogether serious nature of the Medici's artistic interests, it was perhaps inevitable that their most significant contribution to the arts was the encouragement of paintings of secular subject-matter, in particular mythologies.

The category of mythological painting was one of the greatest innovations of the Renaissance. Although a natural accompaniment to the great revival of interest in classical art and culture which took place during this period, it basically provided a very pleasurable alternative to religious painting. As the classical legends are not so familiar to us today as they would have been to a Renaissance public, we tend to take mythological paintings too seriously. Essentially, a mythology offered an exciting narrative content (which was generally lacking in religious paintings) and, most important of all, an erotic stimulus.

The greatest Florentine artist to paint mythologies during this period, and by far the most popular today, was Botticelli. The celebrated *Birth of Venus* was probably commissioned by Lorenzo di Pierfrancesco dei Medici, a cousin once removed of Lorenzo the Magnificent and a friend and pupil of Marsilio Ficino, the founder of the neo-platonic movement in Florence. The fact that Pierfrancesco, who also owned another famous mythology painted by Botticelli, the *Primavera* (pl. 26), was well steeped in neo-platonism has encouraged art historians to search for some obscure philosophical explanation for the work. Although the painting can equally be understood as a straightforward illustration of a classical text, some allegorical significance might also have been intended; but how seriously should it be taken if a convincing explanation was to be found? Neo-platonism could accommodate a considerable degree of light-heartedness, and Ficino's earliest writings had expounded a philosophy in which pleasure was the dominating principle. The sensuous pleasure to be derived from Botticelli's work must at any rate have been far greater than any intellectual one for Botticelli's public; for a painting of a nude figure on such a scale as the Venus was a considerable novelty at the time and thus must have been exceptionally provocative. It is known that in later life Botticelli fell under the influence of Savonarola, and although Vasari's statement that he gave up painting altogether as a

25 Benozzo Gozzoli
The Journey of the Magi (detail),
1459–61
Palazzo Medici-Riccardi, Cappella,
Florence

The fact that this fresco was conceived for a private chapel inside the family palace makes the cheery domesticity of the scene more appropriate.

26 Sandro Botticelli
Primavera, 1477–8
Galleria degli Uffizi, Florence

With no pictorial precedent for this
kind of subject, Botticelli drew his
inspiration from tapestries to
produce this decorative frieze-like
design.

result of this is demonstrably untrue, he certainly would have
repudiated such works as the *Birth of Venus*. His later career was in fact
devoted exclusively to religious works of a spiritual intensity quite
exceptional in the context of Florentine art of this period.

The most bizarre Florentine painter of mythologies of the late 15th
century was Piero di Cosimo. Vasari gives an entertaining description
of Piero as a savage recluse who despised all civilized values, hated the
sound of church bells and the chanting of monks, survived on an
exclusive diet of hard-boiled eggs prepared in great numbers in
advance, and whose life-style was in short 'more bestial than human'.
The mythological world which interested Piero was correspondingly a primitive one; such work as the *Mythological Scene* (pl. 28), which
cannot be satisfactorily related to a specific classical text, is merely a
haunting evocation of life in an almost primeval wilderness. As with
his other paintings Piero displays here his love for animals, and
appropriately a dog is shown to be almost as fascinated by the dead
woman as is the kneeling fawn bent over her. Piero's crude and brutal
outlook on life was shared by at least one of his patrons, Francesco
Pugliese, who owned a very large number of the artist's mythologies
and was later banned from Florence for calling Lorenzo de Medici 'il
magnifico merdo' ('the magnificent shit').

Vasari, writing in the middle of the 16th century, saw the history of
painting as a gradual and logical progression from the works of Giotto
through to those of Masaccio, and finally to the ultimate masterpieces
of Michelangelo. But a survey of 15th century Florentine art shows
that this is clearly not the case: the remarkable variety of paintings of
this period indicates that art takes a number of different courses, some
of which lead nowhere. It is appropriate that this chapter should end
with Ghirlandaio, a painter whose *Adoration of the Magi* (pl. 29)

28 Piero di Cosimo
Mythological Scene, c. 1510
National Gallery, London

The 'Death of Procris' has been suggested as a subject, but many inconsistencies make this unconvincing.

27 Sandro Botticelli
The Calumny of Apelles, 1496
Galleria degli Uffizi, Florence

The idea and subject of this painting are taken from Pliny's description of a lost allegory by the Greek painter Apelles.

29 Domenico Ghirlandaio
Adoration of the Magi, 1485
S. Trinità, Cappella Sassetti,
Florence

The sarcophagus and ruins allude to
the legend that the Nativity took
place on the site of the ruined temple
of Solomon.

summarizes many of the disparate tendencies in Florentine art of this
period. On the one hand it is a slightly old-fashioned work, with
sentimental details such as the grimacing Jesus with a thumb in his
mouth, owing something to Filippo Lippi, and the colourful cavalcade
of the Magi being reminiscent of Benozzo Gozzoli and even of Gentile
da Fabriano. On the other hand it reveals an awareness of the new
fashion for antiquity in its use of severe classical detailing, and also for
Netherlandish painting in its realistic depiction of the shepherds and in
the richness and depth of its landscape background. (This work is in
many ways a paraphrase of an influential altarpiece by the Flemish
artist, Hugo Van der Goes, whose work, together with that of his
northern contemporaries, will be discussed in the following chapter).
But although Ghirlandaio was very responsive to the new artistic
currents of his time, it is strange to reflect that one of his pupils was
Michelangelo, a man whose art seems to have emerged as if from
nowhere and to deny any neat theory of artistic continuity.

Painting outside Italy in the 15th century

Innovation in 15th century Northern painting was derived from the artistic centres of what we now know as Belgium, Luxembourg and Holland, where the prosperity of great mercantile cities such as Bruges, Brussels, Ghent and Tournai made for generous patronage of the arts. The merchants themselves, both as individuals and as members of institutions such as the city councils, religious confraternities and craft guilds, were responsible for the commissioning of some of the most important works of art. But the greatest stimulus to artistic activity was the presence in The Netherlands of one of the most opulent and sophisticated courts, that of the Dukes of Burgundy.

The court of Duke Philip the Bold of Burgundy at the beginning of the century was based in Dijon, which was one of the centres of International Gothic. The wings of the altarpiece the Duke commissioned for the Carthusian monastery of Champmol, for example, were painted by Melchior Broederlam (pl. 30) and show a combination of artifice and beautifully observed detail characteristic of that style. It was Philip the Bold's brother, the Duc de Berry, however, who was the most enterprising patron of his generation. Indeed, International Gothic had reached its most exquisite pitch in the famous work he commissioned from the brothers Limbourg, the *Très Riches Heures* of 1413–16. What makes Broederlam and the Limbourg brothers important in the context of the Netherlandish tradition, with which this chapter is mainly concerned, is the fact that, by an astute combination of diplomatic marriage and alliance, Philip the Bold had extended the compass of his rule beyond the limits of his small duchy to include not only a large part of Northern France, but also the whole of The Netherlands. It soon became clear that the latter was to be the source of ever-increasing wealth and power, and Philip's son and heir, Philip the Good, accordingly made it his place of residence. The Burgundian court there set standards of etiquette and dress for the rest of Europe and most of the greatest musicians, poets and painters of the day were associated with it.

The court artist was not simply a painter of devotional works and portraits. He designed buildings, decorative schemes, furniture, pageants, ceremonial costumes and even armour. Philip the Good's principal painter, Jan van Eyck, was more than equal to all these tasks. He was a highly erudite and cultured man and, according to one source, proficient in geometry, geography and chemistry. But it was his almost magical command of illusionism in art, his ability to deceive the eye into accepting his painted world as a sealed fragment of reality, that was most enchanting to an age captivated by the idea of art as the mirror of nature. Van Eyck was committed to objectivity above all else; he treated the human, animal and inanimate elements of his pictures with exactly the same inscrutable candour and the cornerstone of his art was not some imaginative insight but a technical refinement; though he did not actually invent oil painting – there had been work in this medium long before his time – he was probably among the first to

30 Melchior Broederlam
*The Circumcision and the Flight into
Egypt* (right wing of the Champmol
Altarpiece), 1393–9
Musée des Beaux Arts, Dijon

The 'Rest on the Flight into Egypt'
was at this date rarely depicted. It
became a popular subject with
Gerard David and Joachim Patinir.

31 Jan van Eyck
Arnolfini Marriage Portrait, 1434
National Gallery, London

No other straightforward full-length
portraits are recorded in the
Netherlands in the 15th century, nor
did they become fashionable until the
17th century.

use a mixture of oil and turpentine, which lent itself to rendering the
subtlest natural effects. Certainly, van Eyck's achievement would be
unthinkable without the great precision of detail that oil allows; and
one of the most immediately striking differences between Netherlandish and Italian art of this time lies in the difference between oil and the
most commonly-used Italian media of tempera and fresco.

Netherlandish portraiture of the 15th century is characteristic of the
art of the period in having clearly defined functions. The portrait of a
king, for example, could stand in for him on state occasions. Portraits
were exchanged by friends, carried as souvenirs, talked to, and kissed;
and negotiations for royal marriages were generally preceded by an
exchange of portraits of the would-be fiancés. Van Eyck's *Arnolfini
Marriage Portrait* (pl. 31) is the likeness of an Italian merchant whose
business was conducted from Bruges, with his young wife. According
to religious dogma current at the time, the sacrament of marriage was
not bestowed by the officiating priest but by the couple themselves.
Van Eyck's picture records a marriage being concluded, as many were,
outside the ecclesiastical context. The work is, in effect, a marriage
certificate and a sign of the painter's role as witness to the couple's
vows; above the mirror on the back wall are the words 'Jan van Eyck
was here' written in an elaborate script usually reserved for legal
documents. The single candle lit in the ornate chandelier symbolizes
the presence of Christ, the dog represents marital faith and the
discarded slippers suggest reverence. The *Madonna of Chancellor Rolin*
(pl. 32), also by van Eyck, is an example of the practice by which the
individual who paid for a religious painting (or its 'donor') was
portrayed in it. This notoriously worldly chancellor of the Duchy of
Burgundy is shown in adoration of the Virgin as if already one of the
company of Heaven. If he was too busy with the affairs of state to
bother with religion, at least he could be pious by proxy, by having his
painted representative in constant religious observance.

The art of the Tournai painter Robert Campin makes it clear that
van Eyck's conquest of reality was not an isolated achievement. Yet,
although they shared a fascination for intensely observed naturalistic
detail, Campin differs from the very discreet and undemonstrative van
Eyck in balancing illusionism with an evident desire to present the
meaning of his work in a forthright and moving manner. He invests
the bald narrative of the biblical stories he illustrates with a realism of
characterization and setting that may owe something to the process of
'visualization', an aspect of 15th-century devotional practice whereby
one imagined sacred events as happening in the present and in one's
own everyday surroundings (pl. 33).

Campin's pupil Rogier van der Weyden learnt both from his master
and from van Eyck. In his art, detail is not allowed to possess a
pictorial interest of its own as in that of van Eyck, but is subordinated
to overall design; and narrative is not diffuse as in the art of Campin,
but clearly articulated by means of the composition. Form and content
are in unison in van der Weyden's work. His ability to impose a design
that enhances the drama of his subject and makes the narrative more
commanding made his style the most influential of any Netherlandish
master. The *Descent from the Cross* (pl. 34), an early work, is a play on
levels of illusion of a kind that fascinated this era; for it deliberately
resembles a sculpted wooden altarpiece with figures aligned across a
shallow box-like space to form a frieze. The pathetic, broken figure of
Christ is level with the picture plane in order to maximize the sense of

32 Jan van Eyck
The Madonna of Chancellor Rolin,
c. 1435
Musée National du Louvre, Paris

Utrecht Cathedral has been identified
on the right bank; its setting
however, seems to be imaginary.

confrontation between the spectator and the reality of His sacrifice.
Emotion is registered with consummate subtlety and decorum, as each
of the figures responds to the tragedy in his or her own way. The artist
could also display twists of purely pictorial imagination: the man
behind the cross lowering the body of Christ occupies a space that
could not rationally accommodate him; the way in which his figure is
jammed in between the cross and the back wall has a jarringly
ambiguous effect which imparts a disturbing resonance to the work.

The achievement of van der Weyden set a standard with which
every Netherlandish painter had to come to terms, right up until the
end of the 15th century. Some, such as Gerard David and Hans
Memling (pl. 36), sought to emulate him, bringing his style to a
higher key of sophistication; others determined to surpass him. Van

33 Robert Campin
The Nativity, c. 1430
Musée des Beaux Arts, Dijon

This painting alludes to the legend
that the Christ child gave off a
brilliant light. It is for this reason that
Joseph shades his now redundant
candle.

34 Rogier van der Weyden
The Descent from the Cross, c. 1435
Museo del Prado, Madrid

Close examination of this
composition became *de rigueur*
for all later treatments of the
crucifixion story.

35 Rogier van der Weyden ▷
Portrait of a Lady, c. 1450
National Gallery, London

Van der Weyden's portraits derived
their popularity from their simplicity
of design and pose and the tender
devoutness of their expressions.

der Weyden had ventured into certain areas of artistic exploration, but
had left others undeveloped. The innovators of the next generation
concentrated on expanding the expressive compass of painting and
making it a more telling vehicle for spiritual and psychological truths.
Dirck Bouts was at first strongly influenced by van der Weyden, but
soon evolved a mature style that is highly idiosyncratic. His gaunt,
willowy figures suggest a mood of introspection and emotional
tension. Another very individualistic painter of the period was
Geertgen tot Sint Jans. His *Lamentation over the Dead Christ* (pl. 37)
takes the stylistic example of van der Weyden and transforms it by
simplifying form to the point of abstraction and employing an angular
and incisive line to trace out the scene's expressive essentials. But the
most complex and intriguing artistic personality of the latter half of the
century, and the artist who made the most substantial contribution to
the Netherlandish tradition after the death of van der Weyden, was
Hugo van der Goes.

Having died insane, van der Goes is one of the few pre-Romantic
artists to come close to the modern stereotype of the neurotic and
tormented genius. One must, however, resist the temptation to read
his mental instability into his pictures. Like all painters of his day, he
would have seen himself as a professional working in the service of
society and regarded his inner life as quite irrelevant to his job; it was
only much later, towards the end of the 18th century in fact, that the
artist's own preoccupations and feelings were to become the subject of

36 Hans Memling
Vanity
Musée des Beaux Arts, Strasbourg

The subject of a naked woman
holding a mirror was very popular in
the Middle Ages and Renaissance;
supposedly commenting on the
transience of worldly beauty, it
provided an excuse to portray a
provocative nude.

37 Geertgen tot Sint Jans ▷
*The Burning of the Bones of Saint John
the Baptist by Order of Julian Apostata,*
1480–5
(right wing of the former altarpiece
of the Johanniter convent in
Haarlem)
Kunsthistorisches Museum, Vienna

Geertgen tot Sint Jans was the first
important Dutch painter; his few
surviving works are coarser and
earthier than those of his Flemish
contemporaries.

art. Van der Goes's importance is that he moulded the artistic legacy of
van Eyck and van der Weyden into a far more urgent and vital medium
of expression. His sense of drama and his skill in suggesting emotional
states are well illustrated by the *Portinari Altarpiece* (pl. 38) of around
1475. The Virgin meditates upon the fate of the vulnerable Christ
child, whose ordained death upon the cross is symbolically prefigured
in the still-life, and she is surrounded by adoring angels who attend the
incarnation as if officiating at some solemn ceremony. But this circle of
thought is broken by the jubilant and boisterous arrival of the
shepherds, whose rustic enthusiasm makes a telling contrast with the
insight of those who comprehend the deeper, tragic significance of the
event. In the *Death of the Virgin*, the artist departs from tradition by
showing Christ not standing by the death–bed but levitating above the
Virgin's head, his robes supported by angels and his form enclosed
within an aura of supernatural light. There is no dignity and no

resignation in the attitudes of the apostles at the bedside. Each is completely absorbed in his own thoughts, each a complex study in emotional response. The figures jostle each other in a space that is obviously too small to contain them, and the unease this evokes in the spectator enhances the work's sense of psychological complication.

The history of German painting in the 15th century is the history of a number of independent provincial schools and of the individual

achievements of often isolated masters. Here International Gothic lingered on for much longer. In the hands of a master such as Stephan Lochner, it attained heights of lyrical charm, but by Netherlandish standards the style was already dated. Meanwhile certain artists developed a more forceful manner, influenced by Netherlandish painting but much grittier in its approach to its subject-matter.

One of the first of these was the Swiss painter Conrad Witz, who worked in Basle. His *St. Peter Altarpiece* (pl. 39) of 1444 is in some ways the most 'Eyckian' of German paintings, but is both more realistic and more dramatic than anything by van Eyck himself. Martin Schongauer, who spent most of his career in the town of Colmar in Alsace, may have been a pupil of van der Weyden; and certainly a work such as the *Madonna of the Rose Garden* (pl. 40) of 1475 is indebted to some degree to the rather wistful subtlety of that master. But Schongauer has transformed and made completely his own anything that he may ultimately have owed to the Netherlandish tradition. His work is more tautly composed, his figures are a more articulate rendering of the substance and energy of the human body, and their emotions are described in a more convincing way.

The precarious state of political life in France at this time meant that there was no single all-important centre of patronage such as Paris had been in the past, or Fontainebleau was to become in the next century.

38 Hugo van der Goes
The Adoration of the Shepherds
(Central panel of the Portinari
Altarpiece), 1475–6
Galleria degli Uffizi, Florence

Tommaso Portinari, a Medici agent
living in Bruges, commissioned this
altarpiece and gave it to the church of
the Santa Maria Nuova hospital in
Florence.

39 Konrad Witz
Christ walking on the Water (from the
St. Peter Altarpiece), 1444
Musée d'art et d'Histoire, Geneva

The view of the lake is a
topographical view of Lake Geneva
where Witz lived.

Most artists worked in the provinces, for courts such as that of René of
Anjou at Avignon, or for the key ecclesiastical sees. The impact of
Netherlandish naturalism in France is registered in the *Annunciation* by
the 'Master of the Aix Annunciation'.

But with the work of the unknown master of the Avignon School
who painted the *Villeneuve Pietà* of *c.* 1460, the example of van der
Weyden has been completely assimilated into a highly individual
dramatic mode. The pathos of the work derives from the telling
description of emotional states, which are made all the more moving
by the way they have been rendered in a restrained manner. The most
sophisticated champion of the new realism in France was the court
painter Jean Fouquet. His art has the elegance and suave accomplish-
ment appropriate for a court painter and displays a confidence in the
new idiom that rivals his Netherlandish peers. Fouquet once visited
Italy, where he is reputed to have painted a portrait of the Pope, and
the emphasis upon monumental form and spatial clarity central to the
Italian achievement were important principles in the definition of his
own style; this can be seen in the Melun Altarpiece diptych, *c.* 1451
(pl. 42).

The influence of Netherlandish painting also served as an important
agent for change in the Iberian peninsula. Spain in the 15th century was

40 Martin Schongauer
The Madonna of the Rose Garden, 1473
Saint Martin, Colmar

The art of van der Weyden is the principal source of inspiration for the features of the face and the characteristically long fingers. The Madonna in a garden setting became immensely popular around the end of the 15th century.

a patchwork of contending provinces; it only began to develop any distinct national identity after the marriage in 1469 of Ferdinand II of Aragon and Isabella of Castille. Consequently, as in Germany and France, there was no centralization of art patronage to lend coherence and direction to the endeavours of the country's artists. Each area evolved an individual style contingent upon the degree of penetration of foreign influence (Netherlandish and sometimes Italian too) and the local conditions of taste and patronage. Catalonian painting, for example, was largely impervious to the influence of Netherlandish painting and harks back to the example of International Gothic. In the

41 Nuño Gonçalves ▷
The Veneration of Saint Vincent
(central panel of the São Vicente Altarpiece), 1465–7
Museu Nacional de Arte Antiga, Lisbon

The panels of this polyptich, Gonçalves' only surviving documented work, depict with stunning realism a cross-section of Portuguese society, ranging from humble fishermen to, as in this case, members of the Court.

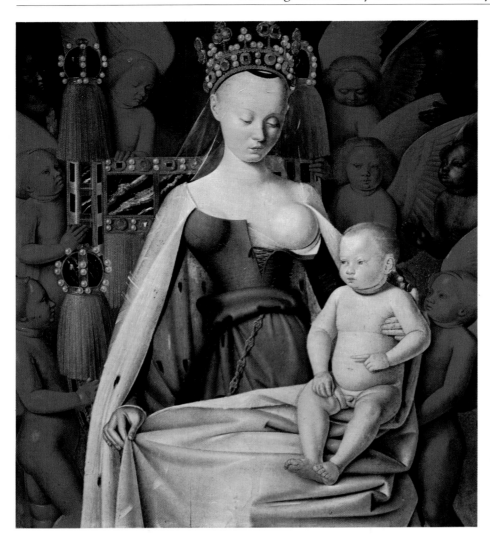

42 Jean Fouquet
Mary and the Child surrounded by Angels (right wing of the Melun diptych), *c.* 1450
Koninklijk Museum voor Schone Kunsten, Antwerp

This voluptuous Madonna is a portrait of Charles VII's mistress, Agnes Sorel.

hands of a master such as Jaime Huguet, the essentially abstract and decorative emphasis of this style could result in works of an ornate and solemn splendour. On the other hand, the art of Luis Dalmau, who was court painter to Alfonso V of Aragon, shows a significant Northern influence, in particular that of van Eyck. The Cordovan painter Bartolomeo Bermejo, who worked in both Aragon and Catalonia, wrought a highly expressive and disturbing art from the example of Bouts and van der Weyden. In the *Pietá of Canon Luis Desplà* (in Barcelona Cathedral) he takes the dignified and restrained *Pietà* of van der Weyden and exaggerates the emotion in a most grotesque and harrowing manner.

Portugal also came under the dominance of Netherlandish painting; as elsewhere the 'Eyckian' tradition could not be ignored, but was given a new identity in keeping with the country's cultural peculiarities. This is well exemplified in the work of Nuño Gonçalves, court painter of King Alfonso of Lisbon, who actually met van Eyck when the latter visited Portugal to paint the portrait of a prospective marriage partner of his patron, Philip the Good (pl. 41). Gonçalves' art is a reconciliation of the new realism with the abstract and hieratic formulae of his native tradition.

Painting in Venice and Northern Italy in the 16th century

In 1548 a Venetian writer called Paolo Pino published a treatise on painting in which he characterized art in terms of the components, *disegno* (drawing) and *colore* (colour); although these terms had been commonplaces of art criticism for many years they had apparently never before been formulated in print. Soon a great controversy arose as to which of these components could be considered as the most worthy. That this debate should have occurred in the first place was indication of the radically new approach to painting that had been evolved by Venetian artists since the late 15th century: for while the Florentine and later the Roman schools had based their art on *disegno*, the Venetians had placed an unprecedented emphasis on *colore*. This debate took at times ludicrous turns, and was generally fired by intense chauvinism. Thus Vasari, a Florentine, considered his compatriot Michelangelo to be beyond criticism and regretted that the Venetian painter Titian had not concentrated more on improving his *disegno*; and Ludovico Dolce, a Venetian writer on art, thought that Titian was the greatest artist who had ever lived and that Michelangelo could not bring his figures fully to life because he had an improper understanding of *colore*. The controversy relating to *disegno* and *colore* was to re-emerge in an even cruder form in the late 17th century, when it centred around a discussion of the relative merits of Poussin and Rubens, and in the 19th century critics would still be arguing over the merits of the linear style of Ingres and the more colourful one of Delacroix.

Although since the 16th century the Venetian painters have been perennially associated with *colore*, it would be wrong to conclude from this, as is invariably done, that they were principally concerned with the rendering of vivid colour. The word *colore* had in fact many implications, most notable among which was a free handling of paint and an intuitive rather than cerebral approach to composition.

Similarly *disegno* did not just suggest good draughtsmanship, but also a meticulous application of pigment, a rational intellectual organization of forms and even a preference for solidity of structure over shimmering pictorial effects. The most striking difference between *colore* and *disegno* is that whereas the one implied an attitude towards painting that could not be governed by strict rules, the other implied one that was carefully regulated. It is symptomatic of this spontaneous and undogmatic approach towards art adopted by the Venetians that an academy of painting was not founded in Venice until 1750, over two centuries after similar institutions had been opened in Florence, Rome and in almost every other art centre in Italy.

The individual style of painting that was evolved in Venice was appropriate to a city which was unique in its setting, government and artistic patronage. Alone among the principal Northern Italian cities, Venice did not have a court, but was ruled by a form of oligarchy, headed by an elected Doge. The unusual nature of Venice's government gave rise to a widespread and misleading notion that the city enjoyed a remarkable degree of freedom, and was a model of the democratic state. This was far from being the case, for the government was exclusively limited to the nobility and few cities could so rigidly have adhered to the class structures.

In the 16th century the state provided one of the major sources of patronage; and the most prestigious position an artist could hold in the city was to be a recipient of one of the *Sensarie* of the Fondaco dei Tedeschi (a type of grant given out by the state), which effectively meant that he was the Doge's official painter. The duties which this entailed included painting a portrait of every newly elected Doge (pl. 43) and helping in the decoration of such public buildings as the Ducal palace. The three principal recipients of the *Sensarie* during the 16th century were Giovanni Bellini, Titian and Jacopo Tintoretto. Another source of patronage which was exclusive to Venice, and resulted in some of the major cycles of painting of the Venetian Renaissance was that of the Lay Confraternities (or *Scuole*). These charitable institutions, originally derived from the flagellant movements of the middle ages, had a particularly strong following in this city, and were exceedingly wealthy. Membership of the *Scuole* was open to both rich and poor, and by joining them one not only enjoyed the pleasures pertaining to a mixed social club, but was also able to give financial assistance to the less fortunate members of the society. All in all the *Scuole* were the most powerful representation of the citizen class in Venice and, more important, embodied a form of religion that was comprehensible to the ordinary individual. Finally one must mention the important role of the private patron, whose principal activity was as a collector: the mania for collecting both antiques and contemporary works of art was in fact more acute and widespread in this city than in any other part of Italy. The function of these collections varied enormously: some reflected a love of scholarship and others were the products of an encyclopaedic mentality, which gave equal prominence, for instance, to botanical or geological specimens as to works of art. There was also considerable social prestige attached to owning a collection. Bartolomeo Odoni's desire to be portrayed surrounded by classical statues does not necessarily indicate that he was a man of great culture; Odoni, who came from the merchant classes, might simply have been trying to disguise his inferior social status. But of course one cannot deny the purely pleasurable side to owning a work of art. Paintings could both afford considerable sensual pleasure and also add to the sumptuous appearance of palaces already decorated with tapestries, brocades, damasks and hangings encrusted with precious jewels.

The first great period of Venetian art, the 16th century, coincided with Venice's pre-eminence as a European power and trading centre. Throughout the century it sustained a heated rivalry with Rome and much of the language and symbols employed by its historians and artists couched propaganda intended to prove Venice's superiority over the southern capital. Like Rome, Venice was relatively unimportant as an art centre in the 15th century, and the great artistic innovations that took place in Florence during this time were largely ignored by the Venetians.

In contrast to Venice, the neighbouring town of Padua, which was one of the major centres of learning in the whole of Italy, was always very susceptible to Florentine influences, and many artists from the Tuscan city, including Giotto and Donatello, came to work here. Any account of Venetian Renaissance painting should in fact be prefaced by

43 Giovanni Bellini
The Doge Leonardo Loredan, c. 1501
National Gallery, London

Venice, as a Republic, severely
curtailed the power of her elected
leaders, the Doges, who tend to be
rather shadowy figures.

a consideration of the work of Padua's first artist of genius, Andrea Mantegna: his paintings are not only interesting for the light they throw on the artistic formation of the young Giovanni Bellini, but they also provide a convenient point of comparison against which the later achievements of the Venetian School can be measured.

Mantegna's most celebrated work in his native city was the cycle of frescoes in the church of the Eremitani. Photographs of this cycle, which was largely obliterated by a bomb during the Second World War, reveal Mantegna's characteristically hard and linear style (a partially Florentine inheritance): in addition the relief-like structure of the compositions and the classical detailing in some of the costumes and settings indicate the painter's very great interest in antiquity.

Later in his career Mantegna became court painter for the Gonzagas in Mantua, and painted for them a series of canvases illustrating the Triumphs of Caesar (now in Hampton Court): these were painted almost as an archaeological reconstruction of classical decorations. More erudite still were two allegories (pls. 45, 46) which he painted for his patron's wife, Isabella d'Este, who was one of the most notorious blue-stockings of the Renaissance, and who spent much of her life trying to enlist the leading north Italian painters to provide canvases for her *Studiolo*.

The *Studiolo* (which literally means small study) was an essential prerequisite of any patron of the Renaissance with cultural pretensions: although it was principally intended as a place of retreat in which to indulge in intellectual contemplation, its decorations also served as the patron's personal manifesto. Isabella, following the ever more popular fashion for humanism, employed a humanist adviser, one Paride da Ceresara, to help her in devising the allegories for her Studiolo. Some idea of the complexity of these is given by a short extract from Paride's description of the work to be painted by the Umbrian artist Perugino: 'These last ('amoretti') will be smaller than the god Cupid and will carry neither gold bows nor silver arrows, but darts of some baser material, either wood or iron as you please. In order to give full expression to the fable and the dawn scene, the olive tree sacred to Pallas will rise out of the ground at her side, with a shield bearing the head of the Medusa, and the owl, which is her emblem, will be seen in the branches of the tree. At the side of Venus her beloved myrtle tree will flower.' Mantegna's *Mars and Venus* shows an equal wealth of

44 Gentile Bellini
Procession on the Piazza San Marco,
1496
Galleria dell'Accademia, Venice

This is a typical example of a *Scuola* painting by Giovanni's brother Gentile, a pedestrian work of art but a fascinating social document.

45 Andrea Mantegna
Balustrade with Women and Putti, 1472–4
Palazzo Ducale, Camera degli Sposi,
Mantua

This, the first fresco to use logical
perspective for a ceiling, is in the
'Camera degli Sposi', or marriage
chamber, of the Gonzagas' Palace.

46 Andrea Mantegna
Mars and Venus, c. 1497
Musée National du Louvre, Paris

The delicate contrapuntal rhythms of
the muses dancing to Apollo's lyre
reveal Mantegna's interest in
bringing to life figures from antique
reliefs.

erudite details, all of which were intended to illustrate the essential
theme of chastity triumphant over the pleasures of lust (a theme of
particular importance to Isabella, whose husband was constantly
absent from Mantua). Although Mantegna seems to have been
mentally pre-disposed to execute such a pedantically-conceived work,
and although, as we shall see, his approach to mythology was
fundamentally different and more serious than that of the Venetian
masters, his *Mars and Venus* is by no means dryly academic: indeed he
responds with commonsensical humour to such ludicrous details of the
allegorical programme as Cupid blowing an arrow at Vulcan's
testicles.

The classical erudition and discipline of much of Mantegna's art is a
similarly misleading front for a painter who also possessed a remarkable emotional range. The anguished intensity of which he is capable is
tellingly revealed in the *Dead Christ* (pl. 47). The foreshortened body
of the Saviour is a startling original conception as is the closeness of the
viewpoint from which we are made to observe the scene: the violent
perspective draws us into the action and in consequence we feel more
intensely the pain of the hysterically weeping Virgin.

It is said that Venetian religious art at its most characteristic radiates
a bland serenity, and that a painter like Giovanni Bellini would have
been incapable of painting such an emotionally charged canvas as
Mantegna's *Dead Christ*. That is blatantly untrue: not only do the
religious works of the Venetian Masters show a great variety of

temperaments, but also Bellini himself executed a number of religious paintings which reveal a quite genuine and disturbing pathos. What is revealing, however, is to compare Mantegna's work with that of Bellini and of subsequent Venetian masters from a purely technical point of view.

Bellini spent several years of his youth in Padua and his early work depicting the *Agony in the Garden* shows a considerable debt to the art of Mantegna in the harsh linear treatment of some of the details such as the ringlets of Christ's hair. But what is special to Bellini and indeed to much subsequent Venetian art is the poetic treatment of the landscape background, in this case the vivid evocation of the sunset. Bellini's *Transfiguration*, (pl. 48) painted *c.* 1487, reveals how the atmospheric quality tentatively conveyed in the *Agony* now permeates the entire canvas, and how much more mellow the artist's technique has become: the whole is invested with an absolute stillness, and the transition between static foreground figures and mellifluous landscape is effortless.

The fluency in the handling of paint as displayed in such a work as the *Transfiguration* seems to us now remarkably fresh and a great advance on the essentially linear style of Mantegna. But the Venetian public of Bellini's time was shortly to witness such dazzling examples of technical virtuosity by other Venetian masters that by the second

47 Andrea Mantegna
The Dead Christ, c. 1480
Pinacoteca di Brera, Milan

This painting seems to have been painted for the artist's own collection; at a later date its height was reduced by about a third.

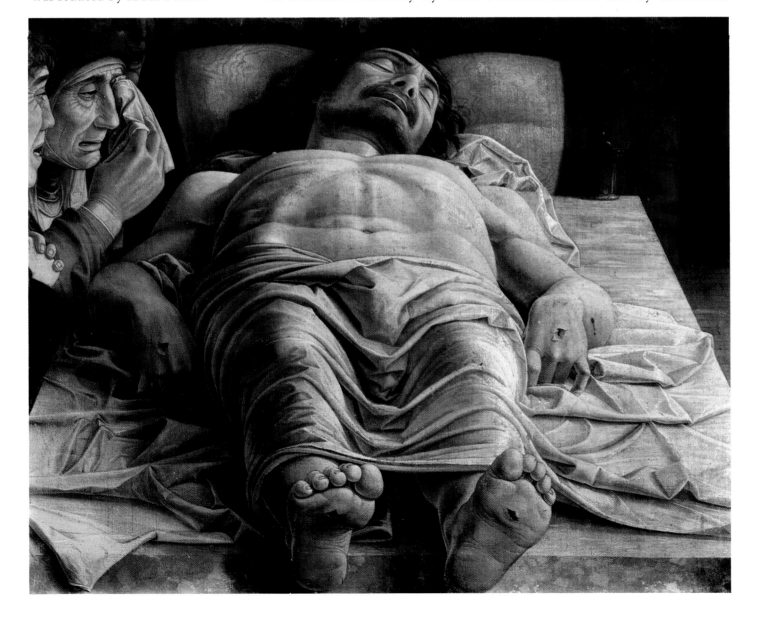

decade of the 16th century Bellini's style was to seem old-fashioned, and by the 1550's it was to be described as 'dry and excessively diligent'. A younger contemporary of Bellini whose work was also to appear similarly antiquated was Vittore Carpaccio. Carpaccio is principally famous for his decorations in the assembly rooms of the *Scuole*. Given the unique status of these institutions, it is perhaps to be expected that the works of art produced for them should have an equally individual character. To illustrate in a series of large canvases the life of the saint to whom the particular *Scuole* was dedicated gave the Venetian artists an excuse to display their love of elaborate narrative. *Scuola* paintings by such artists as Gentile and Giovanni Bellini and even Titian have a colourful vitality and contain much anecdotal detail. Carpaccio's work for the *Scuole* is especially rich in incident and in addition provides a valuable insight into daily life in Renaissance Venice. The so-called *Courtesans* (pl. 49), in fact depicting two Venetian noblewomen, is possibly a fragment of a much larger whole and combines humour with sentimentality in a way that was to make Carpaccio very popular in Victorian times. But in the context of 16th-century Venice, Carpaccio's rambling compositions and meticulous handling of paint would seem increasingly anachronistic even in terms of the idiosyncratic *Scuole* canvases; and after 1510 the artist was to suffer a very significant drop in commissions.

Italian writers on art of the mid-16th century were unanimous in acclaiming Giorgione as the first true innovator of the Venetian Renaissance: in his atmospheric rendition of landscape and in the softness of his modelling of human figures, he indeed went much

48 Giovanni Bellini
The Transfiguration, c. 1487
Museo e Gallerie Nazionali di
Capodimonte, Naples

Bellini, always seeking a naturalistic solution, puts in the sky the fluffy white clouds which Christ, Moses and Elias would normally stand on.

49 Vittore Carpaccio
Two Courtesans, c. 1495
Museo Correr, Venice

Ruskin called this the 'greatest painting ever painted', but he only meant from a technical point of view and besides his judgements were clouded by senility.

further than Bellini. As with Masaccio, his remarkable achievements were contained within a very short working life (he died in 1510 at the age of 32), by the end of which he had attracted innumerable followers. His style was imitated almost immediately and it is now very difficult to distinguish between his own work and that of his acolytes; in fact the canvases that can be securely attributed to him number only a handful. Equally baffling and the source of endless speculation, is the meaning of a fanciful work such as *The Tempest* (pl. 50). Known by this title since the middle of the 16th century, this has sometimes been thought to show the artist responding to the technical challenge of emulating a lost work by Apelles, which portrayed lightning and thunder clouds. In a less prosaic vein, the art critic, Ridolfi, writing in 1648, believed that the painting referred to lines in Lucretius describing the pitiful state of man exposed at birth to the elements. Recent art historians have been more erudite still and have attempted to find complex symbolical allusions in each detail of the composition. This is a particularly futile task, as it is yet to be proved that any of the famous 'problem pictures' of the Venetian Renaissance, such as Giorgione's *Concert Champêtre* (Paris, Louvre) and Titian's so-called *Sacred and Profane Love* (Rome, Borghese Gallery) have any profound philosophical significance. Whereas it is known that Mantegna relied heavily on humanist tracts for a work such as the *Mars and Venus*, Venetian artists seemed to have adopted an altogether more personal and spontaneous approach to secular subject-matter: it is perhaps symptomatic of this attitude that Bellini refused to execute a work for Isabella's *Studiolo*, saying, in the words of a contemporary, that he 'preferred to go his own way in painting'. At all events the pervasive mood of *The Tempest* – the evocation of which would have

50 Giorgione
The Tempest, 1507–8
Galleria dell'Accademia, Venice

The two figures are moved to the sides to allow the landscape to dominate in generating the mood of the painting.

51 Giorgione
Sleeping Venus, c. 1508
Staatliche Kunstsammlungen,
Gemäldegalerie, Dresden

A sleeping nude is always especially
tantalizing because the viewer is
invited to speculate as to her reaction
when she wakes.

been beyond the technical abilities of earlier artists – lives on
independent of any intended meaning: and details such as the child
suckling his mother's breast in a thunder storm have a suggestive
power which affects us and yet cannot easily be rationalized.

Giorgione's *Venus* (pl. 51) offers no such problems of interpretation.
Originally intended as a portrayal of the godess Venus (X-rays reveal a
Cupid by the woman's feet), it is in fact little more than high class
pornography. Art historians coyly refer to the figure's chaste beauty,
but this is certainly not how Giorgione's contemporaries – who were
totally unaccustomed to seeing paintings of almost life-sized recumbent nudes in a landscape – would have reacted to it.

In the same way as Vasari saw Florentine art as leading in unbroken
sequence towards an ideal attained by Michelangelo, so Venetian
writers saw Titian's art as the culmination of a process leading towards
a different, though equally desirable goal. Titian, a pupil of Giorgione
who had actually helped in the completion of the *Venus*, inherited his
master's sensuality in the handling of paint and yet was to evolve a
radical technique of his own which was to seem unsurpassable to his
contemporaries. The speed of Titian's rise to fame was in itself
breathtaking and engendered much hard feeling among Venice's older
artists. When in 1513 Titian was told that he would succeed Giovanni
Bellini as painter to the state, artists such as Carpaccio must have
considered this as the final blight to their hopes and a sign that the old
order was finally overthrown. In every field of painting which he
practised, Titian had something new to contribute, whether as a
painter of religious works, mythologies, portraits and so on. His
essential achievement was summarized by the writer Dolce: 'Titian
alone walks as the equal of nature, so that each of his figures is alive,
moves, its flesh quivering'.

Titian's first major altarpieces in Venice, the *Pesaro Madonna* and the

52 Titian
Crowning with Thorns, 1570–6
Alte Pinakothek, Munich

This is not an unfinished picture, as
some have assumed, but an extreme
example of Titian's late style, painted
for himself and sold after his death to
Tintoretto.

Assumption (both in the church of the Frari), were also the first works
properly to establish his public reputation. Coming after the largely
static altarpieces by artists such as Bellini and Carpaccio, Titian's, with
their symmetrical compositions, sweeping draperies and gesticulating
figures, must have seemed truly dynamic: their effect on the spectator
was not to induce meditation but rather to involve him physically in a
religious drama. The increasingly dramatic quality of Titian's religious
work is accompanied by an ever greater love of violent action. One of
the last, and also the most famous of Titian's Venetian altarpieces, was
his *St. Peter Martyr* for the church of San Zanipolo; the painting was
destroyed by fire in the late 19th century but contemporary copies
show a composition so violent and agitated that the effect on the
viewer must have been truly disturbing.

   After the *St. Peter Martyr*, Titian's public career in Venice came
largely to an end. Although he kept a house in Venice throughout his

53 Titian
*Pope Paul III surrounded by his nephews
(Cardinal Alessandro Farnese and Count
Ottavio Farnese),* 1546
Museo e Gallerie Nazionali di
Capodimonte, Naples

Paul III, who was much sharper than
these sycophants assumed,
recognized the audacious nature of
the portrait but also its justice.

life and continued to be artistic advisor to the state for much of the
century, he spent a great deal of his time travelling around Italy and
elsewhere, and working almost exclusively for private individuals. It
was as a portraitist that he was perhaps most in demand: indeed few
painters before him had been able to achieve such lively renderings of
character, or had evolved such a wide range of poses and expressions.
One of Titian's closest Venetian friends, and the subject of a famous
portrait in the Louvre in Paris, was the infamous hedonist Pietro
Aretino. Aretino, a cruel and brilliant satirist who hated the pedantically erudite and precious prose style of many of his contemporaries,
once wrote that 'I force myself to portray people's character with the
vivacity with which the marvellous Titian portrayed this or that

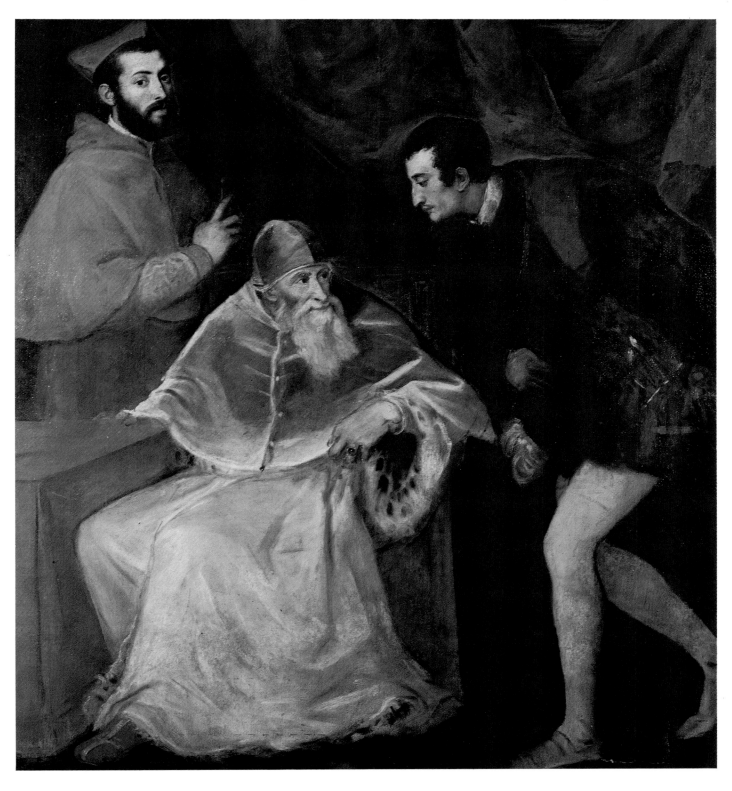

countenance'. But Titian's vivacity as a portraitist was not just limited to representations of close friends and drinking companions such as Aretino: it is also to be found in his portrayal of the two most powerful figureheads in Europe – the Holy Roman Emperor Charles V and Pope Paul III. Titian's relationship with Charles V, which was likened at the time to that of the classical painter Apelles with Alexander the Great, was actually one of some intimacy. This is reflected in Titian's intensely human portrait of him, in which is captured something of the subject's benevolent Erasminism, without any compensating loss of grandeur. By far the most unusual portrait of Titian's career was that of *Pope Paul III surrounded by his nephews* (pl. 53). This work was probably inspired by Raphael's *Pope Leo X* and yet in spirit it could hardly be more different. Whereas Raphael's is static and solemn, Titian's seems almost like a scene from a Victorian melodrama. The Pope is shown as an apparently ineffectual old man being waited upon by deceitful sycophants; even if such a characterization was far from Titian's mind, the way in which he has tried to make a group portrait come alive was in itself remarkable and looks forward, albeit incongruously, to Frans Hals.

The 19th-century essayist Hazlitt considered that no artist other than Titian had given to the nude 'the same undulating outline, the same pulpy tone to the flesh, the same animal spirits, the same breathing motion', had created figures 'in which you saw the blood circling beneath the pearly skin'. Titian's brilliance in the rendering of the nude is already apparent in the so-called *Venus of Urbino* of 1538 (pl. 54). The pose is clearly derived from Giorgione's Venus, but Titian has made her an even more provocative figure: not only are her eyes wide open and staring at the spectator, but she is also conceived within a contemporary interior. In contrast to Giorgione's nude, who lies on a purely decorative arrangement of classical drapery, Titian's is firmly on a bed; moreover the bracelet around her arm, and her elaborate coiffure, only serves to emphasize her actuality. In fact there is no reason to suppose that she was intended as a Venus at all, as the first reference to this painting simply called it 'The Naked Lady'.

The very sensual qualities of Titian's art made him the ideal painter of mythologies. His first major achievement in this field was a series of three canvases for the Studiolo of Alfonso II in Ferrara. In contrast to the decorations of Isabella d'Este's Studiolo at Mantua, none of the ones intended for Alfonso had any allegorical message to impart, and their only consistent feature was a sense of playful revelry. Two of Titian's paintings, *The Garden of Venus* (Prado) and the *Bacchanal of the Andrians*, (pl. 55) were both related to specific classical texts, but these (Philostratus's *Imagines*) were no more than word pictures, evocations of purely sensual scenes that the author thought might interest the painter. Their elusive quality certainly offered a considerable challenge: 'Do you catch something of the fragrance hanging over the garden, or are your senses dull? But listen carefully; for along with my description the fragrance of the apples will also come to you.' This is part of a description that inspired *The Garden of Venus*, and the idea that words can convey smell can be paralleled by the way in which Titian's art seems intended to combine a variety of sensual experiences, that of sight being only an introductory one. This enveloping sensual quality is very evident in the scene of the *Bacchanal* where Titian shows the effect of an unending stream of wine lulling consciousness into a dreamlike state of intense rapture.

54 Titian
Venus of Urbino, 1538
Galleria degli Uffizi, Florence

The eye explores sensuality through
contrasts of texture, the furry dog,
the prickly roses and the profusion of
hair melting into the shoulder.

Almost all of Titian's mythologies in the latter part of his career
were intended for the Spanish King, Philip II. Although based on
stories from Ovid's *Metamorphoses*, the actual subject-matter was often
irrelevant; and Titian simply referred to them as *poesie*, a term
probably intended as a euphemism for erotica. Describing a painting
portraying *Venus and Adonis* (now in the Metropolitan Museum, New
York) Titian explained why he had chosen to show the naked Venus
from the back. Previously he had done another nude for Philip in
which the naked woman was seen from the front; instead, he says, 'I
wanted this other *poesia* to vary and show the opposite part so that it
would make the room in which they are to hang more pleasing to me'.
That such a picture as this invited very immediate sensual responses we
can tell from a long description of it in a letter written by Ludovico
Dolce in 1554. Among other things he notices how the seductively
rounded flesh of Venus's bottom is flattened because of her seated
position. Even a man with the acutest sight might, he says, be deceived
into thinking that she was physically before him and even were he
grown cold with the years he could not help but feel his blood
warming. But what is unique to Titian's mythological nudes is the fact
that they are not just passive objects of sensual contemplation; they are
also trembling, sometimes hysterical, and invariably taking part in
some violent drama. As with Titian's religious work, his mythologies
acquired an even greater element of cruelty as the artist grew older:
their combination of sex and sadism is at times overpowering.

A suitable accompaniment to Titian's increasingly emotional rendering of subject-matter, was a growing freedom of technique.

Titian's working methods in old age were vividly described by the painter Palma il Giovane. 'He laid in his pictures with a mass of colour which serves as a ground work for what he wanted to express . . . with the same brush dipped in red, black or yellow he worked up the light parts and in firm strokes he could create a remarkably fine figure . . . then he turned the picture to the wall without looking at it, until he returned to it and looked at it critically, as if it were a mortal enemy. Thus by repeated re-visits he brought his pictures to a high state of perfection, and while one was drying he worked on another . . . sometimes he used his finger to dab a dark patch in the corner as an accent that would heighten the surface with a bit of red like a drop of blood. He finished his figures like this and in the last stages he used his fingers more than his brush.'

In spite of the very idiosyncratic nature of Titian's late manner, it would be a mistake to be too romantic in one's interpretation of it. The aged Titian was by no means an isolated genius whose work was beyond the comprehension of his contemporaries. Although there were occasionally complaints about the artist's lack of *disegno*, even a writer like Vasari was able to perceive that the apparent facility of his later paintings was belied by the enormous amount of work that had gone into them. One has also to remember that most of the paintings

55 Titian
Bacchanal of the Andrians, 1516–18
Museo del Prado, Madrid

Lest we should feel left out of this scene of intense happiness the nude who has passed out in the foreground makes a gesture of invitation.

56 Titian
Danae, 1553–4
Museo del Prado, Madrid

The pose of Danae is taken from a
Michelangelo sculpture; Titian,
however, corrects Michelangelo's
inability to treat female flesh
convincingly.

from the latter part of his career were intended for private patrons and
would not have been known to the public at large, and others like the
Vienna *Nymph and Shepherd* were definitely unfinished.

Two of the leading painters in the second half of the 16th century
were Jacopo Tintoretto and Paolo Veronese. Tintoretto, who was
born in Venice in 1518, grew up very much under the shadow of
Titian, something of which he was only too well aware. In fact it is
possible to explain his whole achievement, his ever-increasing exag-
gerations of form, movement and life, in terms of an effort to outdo
Titian at his own game. He first achieved notoriety with his *Miracle of
St. Mark* of 1548 (pl. 57), which derived compositional elements from
Titian's *St. Peter Martyr,* but which managed the almost impossible
feat of rendering them in an even more violent manner. Already
criticisms were voiced against the apparent rapidity of his technique;
and it was hoped that this failing could merely be attributed to the
impetuosity of youth. Unfortunately it could not. In later life
Tintoretto was unanimously derided by the critics, most notably by
Vasari who considered his work to be the ravings of a lunatic. It was
only with the writings of Carlo Ridolfi and Marco Boschini in the 17th
century that Tintoretto's work met with a more enthusiastic critical
response. Ridolfi was the more pedestrian of the two men, and
countered criticisms of laziness and lack of *disegno* in Tintoretto's work
by stressing how the artist used to collect antique sculptures and make
careful drawings after Michelangelo and Giambologna. It was also
Ridolfi who was responsible for the silly anecdote that Tintoretto had a
notice pinned on his studio wall which read 'The *disegno* of

57 Jacopo Tintoretto
The Removal of the Body of St Mark,
1562–6
Galleria dell'Accademia, Venice

One of a cycle of paintings ordered
by the Scuola di San Marco depicting
the acquisition by the city of the
body of their patron saint.

Michelangelo with the *colore* of Titian'. Boschini was an altogether more intelligent critic, and someone whose enthusiasm for Tintoretto's work was based on his recognition of the importance of an artist's sense of fantasy; this was an entirely new concept in art criticism. But in spite of Ridolfi's and Boschini's enthusiasms, the most eloquent and influential supporter of Tintoretto was the English 19th century critic John Ruskin. Ruskin considered Tintoretto as a deeply introverted person whose works expressed a tormented soul; while his writings encouraged people to look at Tintoretto's paintings with fresh eyes, they contributed to a popular image of this artist which, as with that of the aged Titian, is thoroughly misleading.

Far from painting solely as a means of self-expression, there is considerable documentary evidence that Tintoretto painted largely for money. The speed at which he worked and his apparent willingness to allow poorly finished works to issue out of his studio, may have made him a target of critical abuse, but it also led to his having a virtual monopoly of all the major religious commissions in Venice and eventually all the state ones as well. Tintoretto was one of the most notorious opportunists in the history of art, and stories abound of his ruthlessness in trying to court favour with both secular and ecclesiastical bodies. In 1571, for instance, he outwitted fellow rivals in a competition to choose an artist to paint a work for the main hall of the Ducal palace by presenting the state with a finished picture; this did not endear him to members of his profession (especially as he submitted the bill afterwards), but it led to his being awarded a *Sensaria* in 1574.

For much of his life Tintoretto was engaged in work for the Scuola di San Rocco. This was always the wealthiest of Venice's lay confraternities: San Rocco was the patron saint of plagues, and to subscribe to his institution was a form of insurance policy against the notorious epidemics that swept through Venice in the 16th century. Tintoretto's enormous canvases for this Scuola cover virtually all the available wall space in the building, and have a dark and melodramatic intensity which is entirely at odds with the colourful anecdotal decorations that one normally associates with the confraternities. The 19th century historian Burckhardt considered that Tintoretto betrayed the 'true genius' of the Venetian school by trying to 'graft a dramatic historical style of painting on to another stem'. But Tintoretto's art cannot be interpreted just as an isolated eccentric phenomenon. In fact it was so much more widely known to the Venetian public in the second half of the 16th century than was that of Titian or of any other contemporary Venetian painter, that it became also the most imitated; and its influence was to be felt well into the early 18th century.

In contrast to Titian and Tintoretto, very little is known about contemporary critical attitudes to Veronese. He did not feature at all in the 16th-century debate concerning *colore* and *disegno*, and the first notices of any length date from the time of Ridolfi and Boschini. Although Veronese could not be compared with Tintoretto, Boschini showed how the former too went beyond the simple imitation of nature, and compared his art to a casket of shining jewels. While Tintoretto was primarily a religious painter, working almost exclusively for business-minded middle-class circles, Veronese relied more on secular commissions from the nobility. Veronese's most important work in Venice – in the Church of San Sebastiano (begun in 1555) – was started immediately after his arrival in the city, at a time when he had yet to consolidate his reputation. His principal excursions into

58 Paolo Veronese
Banquet in the House of Levi, 1573
Gallerie dell'Accademia, Venice

Veronese's colour acquires a special
resonance because it seems to come
from the object depicted rather than
the surface of the canvas.

religious art after that date took the form of enormous banquet scenes,
in which he was able to satisfy his apparently greater concern with
secular subject-matter. This led him into trouble with the Inquisition,
who asked him to explain the numerous profane details which
appeared in his *Last Supper* for the convent of San Giovanni e Paolo.
Veronese excused himself on the grounds that the painter 'takes the
same risk and licence that poets and jesters take', and as a compromise
solution the picture's title was changed to *Banquet in the House of Levi*
(pl. 58). It was perhaps appropriate for a painter whose approach to art
was so much more cheerful and relaxed than was that of Tintoretto,
that his most influential work was for a villa. Veronese's fresco for
Daniele Barbaro's idyllic summer retreat at Maser showed a love of
playful illusionism that was to set the pattern for villa decorations in
the Veneto for the next 200 years: Gods stare down at us from high up
on the wall, and human figures are portrayed with uncanny realism in
fictive doorways.

Whereas in the 15th century Florence had been the leading art centre
in Italy, in the 16th century it was the turn of Venice and Rome. Artists
from Northern Italy were divided in their allegiance between these
two centres, but not to spend a large part of their lives in either one of
them was generally detrimental to their careers. Titian's two major
rivals in the early 16th century, Pordenone and Lorenzo Lotto, had
little chance of gaining a similar reputation to their master's because
they worked largely in small towns in the North Italian mainland.
Pordenone spent most of his life in his native town in the Friuli, and as
a result was never able to overcome his feelings of resentment and
inferiority. Lorenzo Lotto meanwhile was a painter born and trained in
Venice who was forced by the competitiveness of the Venetian art
world to hunt for commissions outside his native city. A well-
documented neurotic, Lotto had actually the most restless of lives, and
ended his days in the Holy House of Loreto; his constant wandering
from one small town to another might explain the bewildering
changes of mood and style in his work. Another Venice-trained
painter who spent much of his time on the mainland, although for
entirely different reasons, was Jacopo Bassano. A native of the sub-
Alpine town of Bassano near Vicenza, he had a definite preference for
the quiet life of the country, and was apparently reluctant to move to

59 Correggio
St. John on Patmos, 1520–1
S. Giovanni Evangelista, Parma

Everything painted here is part of a
vision experienced by St. John who is
portrayed at the bottom of the dome.

less familiar surroundings; his love of the country was reflected in his
work which is particularly noted for its innovatory incorporation of
coarse rustic elements.

By far the most important North Italian painter of the 16th century
who kept away from the major artistic centres of Italy was Correggio.
Born in the Emilian town of Parma, and spending most of his life in
this area, he was hardly mentioned by Vasari who considered him
merely as an interesting provincial. In the 17th, 18th and early 19th
centuries however, his art was to be recognized as one of the major
achievements of the whole Renaissance.

It appears that Correggio did not have any conventional artistic
training; instead he seems to have evolved his very idiosyncratic style

from studying the works of Raphael, Giorgione and Leonardo da Vinci. Perhaps his most innovatory works were his decorations for the domes of both Parma Cathedral and the nearby church of S. Giovanni Evangelista (pl. 59). These frescoes display a type of illusionism that is quite novel for the Renaissance. Instead of relying on a complex perspectival framework, Correggio achieves a remarkable sense of recession through a most suggestive use of light which is made to soften and even dissolve forms. The radiant celestial vision thus created looks forward to some of the major decorations of the Baroque, most notably Baciccia's frescoes in the Gesù.

The 19th century French novelist, Stendhal, claims to have written his culminatory work, the *Charterhouse of Parma*, under the influence of Correggio; for Stendhal, whose aim in life and art was 'the search for happiness', the latter's paintings represented an ultimate state of joy. The ecstatic nature of Correggio's art is apparent not just in his religious works, but also in his mythologies which, in contrast to Titian's, have hardly a hint of violence. Correggio's major works in this field, four Ovidian scenes for Federigo Gonzaga, Duke of Mantua, have a luxuriant sensuality that looks ahead to the Rococo. Correggio's intensely atmospheric use of light made him the ideal painter to depict the maiden being seduced by Jupiter in the form of a cloud: the artist daringly portrays the heroine in the throes of orgasm, and never before or since has this state of sexual pleasure been visualized with such evocative power. As an ironic postscript it is interesting to note that this blatantly pornographic work was commissioned by a man whose mother, Isabella d'Este, had spent her life devising complex allegories in support of the virtues of chastity.

60 Lorenzo Lotto
Portrait of Andrea Odoni, 1527
Hampton Court Palace, Hampton Court

This portrait of a proud collector rivals the brilliant impasto of Titian with its limited but subtle colour range and various degrees of focus.

Painting in Central Italy
in the 16th century

Central Italian painting of the 16th century was dominated by three artists who were accorded an almost God-like status in their time: Leonardo da Vinci, Raphael and Michelangelo. Whereas the art of Titian was regarded by contemporaries as the ultimate expression of *colore*, the work of these three artists represented an ideal of *disegno*. In their very different ways, they brought craftsmanship, rational design, and harmony of pictorial structure to what must have seemed an unassailable height of perfection. But the work of these artists, and of their followers, cannot be rigidly categorized, and is indeed constantly belied by apparent contradictions.

All the major paintings by Leonardo and Raphael, and Michelangelo's most important work (the ceiling of the Sistine Chapel) belong to a period known as the High Renaissance (roughly 1500–1530), when Rome, along with Venice, became the leading art centre in Italy. While in the 15th century papal patronage of the arts had been a relatively limited affair, the reigns of Julius II and of his successor Leo X saw a sudden wealth of papal commissions, largely brought about by the rebuilding of the Basilica of St. Peter's. As the century progressed the threat of the French (who in fact sacked Rome in 1527) and Protestantism diverted the papacy's attention from art patronage; but painters still came here from all over Italy to study the works of the city's two greatest visitors: Raphael and Michelangelo.

Of the three great central Italian artists of the High Renaissance, Leonardo was the only one not to have worked for the papacy. The oldest of the three, he avoided going to Rome in his youth, as this city had then little to offer him in the way of commissions; and later on in his career, he was too independent a genius to work exclusively for any one patron. Born in 1452 in the Tuscan village of Vinci, Leonardo spent his youth in Florence. He worked in the studio of an artist called Verrocchio, a man who practised both as a painter and sculptor, and whose canvases show the decorative and linear style characteristic of much Florentine art of the second half of the 15th century. The first painting to which Leonardo is known to have contributed is Verrocchio's *Baptism of Christ* (pl. 61). Although there is no documentary evidence as to what parts of this painting are by Leonardo, the angel on the left has traditionally been ascribed to him (and supposedly led Verrocchio to contemplate giving up painting altogether). But other details of the picture, such as certain areas of the landscape, and the body of Christ, display a delicate tonality, a subtle modelling, and a grasp of realistic form that must also be attributed to Leonardo.

As Leonardo grew older he devoted less of his time to painting and became ever more absorbed by scientific experiments. His was a restless intellect, easily frustrated, and more interested in the solution of a problem than in the tedious application of that solution. The sometimes cavalier attitude towards execution that resulted meant that he left a number of paintings unfinished, and he also made technical

**61 Andrea del Verrocchio/
Leonardo da Vinci**
The Baptism of Christ, 1470–80
Galleria degli Uffizi, Florence

Fanciful observers have seen in
Verrocchio's angel the 15th century
looking in astonishment at the arrival
of the High Renaissance.

experiments with others that were to prove fatal to their survival.

In 1482 Leonardo moved from his native Florence to Milan. Here he worked for Ludovico Sforza, both as an artist and as a military advisor, and began his celebrated *Last Supper* (pl. 62) on the refectory wall of the church of Santa Maria delle Grazie. For this work Leonardo experimented with a medium which permitted him to paint more slowly than was possible when using the wet plaster technique of true fresco, but which unfortunately began to decay soon after it had been applied. This was especially ironic in view of the fact that the artist had

62 Leonardo da Vinci
The Last Supper, 1495–7
Refectory in S. Maria delle Grazie,
Milan

In spite of the painting's severely
deteriorated condition, its fame still
continues to draw countless visitors.

lavished an immense amount of care on it, and, according to one
contemporary, had even spent whole days contemplating it without
touching a brush. The details are now entirely lost (although a few
preparatory drawings give some inkling of their brilliance), and the
remarkable conviction the work retains is derived entirely from the
overall impression. The subject Leonardo had to paint demanded a
composition – which consisted essentially of a long table with the 12
apostles seated behind it – which was difficult to make exciting. Later
on in the 16th century, the Venetian painter Tintoretto was to give life
to it by placing the table diagonally to the picture surface. Leonardo
instead reduced the composition to its ultimate simplicity, and yet
made it both visually and intellectually satisfying by creating a
harmonious geometrical framework. Christ forms a triangle securely
at the centre of the picture, and the theatrical gestures of the apostles
achieve balance and poise by being played off against it.

The deeply introverted and obsessional nature of Leonardo's art is
fully revealed in the *Mona Lisa* (pl. 64). He kept this picture by him
until his death, and although it may have started life as a simple
portrait of Madonna (Mona for short) Lisa, a Florentine lady, it soon
became the object of a far greater personal concern, a kind of testament
in paint. The sense of mystery which the work emanates is not just due
to the famous enigmatic smile and to the haunting rocky landscape in

63 Leonardo da Vinci
Lady with an Ermine (Cecilia Gallerani), c. 1484
Muzeum Narodowe, Cracow

The sitter cannot securely be identified as the notorious Cecilia Gallerani nor can the symbolism of the ermine be determined.

the background, but also to its novel technique often referred to as 'sfumato' (or 'blurred'): colour has been virtually excluded, and forms are bathed in soft shadows. Leonardo has gone beyond realistic physiognomical observation to create an almost androgynous human being which corresponds to a purely personal ideal.

When the French occupied Milan, Leonardo briefly returned to Florence and thereafter spent the rest of his life in wanderings and frustrated exploits, eventually dying in France in 1519. Although he had a number of pupils and followers in Milan, his genius seems to have been beyond the grasp of most artists of his time, who could copy his gloomy manner of painting, but little else. It is symptomatic of Leonardo's lonely and frustrated life that his greatest commission (to fresco, in 1503, the Battle of Anghiari in the Palazzo Vecchio in Florence) was never completed, and is now known only through copies. It would have demonstrated his ability to make his tremendous knowledge of anatomy serve to represent violent action with horses as well as men fighting to the death. Only in Leonardo's innumerable extant drawings does one find a similar energy, and only in studying these drawings, filled with obsessional apocalyptic visions, caricatural observations of human physiology, and sketches of animals does it become clear how much Leonardo worked simply to please himself. This proto-romantic view of the artist's role naturally led Leonardo into conflict with the clergymen and princes who pressed him continually to complete his works.

Raphael's genius was much more accessible to his contemporaries than was that of Leonardo, yet it is ironically less sympathetic to the tastes of today. His art has a quality of effortless perfection that makes it difficult for us now to recognize how much originality and endeavour have gone into its creation. We are further biased against it by the endless number of bland imitations it spawned right up to the 19th century, and also by the insipid popular image of its creator as someone of almost feminine beauty, who led the most virtuous of lives, and who died in the flower of his youth. This image of Raphael has actually little basis in reality; and the fact that he probably died from syphilis hints at a totally different personality.

His earliest works were painted in Umbria while under the influence of Perugino, who was probably his teacher. Raphael's *Marriage of the Virgin* (pl. 66) is based on a picture of the same subject by Perugino, now in Caen, but it is also similar in composition to the latter's *Delivery of the Keys to St. Peter.* (pl. 65) in the Vatican. A comparison between these two works throws light on the differences which had already become apparent between the two masters. Perugino's painting, one of the Quattrocento frescoes in the Sistine chapel, shows a calm and order that stand out against the frenzied restlessness of works by contemporary Central Italian artists such as Botticelli and Filippino Lippi. Perugino exploits the geometry of the piazza and the discipline of the architecture to the same effect as Leonardo does in the *Last Supper*. He has less grasp of psychological coherence, however, and the background is full of distracting action and purely decorative details such as the elegant silhouettes of the trees. By contrast, in his *Marriage of the Virgin*, Raphael reduces the composition to its essentials, using just the occasional background figure to help define space, and turning the landscape into a hazy generalization. In addition he keeps characterization to a minimum: the gentle inclination of the priest's head suffices to indicate his reverence, and the intent youth breaking

◁**64 Leonardo da Vinci**
Mona Lisa, 1503–5
Musée National du Louvre, Paris

The hold this painting exerts over the imagination was demonstrated when fanatical Italian Nationalists stole it in the belief that it should reside in its country of origin.

65 Pietro Perugino
Delivery of the Keys to St. Peter, 1481
Sistine Chapel, Vatican, Rome

Christ handing the keys of Heaven to St. Peter is a subject much loved of Popes who see themselves as St. Peter's spiritual descendants.

his rod tells the story with poignant economy.

In 1501 Raphael was called to Rome to paint a series of frescoes in the papal apartments of the Vatican, known as the *Stanze*. The first room that he decorated contains the famous *School of Athens*, a work which both in its subject-matter (Plato, Aristotle and other great classical philosophers involved in heated discussion) and in its monumental classical setting is generally considered as the summation of High Renaissance ideals. The harmonious organization of the picture surface that characterized *The Marriage of the Virgin* is here brought to its ultimate perfection, and is accompanied by such massive figures and forms as to make his earlier paintings seem delicate and insubstantial. The artistic influence that can be held largely responsible for the unbelievably rapid evolution of Raphael's style was undoubtedly provided by Michelangelo, who at the time was working only a few hundred feet away from him in the Sistine chapel.

Raphael's extraordinary flexibility as a painter (a quality that somehow contradicts the popular image of him as the serene genius of the Renaissance) led to even further changes of style in the decoration of the subsequent *Stanze*. Whereas the *Schoool of Athens* represented a moment of perfect balance and poise, the frescoes in the *Stanza d'Eliodoro* reveal Raphael to be a restless experimenter. The *Liberation of St. Peter* (pl. 67) has a sensational quality, both in terms of its technical virtuosity and of its treatment of subject-matter, which is not to be found in his earlier work. The wall on which it was painted provided an exceptionally difficult challenge to an artist as it had a window in the middle of it which not only broke up the picture surface but which also let in a sufficient amount of light to impair the spectator's vision. Raphael had a brilliant solution; he divided the painting into three sections and set the story at night. Peter's cell was placed directly above the window, and the luminous brilliance of the angel who has come to free him echoes the real light which enters the room;

66 Raphael
Marriage of the Virgin, 1504
Pinacoteca di Brera, Milan

The flowering of Joseph's rod was
the sign that he had been divinely
selected to marry the Virgin; hence
the disappointed suitor's annoyance
with his rod.

moreover, the way in which the staggering soldier on the left hand side
of the composition shields his glance mirrors the spectator's own
reaction in trying to see clearly what is happening in the central
section. Apart from displaying such considerable ingenuity, Raphael
has represented a nocturnal scene with a degree of realism which one
does not always associate with his work.

In later life Raphael employed an increasing number of assistants.
They helped him with the never-ceasing stream of commissions that
flooded in once he became properly established in Rome, but he still
found time to execute major works himself, so long as they were on a
relatively small scale. One such is the portrait of *Pope Leo, X with
Giulio de Medici and Luigi Rossi*. This early example of a group portrait,
though lacking in psychological unity, perhaps because it is taken from
three separate drawings, is remarkable for the skill with which Raphael
subordinates the heads of the cardinals to that of the Pope. The use of a

very simple range of colour to achieve a genuinely rich effect in this work is characteristic of Raphael at his best.

In Victorian times Raphael was known as the master of the 'Sweet Madonnas'; and it is these works of his that have largely compounded the misleading notion that he was essentially a sentimental painter. Although his Madonnas display a degree of tenderness that is rarely to be found in the work of earlier painters, there is nothing insipid in the boldness of their compositions, or in the liveliness of some of their details. *The Sistine Madonna* (pl. 68) is his masterpiece in this field. The theatrical conception of this picture is not immediately obvious, but eventually it becomes clear that the vision of the Madonna standing on a globe symbolizing the world is bounded by open curtains suspended from a rail at the top, and by a ledge at the bottom. With apparent casualness, Raphael has Saint Sixtus place his tiara on the ledge, but nobody would be deceived into regarding the composition as anything but meticulously thought out. The balance of the picture is exactly calculated so that the two angels look up and down respectively, and even the curtains, although asymmetrically disposed, subtly counteract each other. But in spite of the extreme intellectual clarity of his conception, Raphael showed himself to be sufficiently relaxed in his outlook, both towards art and religion, to incorporate such humorous details as the bemused cherubs.

In contrast to Raphael, Michelangelo was not primarily a painter; his favourite art was sculpture, and he does not seem to have painted for pleasure. When in 1505 he was called from his native Florence to work for Julius II in Rome, he had expected to embark on a monumental

67 Raphael
The Liberation of St. Peter, 1512–14
Stanza d'Eliodoro, Vatican, Rome

Never before has an artist confronted the obvious problem that to see a man in prison you have to look through bars.

68 Raphael
The Sistine Madonna (with the Saints Sixtus and Barbara), 1513–16
Gemäldegalerie, Dresden

In keeping with the Renaissance concern with audience participation, it is we who are granted a vision of the Virgin and not the more worthy figures depicted in the painting.

69 Michelangelo Buonarroti ▷
General View of the Sistine Chapel Ceiling, Vatican, Rome

A comparison of the *Fall of Man* with the later *Creation of Adam* shows Michelangelo developing a greater economy of composition, in this case reducing the design to two gigantic forms confronting one another on a diagonal.

sculptural project. This, however, was shelved, and the story goes that the architect Bramante, a rival of Michelangelo, arranged for him to be given the challenging task of painting the ceiling of the Sistine Chapel in order to bring about his fall from favour.

The Sistine Chapel already contained frescoes painted in the late 15th century, and Michelangelo fitted his work into an existing scheme. The walls were decorated with two complementary narratives, concentrating on Moses and Christ respectively, and dealing in theological terms with Man's life in the Age of Law, and in the Age of Grace. Michelangelo concerned himself with the time before the Law, from the *Creation* to the *Drunkeness of Noah*: by placing the scene of the *Separation of Light from Dark* above the High Altar, however, Michelangelo intended that the whole cycle should be read in a sequence and should illustrate the Neo-Platonic doctrine that life must be a progression from the slavery of the body to the liberation of the soul in God. As a decoration the Sistine ceiling is an outstanding achievement in that Michelangelo was able to place over 300 figures in an architectural framework of extreme complexity and yet achieve a harmonious whole (pl. 69). But what was especially remarkable about the Sistine ceiling was the use of the nude on an unprecedented scale,

◁ **70 Michelangelo Buonarroti**
The Last Judgment, 1536–41
Sistine Chapel, Vatican, Rome

Michelangelo has given to St. Bartholomew the features of his mocking critic, Pietro Aretino, while the flayed skin he holds incorporates a distorted self-portrait.

not just for sensual effect, but to express emotions in the directest possible manner without the distraction of clothing. In 1510, when the first half of the ceiling was completed, the scaffolding was taken down and Michelangelo had the opportunity to study the effect of his work from the ground. This cannot have been as powerful as he had intended, as in the second half he made the figures larger, more dynamic, with even greater animation in their poses.

Over a quarter of a century later Michelangelo executed another fresco in the Sistine Chapel, the colossal *Last Judgement* (pl. 70) on the wall behind the High Altar. By this date, in the more puritanical atmosphere of the Counter-Reformation, the artist's use of nudes in a religious setting had begun to seem offensive, and later in the century a painter called Daniele da Volterra was to be asked to cover the figures' genitalia with draperies. But the controversial reception with which the *Last Judgement* was met at the time may also have resulted from the work's uncompromising severity. Normally artists made the Last Judgement a work of contrast, setting the exultation of the blessed against the misery of the damned. Michelangelo has the mouth of hell rising out of the altar, and the upper part of the wall may be taken as signifying heaven; but the population of both zones is equally and singularly lacking in joy.

The *Last Judgement* reflects the violent pessimism of Michelangelo's religious beliefs, with the Virgin failing to intercede on behalf of suffering humanity, and the Almighty about to destroy his creation.

71 Andrea del Sarto
The Madonna of the Harpies, 1517
Galleria degli Uffizi, Florence

The 'Harpies' of the title, who are the 'Fates' of Greek Mythology, refer to the creatures on the Madonna's pedestal.

The mood of intense despair persisted in Michelangelo's last paintings, the frescoes of the *Crucifixion of St. Peter* and the *Conversion of St. Paul* in the Cappella Paolina in the Vatican. Only in his final sculptures of the Pietà and in his last drawings of the Crucifixion did his art become at once more compassionate and less devoid of hope.

Although they are sometimes regarded as showing a radical break

73 Jacopo Pontormo
Lamentation over the Dead Christ,
1525–8
S. Felicita, Cappella Capponi,
Florence

It is typical of the way in which
Pontormo constructs his
compositions solely with figures that
the cross should be omitted from his
'Deposition'.

◁ **72 Rosso Fiorentino**
Moses defending the Daughters of Jethro,
c. 1523
Galleria degli Uffizi, Florence

Figures in mannerist paintings such
as this seem to struggle more with
some anguish within themselves than
with their assailants.

with the generation of Michelangelo and Raphael, the painters who
followed them actually represented a perfectly consistent development
of their ideas in one of two directions: either towards an extreme of
violence or towards one of elegant refinement. In considering the
Florentines of the succeeding generation, however, it is best to set the
scene by looking first at the work of a contemporary of Raphael and
Michelangelo who was active entirely in Florence. Andrea del Sarto,
even more than artists like Fra Bartolomeo and Albertinelli, represents
the point of departure for Rosso and Pontormo; his *Madonna of the
Harpies* (pl. 71) is, in a sense, the Florentine equivalent of the *Sistine
Madonna*. The details which attracted Rosso and Pontormo are the
lively grimaces of the red-faced angels, the mannered poses of the
saints, and the rich colour and intricate folds of the drapery. What

these later artists lost was Andreas' clarity of pictorial construction, and his combination of intimacy and monumentality.

An extreme example of the violent tendency in Italian art of this later period is Rosso's picture of *Moses Defending the Daughters of Jethro* (pl. 72). Enthralled by Michelangelo's muscular renditions of the male nude, most readily available to him in a cartoon of the Battle of Cascina in the Palazzo Vecchio in Florence, he fills the canvas with violent action. Conventional perspective and spacing are ignored in a conscious attempt to crowd the picture, and forms deliberately burst beyond the the confines of the frame.

Pontormo's *Lamentation over the Dead Christ* (pl. 73) displays a similar restlessness and emotional intensity, but he achieves this effect in an entirely different and more elegant way. Whereas Rosso's figures are firmly rooted to the ground, Pontormo's seem almost to float in the air with balletic grace. The startling use of light blues and pinks (an effect which has admittedly been exaggerated in recent years by the oxidization of certain of the colours) only serves to heighten the unreal, mystical quality of the work.

The eccentric style shown by such paintings, often called Mannerism, is sometimes given a cultural and historical explanation which specifically links it with the Sack of Rome in 1527. Certainly this must have had a profound effect on the lives of everyone living in the city at the time. Whether it provides an adequate explanation of the development of Mannerism must be doubted, however, in view of the fact that many artists, including Raphael in his irrationally-composed *Transfiguration* which was left unfinished at his death in 1520, had begun to reject the values of the High Renaissance before the Sack, and many other artists were in any case not resident in Rome.

The danger of relating historical events, or even incidents in an artist's life, to his art is also illustrated by the general tendency to describe Mannerism as the product of neurosis. Both Pontormo and Parmigianino were reputedly insane, but it is not clear why one should attribute either the careful deliberation of the former's *Lamentation* or the refined elegance of the latter's *Madonna with the Long Neck* (pl. 74) to the workings of deranged minds. Parmigianino, as his name suggests, came from Parma, and if his style owes something to the early influence of Correggio, it is Raphael who had a greater influence on his mature manner. He may well have seen Raphael's *Sistine Madonna* in Piacenza before he ever went to Rome, but his journey to the southern capital was to induce that classic and grandiose expression of his debt to Raphael, his *Vision of St. Jerome*, now in the National Gallery, London. Parmigianino's later works such as the *Madonna with the Long Neck* show the artist developing a more independent and personal style. Although the head of the Madonna, with her eyes looking downwards and her hair tied in an elaborate coiffure, is ultimately derived from the head of St. Barbara in the *Sistine Madonna*, other aspects of the picture such as the elongation of the proportions, the compressed row of angels' heads and the juxtaposition of large foreground figures with a minute one in the background, are entirely personal to Parmigianino.

The Mannerist style, although rather strange to the modern eye, was immediately popular and spread out from its beginnings in Rome both widely and rapidly. Even Siena, for so long an artistic backwater, was ready and willing to accommodate the singular talent of Domenico Beccafumi. Perhaps Sodoma, a slightly older Sienese who worked

74 Parmigianino
The Madonna with the Long Neck,
c. 1534
Galleria degli Uffizi, Florence

The elongated column in the
background is a deliberate jibe at those
theorists who maintained that columns
should reproduce human proportions.

75 Angelo Bronzino
The Princess Isabella de'Medici, 1542
Galleria degli Uffizi, Florence

Bronzino, who in his portraits
usually endows the sitter with frosty
aristocratic elegance, unbends
slightly in this rendering of a child.

with Raphael in Rome and who was reputedly depicted in the *School of Athens*, paved the way for Beccafumi by bringing the modern style back to Siena; but Beccafumi was responsible for taking it a good deal further. It may be that on occasion he went too far even for contemporary tastes. The *St. Michael Routing the Rebel Angels* is a second version which the artist submitted to the Church of San Niccolò after the rejection of an earlier and even more violent interpretation now in the Siena Pinacoteca. Here, in contrast to the first version, a deliberate division is set up (in imitation of Last Judgement imagery) between the twisted sufferings of the damned and the seraphic ranks of the blessed. Stunning effects of fire and darkness are similarly contrasted with the bright colours of the heavenly host. These very light tonalities are a speciality of Beccafumi's and he uses them to particularly spectacular advantage in his frescoes, the best of which are in the Siena Town Hall.

The danger of a style aiming to achieve an elegant artificiality is that it will completely lose touch with the emotional foundations which it is meant to be refining. This is precisely what seems to have occurred in the later works of Bronzino, Pontormo's adopted son and artistic heir, which are characterized by a profusion of nudes painted in feeble imitation of Michelangelo. As a portraitist, however, Bronzino's achievements are considerable. He replaced the disturbing psychological intensity of Pontormo's portraits with a bland and more straightforward mode of representation that has been favoured by stately homes and boardrooms ever since. He was the favourite artist of the Grand Duke of Florence, Cosimo de'Medici, a man who had inherited few of the intellectual interests of his 15th-century predecessors. The main characteristic of Cosimo's artistic patronage was the commissioning of works to strengthen the dynastic image of the Medicis: and Bronzino's impassive icon-like portraits were ideally suited for this task. Even when painting a child (pl. 75), as in his picture in the Uffizi (which probably depicts Cosimo's daughter Mia), Bronzino did not indulge in the sentimentality generally reserved for portraits of this sort, but rather showed an aloof and unsmiling figure constrained by a stiffly elegant costume, with a Medici emblem.

If artificiality could lead to an impasse by excluding emotion altogether, then at the other end of the scale violence was equally difficult to sustain. A dynamic manner of painting, if carried to excess, could result in sheer vulgarity, as is exemplified in many of the late works by Giulio Romano. Romano had in fact started his career as a leading assistant to Raphael and had contributed to the *Stanza Eliodoro* and the *Transfiguration*. His style had changed dramatically, however, by the time he became court painter to the notoriously pleasure-seeking Federigo Gonzaga, Duke of Mantua. Federigo's main interests in life and art were summarized in a favourite emblem of his in which a

76 Giulio Romano
The Bath of Cupid and Psyche (detail), 1527–31
Palazzo del Tè, Sala di Psyche, Mantua

This light-hearted treatment of an erotic story owes much to Raphael's example in the 'Loggia di Psyche' of the Farnesina Palace in Rome.

lizard was accompanied by the words 'what does not affect him, tortures me', an allusion to this animal's apparent ability to withstand love. The exuberant frescoes which Giulio Romano painted of the story of Cupid and Psyche (pl. 76) for Federigo's country retreat, the Palazzo del Tè, have a coarse vitality, and are appropriately full of explicit pornography. Equally entertaining are his frescoes in the Sala dei Giganti (pl. 77) in the same palace. It is only possible to show a detail of this decoration, because Giulio's illusionistic horror show of the Fall of the Giants from Olympus covers the walls, doors and ceiling of this comparatively small room. The overall effect is one of lumbering comedy and caricature, but one is also made to feel quite genuinely that the world is crashing in ruins about one's head.

The state to which Italian art was reduced to at the end of the 16th century is reflected in such paintings as Jacopo Zucchi's *Cupid and Psyche* (pl. 78). The pose of the Cupid is probably derived from the statue of Dawn from Michelangelo's Medici tomb in Florence; but the erotic and humorous context in which it is used is entirely different. It is interesting to compare Zucchi's painting with another by an artist working twenty years later: the *Victorious Amor* by Caravaggio (pl. 92) is no less salacious or witty, but it has an immediacy which is entirely lacking in Zucchi's supremely elegant and artificial creation. Artists of Zucchi's and Romano's generations had been overwhelmed by such geniuses as Raphael and Michelangelo, and had reacted by taking elements of these artists' styles to their ludicrous conclusion.

77 Giulio Romano
The Fall of the Giants, 1532–6
Palazzo del Tè, Sala dei Giganti, Mantua

Giulio Romano belongs to that unfortunate group of artists who possess genius but no talent, as this detail shows.

78 Jacopo Zucchi
Cupid and Psyche, 1589
Galleria Borghese, Rome

The mannerist enthusiasm for
shimmering unreal surfaces becomes
rather stifling as the century draws to
its close.

The Northern Renaissance

By the year 1500 Italian Humanism had begun to influence advanced intellectual circles in Northern Europe. In Germany, The Netherlands and France, men began to look into the writings of classical authors for alternative sources of scientific knowledge and moral values, not necessarily in rejection of Christianity, but in order to chasten it and arrive at a clearer idea of its real meaning. Christian Humanism sought to go back to first principles and thus secure the Faith on surer foundations, placing an emphasis upon reform that led to the Lutheran Reformation and the rise of Protestantism. In the 15th century, Italian painting had been generally considered less advanced than that of the North; painters had looked to The Netherlands for leadership and had seen the pilgrimage to Bruges, Brussels and Ghent as an essential aspect of their education. But during the first half of the 16th century, the situation changed. The focal point of European art was now Italy, and Italian painters set the standard against which all art was judged. 'From Rome bring home skill in drawing, and from Venice the ability to paint' the artist Karel van Mander advised in 1604, defining a programme of training that had been common among young Northern artists since the middle of the 16th century.

The wide range and contrast of styles in 16th-century German painting was a reflection of the fragmentary political state of the nation, which was split up into small principalities and Free Cities. Art patronage centred upon such provincial courts as that of the Elector Frederick the Wise of Saxony and his successors, who maintained Lucas Cranach as their court artist, or that of Albrecht of Brandenburg, Archbishop of Mainz, who employed Mathis Niethardt Gothardt, commonly known as Grünewald.

In Grünewald's hands a late Gothic style of painting became a vehicle for the expression of visionary excitement. The crowning work of his career, the *Isenheim Altarpiece* (pl. 79, 80), completed in 1515, is saturated with the at times harrowing, at times seraphic imagery of the 14th-century mystic St. Bridget of Sweden. In the morbid realism with which Christ's wounds are catalogued, so that each trace of suffering will tell, and the almost unendurable intensity with which his death agonies are expressed, the Crucifixion relates closely to her vision of Christ on the cross: 'His feet were curled around the nails as round door hinges, towards the other side . . . the Crown of Thorns was impressed on his head; it covered half his forehead. The blood ran in many rills . . . then the colour of Death spread.' Such imagery could only be given palpable and shockingly convincing form by an artist in command of the naturalistic idiom of the North. Yet the artist's personal involvement with his subjects has led him to deform the laws that govern the temporal world, in order to suggest the supernatural. The landscape is sunk in a primal darkness and yet the scene of the sacrifice is lit by a harsh and penetrating radiance, which reveals the gigantic figure of Christ twice the size of the other protagonists. This is a literal expression of the words of the

79 Matthias Grünewald
Christ on the Cross with the Virgin, St John the Evangelist, St Mary Magdalen and St John the Baptist (the Isenheim Altarpiece, central panel), 1512–16 Musée d'Unterlinden, Colmar

The chief saints of the Antonite order were invoked against specific diseases: St. Anthony for fever, St. Sebastian for the plague and St. John the Baptist and Evangelist for epilepsy.

Baptist inscribed on the panel, 'He must increase as I must decrease'; the scale of the figure also serves as a jolt to the viewer, making it clear that the work is dealing with a region of experience beyond Nature. In the *Resurrection*, Christ is transfigured by light; the shot rays of the aureole that surrounds him blur his human likeness, and turn the shroud that winds up after him into a riot of coloured light. The dynamic interpretation of the scene, with Christ appearing to explode out of the tomb and send the Roman guards reeling, was unprecedented both in art and in religious literature. Moreover, whatever Grünewald took from other artists, Netherlandish and Italian alike, has been forged in the white heat of his imagination into something completely unique and personal.

Like Dürer, Grünewald seems to have been caught up in the fervent religious climate of the day and to have become a committed Lutheran. He was probably involved in some way in the Peasants' Revolt of 1525, one of the more extreme breakdowns in the social order provoked by the Reformation; this may in fact have been what lost him his job as court painter to the Archbishop of Mainz in 1526. He spent his last years in Halle, a city sympathetic to Protestantism, and amongst effects found on his death was 'much Lutheran trash'. The

80 Matthias Grünewald ▷
The Resurrection of Christ (right wing
of the Isenheim Altarpiece, first
opening), 1512–16

Johann von Orlineo and Guido
Guersi, the donors of the altarpiece,
belonged to the Antonite monastery
in Isenheim, the hospital of which
treated epilepsy, blood and skin
diseases.

subjectivity of Grünewald's art and the visionary cast of his imagination are both the product of troubled times, and the expression of a
particularly urgent brand of faith.

Another German artist, Albrecht Dürer, was the pivotal figure in
Northern painting at the beginning of the 16th century. His insatiable
thirst for experience, his curiosity and his desire to record his
knowledge in theoretical writings mark him out as one of the first
'Renaissance' personalities of the North. Dürer owed much to the
Italian achievement, but his reasons for visiting Italy as a young man
and later actually taking up residence in Venice (at a time when most
German artists still bowed to Netherlandish rather than to Italian art)
reflected a desire to confirm and encourage artistic tendencies he had
already shown during his early career Nuremberg, where German
humanists and antiquarians had stirred his interest in the art and
literature of the classical past. Dürer consciously matched himself
against the standards of Italian painting. His *Feast of the Rose Garlands*
of 1506 owes its splendour of colour to Venetian art and displays a
grasp of the formal qualities of Italian art as a whole, yet, in the context
of the Venetian painting of the day, it stands out as a remarkably
mature example of High Renaissance classicism. Dürer was as much a
leader as a follower in these years, exploring new artistic channels even
more avidly than his Italian contemporaries. His *Self-portrait* (pl. 81) of
1500 illustrates the point. In the Prado *Self-portrait* of 1498, he had
painted himself as a dandified and urbane 'gentiluomo', self-consciously reflecting the higher social status enjoyed by artists in Italy. In the
later work this façade has been stripped away to reveal Dürer's
fascination with his own powers of creation; it recalls the traditional
image of Christ as the 'Salvator Mundi', implying that the artist's
genius is an aspect of the creative power of God. The concept of the
artist as creator rather than craftsman was new in Northern painting;
and the concept of the work of art as a personal statement was
unprecedented even in Italian art.

The first years of the new century were those of the artist's
maximum absorption with Italian art. The influence of Leonardo, for
example, is apparent in the stress upon harmonious formal values in
the *Adoration of the Magi* of 1504. Dürer interested himself in the work
of his Italian contemporaries as part of a larger programme of study
embracing the whole classical tradition and designed ultimately to
revive the true spirit of Antiquity. Such a work as the *Adam and Eve*
engraving of 1503 shows him returning to the most basic and time-
hallowed principles; the figures were constructed with ruler and
compass according to the proportional system of Vitruvius. The
artist's stay in Venice in 1505–6 was partially inspired by a desire to
research literary sources on the lost paintings of Antiquity. He believed
that the Italians possessed secrets concerning the laws of geometry,
proportion and perspective that he must wrest from them. Hence the
importance of his theoretical writings, initiated with the *Four Books of
Human Proportion* in 1512, which were intended to inform the artists of
Germany of the true principles upon which art must be based.

The adoption of Italian ideas by Northern artists generally resulted
in a somewhat uneasy synthesis. Even Dürer's work has a certain
tension, as if the artist's choice of style were more a matter of will than
innate sympathy. Yet one painter of the next generation achieved a
stylistic balance which suggests that, in principle, the two traditions
were not incompatible. Hans Holbein the Younger was the most

81 Albrecht Dürer
Self-portrait, 1500
Alte Pinakothek, Munich

Although commentators have seen
narcissism in Dürer's personality
especially because of the existence of
a nude self-portrait, self-
consciousness is part of humanism.

accomplished painter of the High Renaissance in the North. He spent
his early years in one of the first cities to be affected by Italian
Humanism, Augsburg, and received his training in one of the most
innovatory workshops there, that of his own father. Yet his response
to Italian ideas was generally more reflective than that of his
contemporaries, and even after his probable visit to Northern Italy in
1518–19, the essential character of his style remained indebted above
all to Dürer and Grünewald. His *Dead Christ* of 1521 recalls Grünewald
in particular, yet the harsh reality is observed with an emotional
control that is Holbein's own. It is this objectivity that enabled him to
assimilate High Renaissance classicism more fully than any other
northern master. In the *Madonna of Burgomeister Meyer* (pl. 83) of 1526–
8, northern realism has been combined with an Italian sense of
monumental design. Figures are organized and controlled within a
closely-knit triangular composition reminiscent of Leonardo, and the
younger children have an athletic grace which recalls the putti of
Raphael. But it is the sheer visual accuracy of Holbein's work that
defines his position in the art of the period. The 'donor' portrait in the
Madonna of Burgomeister Meyer, clearly illustrates his ability to seize a
likeness with disarming objectivity; the painter's personality and
attitude are not allowed to obtrude upon the process of making a
record of his sitter's features. The portraits of Holbein, unlike those of
other great 16th-century masters, do not generally attempt to characterize the sitter or cast him within a definite mood or situation; they
maintain a strong sense of decorum and restraint, capturing him in a
state of static self-composure. Our idea of Holbein's artistic and
imaginative range is distorted by the fact that it is as a portraitist (above
all as court portraitist to Henry VIII) that he is most famous. It should
be remembered that he also painted monumental murals and decorative house-façades, made book illustrations, and even designed jewellery and furniture. Most notably, he was active as a religious painter,
but this aspect of his career was blighted by the iconoclastic tenor of
the Reformation, which dramatically removed the demand for religious images.

Not all German artists felt it necessary to come to terms with the
Italian achievement and many asserted their independence and originality by deliberately espousing the indigenous late Gothic tradition.
Dürer spoke of such artists as growing up like 'wild ungrafted trees'.
The early art of Lucas Cranach, for example, shows a markedly
subjective interpretation of biblical themes. Like Dürer, Cranach
considered himself a creator not a craftsman, not humbly mirroring
the natural world but seeking to galvanize and transform it in the heat
of his imagination. His early work, conceived in Vienna before he took
up the position of painter to the Saxon court in 1505 (see below),
illustrates this attitude. In such works as the *Rest on the Flight to Egypt*
(1504) and the *Crucifixion* (1503), a restless linearity, suggesting inner
agitation, is fused with a highly sensitive, painterly rendering of the
light and colour of the Danube valley.

Cranach's early work, along with that of Dürer, was the foundation
of the so-called 'Danube School', a group of artists who shared a
fascination for the landscape along the Danube. The key members of
the group were Wolf Huber and Albrecht Altdorfer. Altdorfer, who
worked mainly in the city of Regensburg, developed a highly
idiosyncratic style, with odd proportions and glaring colours. But his
most original work was his landscape painting; indeed, his *Danube*

Landscape of *c.* 1500–10 may be the first pure landscape in the history of painting. This work captures the spirit of the region and yet the landscape is highly stylized, with trees of no identifiable species made the pretext for strange calligraphic displays. Altdorfer's manipulative attitude towards landscape is evident too in the central work of his career, the *Battle of Issus* (pl. 85) of 1529. This was one of a series of battle-pieces commissioned by William IV of Bavaria for his palace in Munich. In an age fascinated by the artist's capacity to seize the varied aspects of natural phenomena, and ascribing an almost God-like power to the artist who could conjure up effects that vied in grandeur with those of creation itself, Altdorfer's picture was a *tour de force*, intended to stagger its audience. The artist shows a panoramic view from high above the warring parties in order to stress the insignificance of Man's aspirations when set against the vastness of the universe. The battle is a swarm of figures and even Alexander the Great is only identified by the tassel of the plaque that points straight down at him. Even his supreme ambition is frail in comparison with the mysterious forces that govern the natural world. The landscape, in unison with the human event, seems to undergo some cosmic disturbance; the clouds

82 Albrecht Dürer
The Four Apostles, 1526 (left-hand panel: St John the Evangelist and St Peter; right-hand panel: St Mark and St Paul)
Alte Pinakothek, Munich

Part of a project for a *Sacra Conversazione* which was shelved in 1525 when outdated by the Reformation.

83 Hans Holbein the Younger
Madonna of the Burgomaster of Basle, Jakob Meyer zum Hasen, 1526/8
Schlossmuseum, Darmstadt

The Burgomeister, Jacob Meyer, requested that Holbein should include in this devout family group not only his living wife, Dorothea, but behind her, his dead wife, Magdalene.

85 Albrecht Altdorfer ▷
Victory of Alexander the Great over Darius, King of the Persians, at the Battle of Issus, 1529
Alte Pinakothek, Munich

Altdorfer combines the information contained both in a map and a plan of a battle with a convincing atmospheric landscape.

84 Lucas Cranach the Elder
The Nymph of the Spring, c. 1537
Musée des Beaux Arts et d'Archéologie, Besançon

Cranach's figure combines a pose derived from classical representations of Venus with the coarse features and angular anatomy wholly characteristic of Nordic art.

break apart to send a slanting beam of sunlight over the victorious army of the Greeks as if God had ordained Alexander's victory. The pantheistic response to landscape is fundamental to the Danube School. As a later 16th-century German mystic expressed it: 'As the air fills everything and is not confined to one place, as the light of the sun overfloods the whole earth, is not on earth and nonetheless makes all things verdant, thus God dwells in everything and everything dwells in Him.'

The turning point in Cranach's career came in 1505 when he was appointed court painter to Duke Frederick the Wise of Saxony and his successors. His new role presented him with much greater demands than he had so far had to face, and required a more pragmatic and flexible approach. He was called upon not only to create religious works, mythologies and dynastic portraits, but also to decorate castles with allegorical murals, to make pictorial records of celebrated hunts, and even to paint each day's catch in water-colours; and in 1542 he executed 2000 shields for the Saxon army. The sheer scale of work demanded of him required that much of it be delegated to assistants, and the artist accordingly modified his style so that it would be easier to copy and lend itself to mass-production. The rich colouristic and tonal variation of his earlier period are chastened and the emphasis placed upon line; interior modelling of forms is reduced to the minimum required to suggest volume, and the figures have the graceful weightlessness of silhouettes. Cranach's scenes from mythology, his Judgements of Paris, Venuses, Cupids and Sleeping Nymphs illustrate the fact that the Renaissance made not only the learned classical texts fashionable but also the salacious and erotic ones. The pert Saxon beauties who populate these works are artistically far removed from the classical models that so deeply influenced Italian

86 Hieronymus Bosch
The Garden of Earthly Delights
(central panel), 1503–4
Museo del Prado, Madrid

Bosch taxes both mind and eye. The
meaning is obscure and visually the
juxtaposition of figures, animals, and
semi-organic inventions remains
irrational and inexplicable.

mythological painting. Their figures are shaped by his incisive line into
sinuous, elongated forms that are all the more sensuous for their
artificiality.

In The Netherlands of this time painters were split between the
'Romanists', who elected to emulate the example of Italy, and the
Realists, who chose to mine the still rich resources of the native
tradition. For some, such as Jan van Scorel, Bernard van Orley and
Martin van Heemskerck, Italian art became something of a cult, and
certainly by mid-century the pilgrimage to Italy became the pivotal
point of the young painter's education. The 'Romanists' believed in the
Italian credo of the artist as genius, and would have confined
themselves to religious and mythological subjects, had not portraiture
been the only safe way of earning a living. This faction found

particular favour at the court of the Hapsburg Regent of the Netherlands, Margaret of Austria, who ruled the country from 1494 to 1530, and her successor, Mary of Hungary. Here the cultural climate encouraged the dominance of 'Romanistic' painting because Italy was considered as a model to be emulated in all aspects of art and life.

The unique cast of Hieronymous Bosch's imagination led him to very different sources, not in Italian art but in the backwaters of the Netherlandish tradition that his contemporaries would have considered retardataire and eccentric. His work owes its unusual imagery to the drolleries and grotesques that creep around the edges of medieval manuscripts and the gargoyles that leer at mankind from the heights of Gothic cathedrals. Yet he invests these fabulous inventions with an uncanny vitality, realizing them with a precision that reveals him as the heir of van Eyck. In his scenes of daemonic torment, such as the *Temptation of Saint Anthony* or the hell scene from the *Garden of Earthly Delights*, Bosch is able to make the activities of diabolical forces all the more palpable and harrowing by contradicting the laws that govern commonsense reality without abandoning highly naturalistic detail. *The Garden of Earthly Delights* (pl. 86) is an elaborate example of the moralizing genre that was a speciality of the painter. The central panel illustrates humanity's bondage to the pleasures of the flesh, alluding by a variety of literal and symbolic means to the ways in which the fleeting satisfactions of sin blind mankind to the world of the spirit.

The increasing popularity of art-collecting at this time resulted in a broadening of the range of styles and types of subject-matter. Many painters became specialists in a particular genre and explored new

87 Pieter Bruegel the Elder
Hunters in the Snow, 1565
Kunsthistorisches Museum, Vienna

This astonishingly tangible and atmospheric landscape represents February in a cycle of the twelve months.

subject-matter, in a speculative fashion, in order to open up new areas of the market. They could now focus on the particular branch of painting that they found most sympathetic, rather than allowing their work to be determined by commissions. Pieter Breugel began his career following in the footsteps of Bosch, but eventually abandoned the fantastic world of the older master in favour of a more realistic, if equally idiosyncratic vision of the world. Though depicted with candour and some sympathy, incisive observation and an evident relish for the seamier side of life, the peasant scenes that were his speciality were in fact probably designed to give amusement to rather supercilious middle- and upper-class connoisseurs.

The most important painters of Eastern Europe in the 16th century were Bartolomeus Spranger and Guiseppe Arcimboldo, who both worked for the court of the Hapsburg King Rudolf II of Bohemia. Arcimboldo was a court favourite and artistic impresario who spent most of his energy searching for works of art, jewels, curiosities for the King's art collection and the intriguing display of human and natural miracles he kept in his private 'Kunstkammer'. The fecundity of his imagination made Arcimboldo the ideal court artist, since he could always come up with some outlandish and amusing invention to delight his patrons. His speciality was abstruse allegory that tested the spectator's erudition, and 'composite heads', which are ingenious portraits created out of inanimate objects. Rudolf's father had ordered all the characters of the court to be recorded in this way; the cook's features, for instance, were built up out of pots and pans.

Spranger had received his training in what was now the most lively artistic centre in The Netherlands, Antwerp, and like all ambitious Netherlandish artists he had travelled to Italy in order to give his style a

88 Pieter Bruegel the Elder
The Peasants' Dance, c. 1568
Kunsthistorisches Museum, Vienna

Bruegel includes in this 'Kermesse', or carnival, a chastisement of human sins by hanging an unheeded image of the Madonna on a tree.

89 Giuseppe Arcimboldo
The Fire, 1566
Kunsthistorisches Museum, Vienna

Part of a series representing the four
elements where grotesque heads are
constructed of objects appertaining
to each element.

90 Bartholomeus Spranger
Hercules and Omphale, 1575–80
Kunsthistorisches Museum, Vienna

So subjected is Hercules by his love
for Omphale that he agrees to
exchange his club and lion skin for
her dress and distaff.

final polish. He arrived there in 1565 and spent the next ten years in Parma, Milan, and Rome studying not antique art, but that of Correggio and Parmigianino, and blending their styles into an extravagant and sophisticated hybrid. His elegant and courtly Mannerism is an example of the self-consciously 'stylish' style which had been evolved in Italy during the 1520s and had progressed over the next two decades to dominate art – especially court art – both north and south of the Alps.

The Western Hapsburgs, and in particular the Emperors Charles V and Philip II of Spain, were also distinguished patrons of the arts. Both monarchs amassed fine collections of Netherlandish paintings, by both contemporary and earlier masters; but it was above all Italian art, and especially that of Titian, that caught their imaginations. The most important painter actually to spend most of his career in Spain in this period was the Cretan El Greco. El Greco was not a court painter; his enraptured, visionary style did not accord well with the grave and decorative naturalism favoured by Philip II. It was rather in Toledo, a central power house of Catholic reform in Spain and a focus for the more progressive and articulate factions of religious thought, that he found the kind of sophisticated patronage he required. His work is a highly personal and introspective response to the problem of creating art to express the tenets of the Counter-Reformation. His painting of *The Burial of Count Orgaz* (pl. 91) of 1586–8 commemorates a miracle;

91 El Greco
The Burial of Count Orgaz, 1586
S. Tomè, Toledo

The human reality portrayed in the lower half of the painting, which contrasts with the fantastic vision above, is emphasized in such details as the figure of St. Stephen being reflected in the Count's armour.

in 1323, at the Count's burial in S. Tomè, the Saints Augustine and Stephen appeared and, before the eyes of the stunned congregation, lowered the body into the tomb. In this work the cream of contemporary Toledo society affects various levels of restrained surprise at the miraculous event, as above their heads the sky opens to reveal the Count's soul being carried upwards into the celestial hierarchy. The painting of the divine intervention above is carried out expressed in a style deliberately at variance with that of the temporal reality below.

Baroque Painting in Italy

Around 1600 Rome emerged as the leading art centre in Europe and remained as such throughout most of the 17th century. Artists were attracted here not only from all over Italy but also from France, Germany, Spain, Holland and Flanders. Never before had a single city known such an intensive period of artistic activity, and it was only in Paris during the 19th century that the phenomenon was to be repeated.

Rome's cultural supremacy at this time can partly be interpreted as a triumphant assertion of the Catholic faith after many years of challenge and uncertainty. The defeat of the Turks at Lepanto in 1571 and the increasingly defensive position of Protestantism after the 1570s, meant that the Church's two greatest threats had been contained. From then onwards the papacy could again devote much of its attention to patronage of the arts; and simultaneously the funds at its disposal grew to enormous proportions. This new era of papal patronage began with the election of Sixtus V in 1595. But neither he, nor his two successors, Clement VIII and Paul V, were as enlightened in their artistic tastes as some of their cardinals, most notably the latter's brilliant and gregarious nephew, Scipio Borghese. The outstanding papal patron of the 17th century was Urban VIII. In his passionate enthusiasm not only for art and architecture, but also for scholarship, poetry and music, he had superficially much in common with his humanist forerunners; and his long reign (1624–44) marked the high point of Rome's artistic revival. The artist with whom he was most closely associated, and someone who proved the ideal executant for his ambitious projects, was Gian Lorenzo Bernini; the work of this architect, sculptor and painter is characterized by its stunning virtuosity and has come to represent the most flamboyant expression of the style of art known as the Baroque.

The term Baroque is in many ways a misleading one when used with reference to the great artistic developments which took place in Rome in the first half of the 17th century and which had a profound influence on the art of the next two hundred years. The word was in fact originally coined as a term of abuse to describe architecture that was irregularly shaped and grotesque. Today, it is used indiscriminately for both architecture and painting, and carries connotations of the spectacular and the profusely decorative. While these latter features are present to an unprecedented degree in the Italian art of the 17th century, they are only one aspect of the style. One is struck more by the great variety of paintings in this period, a factor partly explained by the complex, wide-ranging tastes of the patrons. What the works of such disparate artists as Caravaggio, Annibale Carracci, or Domenichino have in common is the least obvious characteristic of the Baroque: namely its reassertion of classical values. Far from wilfully distorting forms or aiming at mere extravagance, the artists of this time rejected the precious and unnatural style adopted by their Mannerist predecessors in favour of an art of emotional directness. This directness was equally expressed in the disconcerting realism of

92 Caravaggio
Victorious Amor, 1596–8
Staatliche Museen, Gemäldegalerie, Berlin West

This painting was intended as a pair to a 'Divine Love' by an incompetent called Baglione – the Devil always gets the best tunes.

93 Caravaggio
The Calling of St Matthew, 1599–1600
S. Luigi dei Francesi, Cappella
Contarelli, Rome

Caravaggio uses the art of the past to
establish the status of the divine
figures in common surroundings;
Christ's gesture recalls that of God
the Father in Michelangelo's *Creation
of Adam.* (cf. pl. 000)

Caravaggio as in the measured simplicity of Domenichino and the
theatrical dynamism of Bernini. A parallel can be found in Catholic
thought of this period, especially in the spiritual outlook of the
recently founded religious orders of the Jesuits and the Oratorians.
Both these Orders opposed monastic withdrawal in favour of an active
participation in the affairs of the world; and instead of holding purely
abstract mystical notions, they believed that man could shape his own
destiny, and that art could vividly render the immaterial.

At the beginning of the 1590's a young painter called Michelangelo
Merisi, originating from the North Italian village of Caravaggio,
settled in Rome after a period of study in Milan. This man, later to be
referred to after the name of his native village, was soon patronized by
the notorious Cardinal Del Monte, who introduced him to what
appears to have been an exclusively homosexual circle of noblemen.
Del Monte himself – who later in life was to repent of his past
behaviour – largely spent his youth in organizing banquets, theatrical
entertainments, and parties where, 'as there were no ladies present, the

dancing was done by boys dressed up as girls'. Much of Caravaggio's earlier art catered in fact for paedophiliac tastes and was largely comprised of portraits of effeminate boys. The most erotic of these portraits was the *Victorious Amor* (pl. 92), a work which one contemporary suggested should be hidden by a curtain. The naked boy's legs are splayed in provocative fashion to offer an unusual glimpse of buttocks and a penis which forms the apex of the composition. Other titillating details include a ruffled bedsheet on which the boy is seated, a feather which brushes gently against his thigh, and a suggestion of discarded clothes in the armour lying on the floor. The work's erotic impact is heightened by the artist's novel technique, which combines extreme realism with a dramatic use of light and shadow.

It was through the intercession of Cardinal Del Monte that Caravaggio obtained his most important Roman commission – the decoration of the Contarini Chapel in San Luigi dei Francesi. The two principal canvases of this Chapel were devoted to the life of St. Matthew. The one representing the saint's martyrdom is the more mannered and conventional of the two, but it displayed yet again the powerful originality of the artist's technique; in addition, X-rays of this work reveal how the artist painted directly onto his canvases without apparently any previous drawing or careful planning. The *Calling of St. Matthew* (pl. 93) is unlike any other previous religious painting. The saint is seen in what appears to be an ordinary Roman tavern of the time and in the company of the fancifully dressed boys associated with the circle of Cardinal Del Monte. The novel idea of rendering a religious scene in contemporary terms is matched by the stark forcefulness of the technique: a vivid band of light breaks into the room at the right hand corner and neatly divides the work in two.

Caravaggio's life was as orthodox and uncompromising as his art; and much of what is known about it comes from police records of the time. A succession of assaults, and such acts as throwing stones against a former landlady's venetian blind, culminated in the killing of a young man in a brawl over a ball game. Two days later, on 31 May 1606, Caravaggio fled from Rome, and thereafter led a peripatetic existence, which took him to Naples, Sicily and even to Malta. His short but eventful life ended with his death from malaria in the summer of 1610.

Not surprisingly Caravaggio's powerful personality, both as a man and as an artist, left a deep impression on his contemporaries. A group of admirers from among his immediate circles in Rome and Naples began to imitate his realism and dramatic lighting; soon the 'Caravaggesque' manner caught on in other parts of Italy and eventually was disseminated throughout Europe. However, few of the artists who are now called the 'Caravaggisti' attained the same degree of subtlety as had Caravaggio himself. For in spite of the latter's shock tactics, his was also an art of exceptional profundity and depth of emotion; these qualities become increasingly apparent in the religious work done after his departure from Rome in 1606. Some of his followers, such as Gentileschi, softened and sentimentalized his manner; and others, such as Ribera (pl. 104), exaggerated and distorted it. And the most lasting legacy of Caravaggio's art was to inspire a widespread fashion for scenes of low life. This had been only a minor and superficial aspect of his work, yet it was the one that could be most easily understood by the public and artists of his time.

It is ironical that Caravaggio's paintings, which to us now make religious subject matter so immediately accessible, had by no means a universal appeal to his contemporaries; in fact they were only appreciated by a sophisticated and enlightened minority. Ironically the peasants, with their lined faces and grime-covered feet, who so often appear in Caravaggio's religious scenes, would themselves have preferred the very different and to us now more academic art of Caravaggio's great rival, Annibale Carracci.

Carracci came to Rome in 1595 from Bologna, having been summoned to fresco the gallery of one of the city's leading palaces, the Palazzo Farnese (pl. 94). Together with his assistants, he was engaged on this decorative scheme for much of the next decade, and the resulting work became for many years one of the most admired sights in all of Rome. Although it was the first of the major fresco cycles of the Baroque, it has none of the unity of composition that characterizes many of the great decorations to come. It is in fact a hybrid work, combining obvious references to Michelangelo's ceiling in the Sistine Chapel, with an irrational decorative scheme that has much in common with many mannerist decorations. What does, however, hold the work together, is its extraordinary energy and the lifelike quality of the figures.

Annibale Carracci was discussed by 17th century writers very much as was Giotto by Vasari – in other words as a painter who had rescued art from the decline into which it had fallen by bringing naturalism back into it. While his art was so much more vital and less mannered than that of his immediate predecessors, it was not of course naturalistic in the sense that Caravaggio's was: the nature that he imitated was an ideal one based on harmonious proportions and a vision of antiquity and the High Renaissance. The fact that his art had so much in common with his great Italian predecessors explains why he enjoyed a wider popularity at the time than did his rival. But his achievement as an artist was a diffuse one. Apart from giving new life to fresco painting and executing a series of religious works that were worthy of Raphael in their fresh simplicity and dignity, he was also capable of portraying modest genre scenes, was a pioneering caricaturist, and played a vital role in the history of landscape painting. In respect of this latter achievement, special mention must be made of four lunettes which he executed for the Chapel of the Palazzo Aldobrandi (now in the Doria-Pamphili Gallery in Rome). In these he subordinated the religious subject matter to an enveloping landscape, which is neither a direct transcription of nature, nor a purely decorative fantasy as is found in the work of many of Carracci's contemporaries: instead it takes its initial inspiration from the countryside near Rome and renders this in a carefully composed and idealized manner. What Carracci achieved in the Aldobrandi lunettes was to be of profound significance for the two most famous French landscapists of the 17th century – Nicolas Poussin and Claude Lorraine.

In about 1605 Carracci suffered a severe nervous breakdown, and painted little during the remaining four years of his life; but his overtly classical and Raphael-inspired style was disseminated by the many Bolognese painters who followed him to Rome. In the first quarter of the 17th century, these Bolognese classicists were indeed to dominate artistic life in the city; and they were in undisputed command during the brief reign of the Bolognese Pope, Gregory XV (1621–23). One of the first of these artists was Guido Reni, who arrived in Rome in 1600. Although it was inevitable that a Bolognese artist should be drawn on arrival in the city into the powerful orbit of Carracci's studio, Reni was

94 Annibale Carracci
Triumph of Bacchus and Ariadne 1597–1604
Palazzo Farnese, Galleria, Rome

The Farnese decorations were executed in celebration of a marriage in the family – hence the riotous jubilance of the scenes.

far less dependent on it than were many of his fellow citizens. From the start he received important commissions of his own, including the *Crucifixion of St. Peter* (1605–6; Vatican Gallery) in which he perversely imitated the dramatic lighting and realism of Caravaggio. This painting represented in fact the closest approximation reached by Reni, or indeed by any Bolognese classicist, to the art of Caravaggio, and differs significantly from the latter's work in its carefully considered classical composition. Reni's major Roman work was his ceiling fresco of *Aurora* for the Casino of the Palazzo Rospigliosi–Pallavicini. As a decorative scheme it is much more unified than Carracci's in the Palazzo Farnese in that it consists of a single *quadro riportato* in a subdued stucco setting. Such simplicity looks forward to the Neoclassical decorations of the 18th century; but the work is by no means austere, being lively, colourful and sensual in its details. In 1616 Reni returned to Bologna where he spent the rest of his life, gambling, notoriously maintaining his virginity, and painting in a sometimes mechanical fashion a whole series of sweetly sentimental devotional pictures which earned him for many years a reputation as one of the greatest artists of all time.

Reni's departure from Bologna left his fellow countryman, Domenichino, as the leading painter in Rome. Domenichino came to the city in 1601, and soon became a favourite pupil of Annibale Carracci. He derived his inspiration from the more austere and disciplined side of his master's art, and like him devoted much time to careful preparatory drawing. In 1608 he found himself in competition with Reni, each artist having to paint a scene from the life of St. Andrew for an Oratory attached to the Church of Gregorio Magno. The works clearly brought out the differences between the two painters, and there was much critical debate at the time as to which was the better; silly stories were even circulated about women who burst into tears in front of Domenichino's fresco while being completely unmoved by Reni's. The fact is that Reni's approach to painting was that of an artist more interested in colourful effects than in intellectual analysis, whereas Domenichino aimed for the greatest economy of composition. It was at about this time that Domenichino entered into a very close friendship with Monsignor Giovanni Battista Agucchi, an amateur art theorist, who advocated classical simplicity and intellectual discipline. Perhaps under the latter's influence the austere side to his art as revealed in the Oratory fresco became more pronounced in later years, culminating in his frescoed scenes of the life of St. Cecilia in the Church of San Luigi dei Francesi, and in his altarpiece *The Last Communion of St. Jerome* of 1613 (pl. 95) in the Church of San Gerolamo della Carità. This latter work, another of the much-acclaimed masterpieces of the 17th century which fell out of fashion during the 19th, represents an extreme moment of classicism in the religious art of this period. The flying putti do not detract from the overall solemnity of the composition; the story is told with the utmost simplicity and directness, with each gesture and expression contributing something to the whole. One should also mention the glimpse of countryside in the background, which is a reminder of the artist's remarkable achievement as a landscapist. An assistant to Carracci in the Aldobrandi lunettes, Domenichino went further than his master in developing an ideal nature reduced only to essentials and yet emanating a haunting and poetic mood.

A very great admirer of Domenichino, and for a short while an

95 Domenichino
The Last Communion of St Jerone, 1614
Pinacoteca Vaticana, Vatican, Rome

Scenes of St. Jerome receiving the
sacrament just before death provided
the Catholic church with propaganda
in favour of the efficacy of Extreme
Unction.

assistant in his studio, was Nicolas Poussin. Poussin, along with
Claude Lorraine, was the major French painter of the 17th century; yet
both he and Claude spent most of their working lives in Rome.
Poussin settled there in 1624, and after a period of real poverty soon
attracted a much sought-after commission to paint an altarpiece for the
Basilica of St. Peter's. Important though this commission was,
however, it was really unsuited to Poussin's talents. He felt simply ill
at ease in these big compositions in which the Roman artists of his day
scored their greatest success. The work was not well received, and it
was to be his only public picture painted in Rome. Whether as a result
of its failure or of a serious illness which he suffered around this time,
Poussin's art subsequently underwent a change of direction. The artist
now began to concentrate exclusively on small-scale horizontal works,

generally of mythological subject matter and with a predominantly landscape background. He even had a change of patrons. Whereas previously he had the support of influential cardinals and aristocrats, he now worked entirely for an elite group of unostentatious middle-class intellectuals, most notable among when was Cassiano del Pozzo, a discerning patron of the arts with a special passion for classical archaeology. Unable to buy any original antiques himself, he commissioned a whole team of artists, including Poussin, to record all the Roman remains that were excavated. Del Pozzo's classical enthusiasms were an undoubted stimulus for an artist who, more than any previous painter, immersed himself in the ancient world and acquired a profound understanding of it.

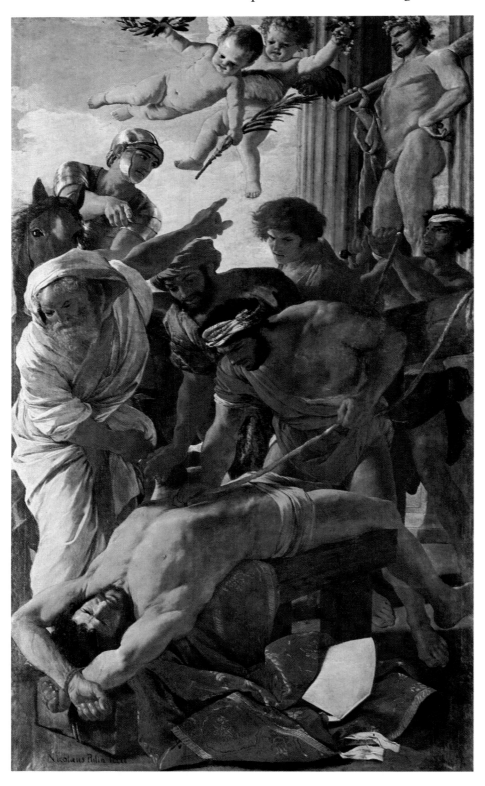

96 Nicolas Poussin
The Martyrdom of St. Erasmus, 1628
Pinacoteca Vaticana, Vatican, Rome

The saint is having his entrails dragged out by a winch for refusing to bow down to a pagan image of Hercules.

97 Nicolas Poussin

Autumn, or: the Spies with the Grapes from the Promised Lands, 1660–4
Musée National du Louvre, Paris

One of four paintings of the 'Seasons' for the Duc de Richelieu; each season is envisaged as a Biblical narrative.

Whereas Poussin always revered the austerity of Domenichino's designs, he was also enamoured in his youth with the art of Titian, and the *Martyrdom of St. Erasmus* (pl. 96) shows how much he gained from the Venetian Master in the way of sensual colour; this same influence makes his early mythologies the most immediately appealing in his career. But gradually Poussin suppressed any hint of sensuality in his paintings. What they then lost in charm, they gained in profundity, eventually becoming philosophical enquiries into the nature of the universe. At this date, Poussin was a virtual recluse, and the recondite symbolism of much of his work could only have been understood by a privileged and enlightened minority.

In contrast to Poussin, Claude Lorraine was exclusively a landscapist who attracted aristocratic and not especially intellectual patrons. Following in the ideal landscape tradition which originated in Annibale Carracci, Claude's works were evocations of a world of antiquity. Less concerned with rigid structure than either Domenichino or Poussin, Claude delighted in the rendering of mood and subtle light effects. In this he is said to have been influenced by the short-lived German painter Elsheimer; but Claude was the first painter meticulously to evoke over a large area of canvas the effect of sunlight on a landscape. Contemporary accounts relate how the artist spent much of his time sketching and even painting in the countryside near Rome. But whatever the realistic basis for Claude's art, it is an imaginative transformation of nature which in its serenity approximates to the pastoral idylls of Virgil.

Whatever their differences, Annibale Carracci, Guido Reni,

98 Claude Lorraine
Ulysses restores Chryseis to her Father, 1644
Musée National du Louvre, Paris

The magic of Claude's many port scenes inspired the 'Invitation to a Voyage' poems of the French poets Gautier and Baudelaire.

Domenichino, Nicolas Poussin and Claude Lorraine represented the overtly classical tendencies in the Roman art of the 17th century. Such artists, defended by contemporary theorists like Agucci and Bellori, were in fact the dominant forces in Roman painting at this time. Meanwhile the spectacular illusionistic decorations one imagines to have been a major feature of contemporary Roman art were a relatively short-lived phenomenon. The fashion for such decorations reached its peak during the reign of Urban VIII, who, as we have seen, favoured the theatrical exuberance of Bernini. Another artist of similar virtuosity was Pietro da Cortona, who practised both as an architect and as a painter. One of his greatest works was executed for the palace of Urban's nephew, Cardinal Barberini. The frescoed ceiling of the Palazzo Barberini (pl. 99), painted only ten years after the *Aurora*, reveals a basically different approach to decoration. The assurance of the *quadro riportato* is replaced by a struggling mass of bodies which recedes to a triumphant celestial vision in which bees symbolizing the Barberini family play a prominent part. Some measure of Cortona's achievement can be had by comparing his ceiling to a nearby one in the same palace, executed by a pedantically classical painter called Andrea Sacchi. Sacchi's *The Divine Wisdom* is a much more intellectual scene than Cortona's, containing no more figures than were strictly necessary, and, in common with most classically-inspired decorations, making little concession to illusionism. There was actually a considerable academic controversy in the 1630s as to which manner of painting was to be preferred. Sacchi, supported by Poussin, maintained that 'a picture should be likened to a tragedy, which was better when the greatest effect was achieved by the smallest number of players'. Other writers meanwhile argued that painters like Cortona 'did not expect the spectator to examine minutely the details of their pictures; in fact, to prevent them from doing that, they set before them a splendid, harmonious, lively general effect, which would provoke marvel and surprise'.

Apart from its aesthetic qualities, Cortona's ceiling in the Palazzo Barberini was an unprecedently grand piece of propaganda for a single family and testifies to the supreme power which the Barberini enjoyed at the time. Their dominance over political and cultural life in Rome was naturally a source of mounting criticism and hostility. There were certain grounds for complaint: by the time Urban VIII died in 1644, the funds of the papacy had been severely diminished through his lavish expenditure. Thereafter papal patronage of the arts was on the decline. The reign of Urban's successor, Innocent X, a man with few cultural interests, was one of austerity. Alexander VII, who followed him, inherited many of Urban's intellectual enthusiasms, and under his rule Rome enjoyed a brief flourishing of the arts. But dwindling finances, and the increasing threat of Louis XIV in France, ensured that when he himself died in 1677 even an artist of the calibre of Bernini was to find himself starved of commissions.

Ironically, two of the best known illusionistic decorations of the Baroque date from this later period. Both Baciccia's *Worship of the Name of Jesus* in the Church of the Gesù and Pozzo's *Triumph of St. Ignatius* in the Church of S. Ignazio (pl. 101) were Jesuit commissions, and both reflect a change of artistic policy within the order, partly

99 Pietro da Cortona
Allegory of Peace (detail), 1633–9
Palazzo Barberini, Salone, Rome

With typical wit Cortona makes the falling giants of the scene collide with the false marble figures of the frame.

100 Baciccia (Giovanni Battista Gaulli)
The Worship of the Name of Jesus
(detail), 1676–9
Il Gesù, Rome

Bernini was a friend of Padre Oliva and was so keen that Baciccia should get this commission that he offered himself as a guarantor.

brought about by the new general who was elected in 1664, Padre Oliva. The church of the Gesù was originally bare and simple until the late 1660s when it was decided to adorn it with a rich revetment of stucco and fresco. Although the ceiling of the nave was painted by Baciccia, the overall design was almost certainly by Bernini. It is a conception of extraordinary theatricality: the gold light emanating from the name of Jesus binds together a rich confusion of figures, some of whom are half-painted on stucco so that they appear convincingly to hang in space. A very different illusionistic scheme is Padre Pozzo's

101 Andrea Pozzo
The Triumph of St Ignatius of Loyola
(detail), 1691–4
S. Ignazio, Rome

Pozzo was a member of the Jesuit
order and could therefore be
prevailed upon to offer his services at
a cheap rate.

102 Guercino
The Incredulity of St Thomas, c. 1621
Pinacoteca Vaticana, Vatican, Rome

Although the composition of this
early Guercino owes much to
Caravaggio, the flurry of the
treatment is however totally
different.

which consists of an extremely heavy architectural framework (*quad-ratura*) seen in acute foreshortening. *Quadratura* of this type was not popular in Rome, and the work met with negative critical response. But the new Jesuit taste for the ornate was in itself an anachronism at a time when Roman art and architecture had succumbed to a dry and uniform classicism. The most successful painter of the second half of the century was Carlo Maratta, a man with a deep respect for Raphael and for the artistic theories of Poussin's apologist, Pietro Bellori.

The story of 17th century Italian painting outside Rome is exceedingly complex. Whereas little of interest was produced in what had once been two of the leading art centres in Italy – Florence and Venice – new centres emerged. The most important of these was perhaps Bologna, which, as we have seen, fostered some of the major classically-orientated painters of the Baroque; the strongly academic bias of Bolognese art was maintained right into the 18th century.

Just to the North of Bologna is the Emilian town of Cento, which gave birth to one of the more individual geniuses of the Italian Baroque, Giovanni Francesco Barbieri, called Guercino. Much of Guercino's early work combines realistic observation with a Correggio-like blurring of outlines; the compositions are melodramatic and the lighting strange and irrational. In the the early 1620s he spent a short period in Rome and became friendly with Monsignor Agucci, who encouraged him to modify and rationalize his style. The paintings which he produced on his return to Cento were in consequence blander and more attuned to the ideals of the Bolognese classicists. Another interesting Emilian painter of more provincial significance was the Parma artist, Bartolommeo Schedoni. His early works show the influence of Correggio, the Carraccis, and Caravaggio; but a handful of large pictures painted in the last three years of his life (pl. 103) are entirely personal.

Another new centre of painting was Naples, the city to which Caravaggio had fled after leaving Rome. Caravaggio's dark and brutally realistic style met with extreme enthusiasm here and affected the artists in this city to a much greater extent than it had done in Rome. Naples was under Spanish rule throughout the 17th century, and one of the leading painters to work here was a Spaniard, Jusepe Ribera. Many of Ribera's paintings, like *The Boy with the Club Foot* (pl. 104) are intentionally repulsive, interpreting Caravaggio's realism as an excuse to dwell on human deformities. There was a considerable market for scenes of this sort: one of Ribera's main patrons, a Flemish merchant called Gaspard Roomer, had an especially large collection of paintings with horrific subjects, including one by Ribera which depicted the Greek philosopher Cato 'who lies in his own welling blood after committing suicide and tears his intestines into pieces with his hands'.

The early works of another Neapolitan painter, Luca Giordano, showed a close assimilation of Ribera's style. Remarkably adaptable as an artist, Giordano had also a brilliant gift of painting at speed which earned him the nickname of 'Fa Presto' ('do it quickly'). In his extensive travels throughout Italy, he learnt much from being confronted with different local styles of painting; and in Venice he fell

103 Bartolomeo Schedoni
The Three Marys at the Tomb, 1614
Galleria Nazionale, Parma

Experiment with the expressive properties of drapery was common at this time – the jagged, icicle-like shapes here show an extreme solution to the problem.

105 Luca Giordano ▷
The fall of the rebel Angels, 1666
Kunsthistorisches Museum, Vienna

In this painting we seem to see the
airy lightness of the Rococo
emerging from the prevailing
sombreness of the Italian Baroque.

104 Jusepe de Ribera
The Boy with the club foot, 1652
Musée National de Louvre, Paris

This young beggar carries a plea for
alms somewhat inappropriately in
Latin: 'Da mi elimosinam propter
amorem dei' (Give me alms for the
love of God).

heavily under the influence of the colourful manner of Veronese. This
influence is very apparent in a series of altarpieces he painted for the
Venetian church of the Salute. Most contemporary painters in this city
were working in a dark and mannered style indebted to Tintoretto; but
Giordano's example opened their eyes to the lighter, more colourful
Venetian masters of the past. This was to have repercussions in the
18th century, when Venice was to emerge yet again as a leading
cultural centre and indeed to witness the last great moments of Italian
decorative art.

Painting in France, Flanders and Spain in the 17th century

Italy exerted a dominant influence on European art and architecture throughout much of the 17th century. Artists from countries like France, Flanders and Spain not only reacted to the great developments in painting which took place in Rome at the beginning of the century, but also to earlier periods in Italian art. The 17th century saw, in fact, a growing interest in the painting of the past, and the collecting of old masters was practised on an unprecedented scale. Venetian Renaissance painting was particularly popular at this time, and Venice, though producing little of interest in the way of contemporary art, became a mecca for collectors or their envoys from the most distant countries of Europe. It was partly as a result of this great trade in works of art that a knowledge of Italian painting was disseminated throughout the Continent, and that, in consequence, the currency of European paintings became more international than ever before. In spite of Italy's dominance over the arts, however, each of the major European countries continued to make very individual contributions of their own and produced such idiosyncratic geniuses as Rubens, Velazquez and Rembrandt. Moreover, by the end of the century, Italy was superceded by France which was thereafter to enjoy a supremacy almost unchallenged until very recent times. But long before this happened, the small and recently formed Protestant country of Holland (or more accurately, the United Provinces) produced a school of painters which was almost entirely independent of Italy, and which was indeed to be of immense significance for the art of future generations.

The great cultural revival which France experienced in the 17th century coincided with the country's growing political importance. Throughout the second half of the 16th century France was divided by civil war, and it was not until Henry IV had acceded to the throne in 1594 that a certain degree of stability was achieved. But France's emergence as a major European power dates properly from the time of the dynamic ministries of the Cardinals Richelieu and Mazarin (that is to say roughly from 1630 to 1660); this was when the last forces of internal religious and social discord were finally crushed and a victory scored in a long drawn out struggle with Spain. On the death of Mazarin in 1661 the youthful Louis XIV decided to govern the country himself without the aid of any first minister. Convinced that he was the greatest monarch of the century, Louis XIV built a court at Versailles unequalled in Europe and which eventually dictated social and cultural fashions not only all over France, but also throughout the Continent.

The most striking characteristic of French art and literature in the 17th century is its pronounced classicism. The two leading classical painters of the time, Nicolas Poussin and Claude Lorraine, were also the two major French painters of the century, but they spent most of their lives in Rome. Their only serious French rival as a classically-inspired painter was Simon Vouet, an artist who likewise spent a

106 Simon Vouet
Psyche looking at the Sleeping Amor,
1626
Musée des Beaux Arts, Lyon

This rather precious eroticism,
typical of its time, is a combination
of a taste for Caravaggio, the
pederast, and Guido Reni, the
mysogynist.

period of time in Italy but who afterwards returned to settle in his
native country. While in Rome, where he resided for much of the first
and second decades of the century, Vouet painted initially in a
Caravaggesque manner before succumbing to the art of the Bolognese
classicists. The classicism of Vouet, who returned to Paris in 1627 to
become the city's most important artist specializing in ambitious
figurative scenes, was nonetheless never as extreme as that of Poussin
and was always tempered by a great love for Venetian colouring.

Even though the ministries of Mazarin and Richelieu saw some of
the greatest monuments of French classical culture – the works of
Claude and Poussin no less than the plays of Corneille and Racine – the
arts in France were by no means as unified at this time as they were to
be under Louis XIV. In addition, there was a marked discrepancy
between the styles of painting that were fashionable in Paris and those
that were current in the provinces. The principal difference consists in
the fact that the influence of Caravaggio's art, despite Vouet's brief
flirtation with it during his stay in Italy, never penetrated as far as
Paris, and yet affected the whole development of painting elsewhere in
the country.

In what manner French provincial painters came to acquire a
Caravaggesque idiom is often the cause of speculation. Especially
puzzling is the artistic formation of perhaps the greatest of these artists
– George de La Tour. La Tour, who was born in 1593, worked all his
life in the small but prosperous town of Lunéville in the Duchy of
Lorraine. Although it has been suggested that he might have paid a
visit to Italy in his youth, a more likely point of contact with
Caravaggio's art would have been through the latter's Dutch imitator,
Terbrugghen. At all events, a painting like *The Card Players* (pl. 107)
shows both the similarities between his and Caravaggio's work and

107 Georges de La Tour
The Card Players, 1619–20
Private Collection, Paris

The bland-looking nobleman on the right is about to be robbed both by the cheat and the procuress.

also the great differences. While the subject matter is obviously related to the latter's scenes of Roman low life involving fancifully dressed boys, the figures in La Tour's work have a motionless puppet-like quality that makes them very different from the warm-blooded creations of the Italian. In later life La Tour developed an even calmer and more detached interpretation of Caravaggio's naturalism; this was given its fullest expression in his religious works. In the famous *St. Sebastian* in the church of the Broglie (a contemporary copy of which is in the Staatliche Museen, Berlin) the artist does not dwell on the gruesomely realistic details of the saint's martyrdom, but instead shows just a single drop of blood emanating from his body: the work's motionless forms, generalized to their greatest degree and illuminated by a flaming torch, give the whole a quality of intense silence and solemnity.

A similar quality is found in the works of La Tour's most original Parisian contemporary, Phillippe de Champaigne. Champaigne's art, however, does not have its roots in that of Caravaggio or indeed in that of any contemporary Italian master, but instead owes much to Flemish painting. The artist was in fact of Flemish origin, and studied as a landscape painter in Brussels before settling in Paris in 1621. Here he established an important position for himself as a painter of portraits and religious subjects, many of which betray a certain influence of the early works of Rubens and van Dyck. But no artist before him attained such a degree of severity and coldness in the portrayal of the human figure. In the 1640s he became involved with the religious sect of the Jansenists, which was principally based at the convent of Port-Royal just outside Paris and which advocated a severe way of life, a complete sincerity in religious beliefs, and a rejection of everything that was worldly; the effect of its teaching was fundamentally to change Champaigne's life. It was for the Jansenists that he executed his most uncompromisingly austere work (pl. 108). The *Ex-Voto* was painted in thanksgiving for the miraculous cure of Champaigne's daughter, a nun at the convent, who had been struck down by paralysis in 1661 and for a while had been totally unable to walk. Almost entirely in monochrome with only a single ray of light to suggest a supernatural event, Champaigne's rational portrayal of a miracle is entirely Jansenist in inspiration, and differs radically from the rapturously ecstatic representations which characterize much Jesuit-inspired art of the Roman Baroque. The Le Nain brothers are the other great French painters of the middle of the century and, like Champaigne's, their art owes more to Netherlandish painting than to Italian. The question of what pictures can be attributed to which of the three brothers is a vexed one, but in general it could be said that the ones depicting scenes of rural life are by Louis Le Nain, who also appears to have been the most outstanding of the three. Louis's rural scenes have generally been thought to portray peasants, but recently it has been suggested that they might be representations of the new class of bourgeois landowners, people often with small amounts of liquid capital who acquired little plots of land in the hope of building up country estates. If this identification is correct, it would solve the controversial issue as to what constituted the appeal of works of this sort, or what type of patron would have been attracted to them. For if they were peasant scenes, they had a seriousness and dignity incompatible with this *genre*

108 Philippe de Champaigne
Ex Voto (Abbess Agnès Arnauld and Sister Catherine de Sainte-Suzanne), 1662
Musée National du Louvre, Paris

Champaigne clearly felt harmonious composition to be too stylish and therefore too worldly a virtue; he also includes a written thanksgiving without embarrassment.

of painting, a *genre* which normally made fun of its subjects and appealed to sophisticated tastes. On the other hand if they represented these middle-class small holders, they might have been bought by them as well: this new social class was proud of the simple country life and was anxious to demonstrate its virtues.

The age of Louis XIV, as we have seen, saw a much greater unity in French painting; in fact the 'Sun King', aided by his able assistant Colbert, exerted a virtual dictatorship over the arts. Strict rules on how and what to paint were laid down by the French Royal Academy, and even treatises appeared outlining the correct way of rendering human emotions. The Academy's leading painter at this time was Charles le Brun, a man who had spent many years in Italy where he had benefited greatly from the guidance of Poussin. Le Brun's reverence for this master, which led to a very pedantic attitude towards classical archaeology and to a dry formal manner of painting, is typical of most official French art of this period. Yet a pronounced severity, even if of a rather different sort, had characterized the work of such disparate artists as George de La Tour, Phillippe de Champaigne, and Louis Le Nain, and can perhaps be attributed to the same phenomenon – the triumph of rationalism in the French culture of the 17th century.

Painting, as it developed in 17th-century Flanders, though occasionally influencing certain French artists, was of a fundamentally different nature; and it was dominated by just one figure, Peter Paul Rubens, a

109 Charles Le Brun
Chancellor Séguier, c. 1660
Musée National du Louvre, Paris

This self-satisfied chancellor conceives of himself as Apollo with a horse instead of a chariot and with boys as the Hours dancing in attendance.

110 Peter Paul Rubens
The Descent from the Cross (triptych),
1612–14
Onze-Lieve-Vrouwekathedraal,
Antwerp

This is the central panel of a
monumental triptych commissioned
by the Archers Guild for their chapel
in Antwerp Cathedral.

painter whose work has traditionally been considered as diametrically
opposed to that of Poussin. The years immediately preceeding Rubens'
birth were ones of great civic turmoil in the Spanish-governed
Netherlands. During the 1550s and 60s Protestantism was spreading
rapidly throughout the Lowlands, leading to widespread iconoclasm.
The Spanish king, Philip II swiftly retaliated, and his envoy, the Duke
of Alba, carried out a relentless persecution in Flanders. Rubens'
father, one of the many Flemish Catholics who had briefly flirted with
Calvinism, fled to Germany where Peter Paul was born in 1577. On
the father's death ten years later, the family, now reconverted to
Catholicism, returned to the Flemish city of Antwerp, where Rubens
was later apprenticed and where he stayed until his departure for Italy
in 1600.

The nine years Rubens spent in Italy were of seminal importance for
the development of his art. Employed for much of his stay by the
Gonzagas at Mantua, he benefited greatly from the study of their
superb collection of paintings by artists such as Mantegna, Titian,
Raphael, Correggio and Giulio Romano. He also paid two significant
visits to Rome. On the first one, in 1603, he was reunited with his
brother Philip, an ardent classical scholar then resident in the city, who
undoubtedly helped foster Rubens' lifelong passion for antiquity. But
Rubens was a man with exceptionally catholic tastes, and his classical
leanings by no means prevented him from admiring the works of an
artist like Caravaggio: his enthusiasm for Caravaggio's work was
greater than that for any other contemporary Italian painter, and led to
his securing one of the latter's more famous paintings, *The Madonna del
Rosario*, for a church in Antwerp.

111 Peter Paul Rubens
Madonna with Saints, 1638–40
Sint Jacobskerk, Antwerp

Painted for Rubens' own funeral
chapel, this work shows his
persistent desire to outdo 16th-
century Italian compositions, in this
case one by Correggio.

In 1609 a twelve-year truce was signed in the Netherlands between
Catholic and Protestant parties. It was significantly in this same year
that Rubens returned to Flanders to become court painter to the
Archduke Albert and the Infanta Isabella, both of whom were clearly
anxious to sustain the new period of peace and prosperity with a
renewed patronage of the arts. Although the Court was situated in
Brussels, Rubens was allowed to live in Antwerp where he soon
settled down to what was, by all accounts, a life of domestic bliss.
Writers on Rubens have invariably tended to eulogize the man; and
indeed it is difficult not to do so. His outlook on life was summarized
in the famous stoic motto which he had inscribed on the portal of his

112 Peter Paul Rubens
Double Portrait *(Rubens and Isabella Brandt in the Honeysuckle Bower), c.* 1609
Alte Pinakothek, Munich

Although the fact that Isabella is seated at Rubens' feet symbolizes obedience, the artist does not present himself as an assertively dominant husband.

house: *Mens Sana in Corpore Sano* ('a healthy mind in a healthy body'). Rubens' life and art were characterized by a remarkable energy and versatility; these same qualities enabled him to combine an exceptionally active career as a painter with a lifetime involvement in diplomacy. His potential as a diplomat was first recognized by the Gonzagas, but it was for the Hapsburg court at Brussels that he undertook his most important missions which took him to England, Holland and Spain. As a true stoic, Rubens believed fervently in peace, and he was able to plead this cause not only in the course of his diplomatic duties but also in his paintings. Describing to a friend a large allegorical canvas portraying the horrors of war, he referred to the 'grief-stricken woman clothed in black, with torn veil, robbed of all her jewels and other ornaments' as 'the unfortunate Europe who for so many years now has suffered plunder, outrage and misery'. As a diplomat Rubens was ultimately unsuccessful, for the peace that he so constantly advocated was essentially the peace that only Spain could bring to Europe. But if the sincerity of his beliefs led to a certain political naivety, it gave his art that remarkable sense of conviction which is apparent even in his most hectic religious and mythological works and in his huge allegories exalting such high-ranking but unworthy subjects as James I of England and Maria de'Medici of France.

113 Peter Paul Rubens
*Het pelske (Portrait of Hélène
Fourment), c.* 1638
Kunsthistorisches Museum, Vienna

Hélène clearly realized the status she
gained by her advantageous
marriage; Rubens here catches her off
guard with the symbol of that status
– the expensive fur – falling from her
shoulders.

Rubens' artistic achievement was so wide-ranging that a small selection of his works can only give a pale reflection of it. Some idea of his stylistic development, however, can be had by comparing two works painted at very different stages of his career. The *Descent from the Cross* (pl. 110) was executed shortly after his return from Italy and displays a certain influence of Caravaggio in its gruesome realism and dramatic lighting. Its impact is due to the overwhelming intensity of the composition, an intensity somehow at odds with the work's cold and almost metallic colouring. The relatively late *Madonna with Saints* (pl. 111) shows in contrast how the artist's habitual vitality is strengthened by the use of the warmest and most vivid colours.

Rubens once wrote 'that I am, by natural instinct, better fitted to execute very large works than small curiosities. Everyone according to his gifts; my talent is such that no undertaking however vast in size or ambitious in subject has ever surpassed my courage'. This is a misleading statement in that Rubens also excelled in works of an intimate and private nature that reflected a deep love of his family. The Munich *Double Portrait* (pl. 112), with the couple placed underneath a honeysuckle which symbolizes fidelity in love, shows the artist in the company of his new wife Isabella Brandt whom he had married in 1609. Isabella died in 1628, and the middle-aged Rubens subsequently married a 17-year-old girl renowned for her beauty – Hélène Fourment. Both marriages were apparently exceptionally happy. The overtly sensual portrait of Hélène (pl. 113), her sensuality heightened by the fur wrap over her shoulders, and her right arm positioned in such a way so as to emphasize her large nipples rather than modestly shield them, was painted solely for the artist's personal pleasure and was kept in his private possession until his death. Both Isabella and Hélène, and the children which they bore Rubens, were a constant source of inspiration to the artist; and they feature not only in works such as these but also in his ambitious multi-figured compositions to which they add an engaging homeliness.

Towards the end of his life Rubens broke off his commitments to the court and retired to his country house at Steen. The landscapes (pl. 114) which he painted of his new surroundings, serve as a perfect coda to his career. They depict nature not just as an object of passive contemplation but as an active and restless force; their apparently spontaneous compositions and vivid, freely painted renderings of natural effects give the spectator the uncanny impression that he is actually walking in a landscape. They have a freshness and originality unequalled in the work of other landscapists of Rubens' time; and their special qualities were not to be recaptured until the 19th century.

Soon after Rubens' return from Italy, a growing number of students and assistants were attracted to his studio, making it eventually the most important in Northern Europe. On Rubens's death in 1640 the studio was taken over by Jacob Jordaens who, together with Anthony van Dyck, was one of the few of Rubens' innumerable followers to have a clearly defined artistic personality of his own. It is not, however, an especially attractive one. Jordaens' coarse and pedestrian imitation of his master's idiom was best suited to *genre* painting (a category which Rubens himself never attempted); and his most original mythological compositions were accordingly those which had realistic contemporary settings. Van Dyck's paintings are entirely different from Jordaen's and show a certain refinement of Rubens' art. Most of his life, however, was spent in England, where he worked

114 Peter Paul Rubens
The Rainbow, c. 1636
Alte Pinakothek, Munich

A scene painted towards the end of
Rubens's life, showing the qualities
of his achievement as a landscapist.

almost entirely as a portraitist. His portrait of Charles I (pl. 115) has a relaxed, fluent quality; but whereas Rubens' would have shown some of the subject's vitality and warmth, van Dyck renders the King as rather precious and aloof. The elegance of van Dyck's manner, so different from the awkward stiffness of so many portraits of the 16th and 17th centuries, revolutionized the art of portraiture in England. Yet only Gainsborough, working in the 18th century, managed a comparably ethereal representation of his sitters.

The wealth of cultural activity in 17th-century Italy, France, Flanders and Holland, was partly related to increased political stability and economic prosperity. No such reason can be given, however, to explain the remarkable flourishing of the arts that took place concurrently in Spain, a country whose political and financial fortunes had in fact declined to such an extent from the late 16th century onwards that by 1619 one of the King's advisors was able to report that five-sixths of the population were without profitable employment or means to support life. The so-called Golden Age of Spanish painting and literature is even more difficult to explain in view of the fact that its leading protagonists worked largely in isolation from the rest of Europe: Spain's greatest painters of this period were little known outside the country until the late 18th century, and similarly, their own knowledge of artistic developments elsewhere was a limited and often second-hand one.

The major centres of patronage in 17th-century Spain were Madrid,

115 Anthony van Dyck
Portrait of Charles I, King of England,
1635–8
Musée National du Louvre, Paris

While the figure of the king
embodies regal nonchalance, his
furiously champing horse, which has
to be restrained, denotes regal
power.

116 Diego Velázquez
Las Meninas (The Ladies-in-Waiting),
1656
Museo del Prado, Madrid

Velázquez, with his uncanny
understanding of optical experience,
sees that the two dwarfs at the side of
our vision appear slightly out of
focus.

where the court was situated, and Seville, which was the country's
commercial and trading capital. Velázquez was born in Seville in 1599
and was trained under one Francisco Pacheco, who at the time was the
city's leading painter and the mainstay of a small cultural and
intellectual circle. Pacheco is mainly interesting to us today not for his
canvases but for his lengthy treatise on the art of painting. Although
this is a pedantically erudite work, full of half assimilated pieces of
information derived from Italian authors, it offers a revealing insight
into Spanish taste in its strong emphasis on realism in art. Pacheco
greatly praised Caravaggio, an artist whom he knew only by report
and whose work he would have known solely through imitations.

At all events, the taste for a sometimes grotesque realism is inherently Spanish and has always inspired the country's greatest monuments of art and literature: in the Renaissance, for instance, Spanish painters reacted with much greater enthusiasm to Flemish painting than they did to classically-based Italian art such as that of Raphael.

Many Sevillian artists of Pacheco's time were in fact working in a dark, realistic manner derived partly from Caravaggio and partly from Netherlandish painting, although few attained the same degree of realism in their naturalistic detailing as did Velázquez. Velázquez's Sevillian period is comprised largely of *genre* paintings in which the artist portrayed, without recourse to sensationalism or grotesque humour, scenes from Sevillian life. Some of these scenes include token biblical stories taking place through a window in the background; although this device can be found in many Flemish paintings of the 16th century, it was somehow prophetic of much of Velázquez's later work in which a sharp contrast is frequently set up between contemporary reality and unworldly events.

Velázquez's outstanding technical abilities were immediately recognized by his teacher and soon led, in 1623, to his being employed by the court in Madrid. Remaining at the court for the rest of his life, he developed what was apparently a very close friendship with King Philip IV, who treated him with a respect generally reserved for the most important courtiers.

Velázquez's principal activity as a court painter was as a portraitist; throughout his long years in Madrid he dutifully recorded the appearance of the King and of his family in a series of works in which

117 Diego Velázquez
The Topers, 1628–9
Museo del Prado, Madrid

Velázquez here incorporates the spectator into the scene; our arrival has been noticed by one reveller who draws the attention of another to us.

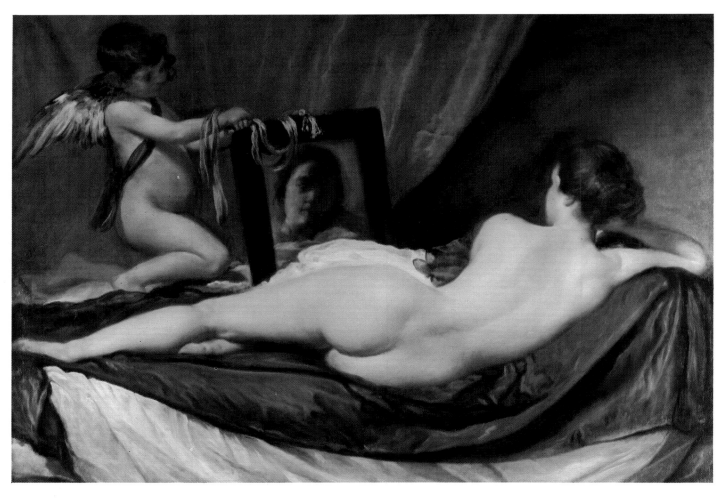

118 Diego Velázquez
The Rokeby Venus (The Toilet of Venus), 1649–50
National Gallery, London

This painting was repeatedly slashed at the beginning of this century by an outraged suffragette – an oblique compliment.

only the subjects' features are shown to change but not their impassive, unsmiling expressions.

Very different are his portraits of other members of the Royal household, and in particular of the court dwarfs, who, unlike their inscrutable superiors, smile, grimace, mock and frown. Seen as a whole, Velázquez's portraits offer an evocative picture of court life which, in its combination of the aloof and the grotesquely satirical, reflects the wide range of Velázquez's own art. All his qualities as a portraitist are to be seen in his largest canvas, *Las Meninas* (or, the *Ladies-in-Waiting*) (pl. 116), a work so famous and so often reproduced that one can easily fail to recognize its originality. *Las Meninas* shows the artist painting a portrait of the king's daughter, who is accompanied by her ladies-in-waiting. In the background can be seen a nun and two courtiers, one of whom hesitates to come into the room, and the faces of the King and Queen, who are actually observing the scene from the spectator's own viewpoint, but who are reflected in a mirror on the back wall. The idea of the picture probably came about as a result of the King's known habit of coming to visit Velázquez in his studio to watch him paint. Apart from the novelty of the work's composition – its abrupt transition in scale and its playful tricks of illusionism – the conception of a royal portrait involving both the artist and other members of the household is quite unprecedented and denotes the degree of freedom Velázquez was allowed. Something should also be said about the artist's handling of paint, which from a distance and in reproduction seems meticulous, yet on close inspection is as bold as every other aspect of the picture: the glittering sheen of silvers and greys is achieved by the minimum of brushstrokes.

Velázquez was exceptional among Spanish painters in not having to spend his life executing religious commissions; during his whole period in Madrid he painted in fact only two altarpieces. Given the freedom to paint imaginative works of his own choice, he seems to have preferred the world of mythology. This taste was in itself an unusual one for Spanish artists, for although the King had an unequalled collection of mythological works by Titian and Rubens, there was no tradition for this type of painting in Spain. Velázquez's first mythology was *The Topers* of 1628 (pl. 117), which shows the god of wine, Bacchus, in the company of drunken revellers. The work could hardly be more different in spirit from Titian's famous *Bacchanal of the Andrians* which had recently been bought by the Spanish court; but in fact certain details such as the recumbent nude on Bacchus's right were certainly derived from it. The dark colouring and the incorporation into a classical story of vividly realistic peasants such as one still finds today in provincial Spanish bars, is, however, more closely related to Caravaggio's art. The work is straightforwardly satirical, and as such lacks the complexity and ambiguity of mood characteristic of many of his later painting.

In 1631 and 1645 Velázquez visited Italy to buy works of art for the royal collection. The experience of seeing this new country and being exposed to such a great variety of art treasures, seems to have encouraged him to adopt a more fluent and colourful manner of painting; in turn Italian artists reacted with equal excitement to his own work, for on his second visit to the country he received the influential commission to paint a portrait of Pope Innocent XI. The so-called *Rokeby Venus* (pl. 118) was probably executed on this visit and only then sent back to Spain where it hung in the house of a private collector. There was as little tradition for the painting of nudes in Spain, as there was for mythologies. But to Velázquez's contemporaries of any nationality, his Venus would have seemed remarkably fresh and naturalistic: not only has the artist used the merest suggestion

119 Diego Velázquez
The Spinners (Arachne and Minerva),
c. 1659
Museo del Prado, Madrid

Velázquez's freedom to conceive one-off compositions such as this for the Royal collection is a further testimony to the favour he enjoyed.

of modelling to create a nude which actually looks like a naked human body, but also his choice of a recumbent backview of the model is virtually unprecedented.

Velázquez's best mythological picture is *The Spinners* (pl. 119), which until very recently was thought to be just a realistic depiction of the royal tapestry factory at Aranjuez. It is in fact based on the legend from Ovid in which the maid Arachne challenges the goddess Minerva to a tapestry weaving contest; for her presumption in so doing, Arachne is later turned into a spider. The choice of subject was an exceptionally unusual one, and so was Velázquez's treatment of it. Rather than just showing the gruesome outcome of the story, Velázquez divides the work into two halves, with the competition taking place in the foreground, and Minerva's triumph shown in the background. Allegorical figures of the arts flanking Minerva on her dais indicate that the work has a deeper meaning, but in spite of innumerable suggestions such as that Velázquez was alluding to a recent petition to have artists exempted from tax, no one has satisfactorily discovered what this is. Whatever the exact meaning of the painting, one is nonetheless aware of some transformation of reality, in which the eye is led from the naturalistic and relatively subdued foreground to a distant and very colourful world of fantasy.

Of the many distinguished Spanish painters of Velázquez's time, special mention must be made of Francisco Zurbarán and Bartolomé Murillo. Both these artists paid long visits to Madrid but, perhaps as a result of Velázquez's dominance over artistic activity in this city, both chose to spend most of their working lives in and around Seville.

120 Francisco de Zurbarán
The Holy House of Nazareth, c. 1630
Cleveland Museum of Art,
Cleveland

The young Christ and the Virgin are surrounded by premonitions of the Passion: the crown of thorns, Christ's pricked finger and the Virgin's bundle of linen, which recalls the shrouded body of Christ.

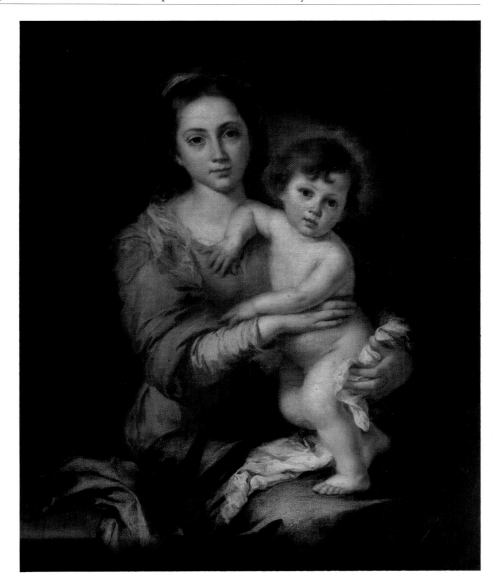

121 Bartolomé Esteban Murillo
Madonna and Child, 1650–60
Palazzo Pitti, Galleria Palatina,
Florence

A perfect example of the 17th-
century cult of Raphaelism; it is this
cult that the Pre-Raphaelites
abhorred even more than Raphael
himself.

Zurbaran's art represents the most austere and morbid expression of the Caravaggesque idiom: the artist places greatly simplified figures in dark bleak settings which have only the simplest of props. His economy of expression and his isolation of individual naturalistic details can create images of great power, such as when he shows black-robed Franciscan monks praying in front of a skull, or a bowl of lemons on a plain wooden table. By the time of his death in 1664, however, his austere art had gone out of fashion and his younger Sevillian contemporary, Murillo, had become the most popular artist in the city. Murillo himself had begun painting in a dark Caravaggesque manner, but in his maturity he evolved a more smiling, brighter and freer style of painting which was to make him one of the most popular artists of the 18th and early 19th centuries, though he is now found to be excessively sentimental.

Dutch Painting in the 17th century

In 1579 seven of the northern provinces of The Netherlands (the most important of which was Holland) were bound together by a political pact known as the Union of Utrecht, and formed into an independent country; this was given *de facto* recognition in 1609, on the conclusion of a twelve-year truce with Spain. Within a very short period of time the United Provinces rose to become a leading European power and trade centre.

The birth of this new nation was suitably accompanied by the development of a flourishing culture, whose independence from the rest of Europe can largely be explained by the fact that the State and the Church, which had been the major sources of artistic patronage in Italy, France, Flanders and Spain, were negligible factors in Dutch life. The Court of the Stadtholders in the Dutch capital of The Hague was modest in scale, playing a relatively small part in the civil administration of the country, and offering few commissions to artists. The decoration of the Stadtholder's country residence, the Huis Ten Bos, was one of these exceptional commissions and significantly was undertaken by a largely Flemish group of artists headed by Jacob Jordaens; the large-scale mythological canvases which adorn the walls of this palace epitomize the spirit of court culture and are antipathetic to most contemporary Dutch tastes. Opposition to autocratic rule from the court came from the ever more powerful middle-classes, whose newly found importance is reflected in the proud Burgher groups as portrayed by artists such as Hals and Rembrandt. The democratic nature of Dutch 17th-century society was matched by an extreme tolerance in religious matters, the majority of the Burghers favouring a very mild and humane form of Calvinism.

One of the most striking aspects of Dutch painting of this period is the fact that it was collected by such a wide selection of the population. An English traveller to Amsterdam in 1640, one Peter Munday, wrote with astonishment: 'As for the art of Painting and the affection of people to Pictures, I thincke none other go beyond them, there having bin in this Country Many excellent Men in thatt Facullty, some att present, as Rimbrantt, etts All in generall striving to adorne their houses, especially the outer or street roome, with costly peeces. Butches, bakers not much inferiour in their shoppes, which are Fairely sett Forth, yea many tymes blacksmithes, Cobblers, ettes will have some picture or other by their Forge and in their stalle. Such is the generall Notion, inclination and delight that these Countrie Native (s) have to Paintings'. The widespread popularity which painting enjoyed in the United Provinces resulted in a work of art having a more modest function: no longer serving principally either as propaganda for the aristocracy and the church, or as a stimulus for an intellectual elite, it could simply be regarded as a pleasant way of decorating one's house. Appropriately there was a predominance of such popular straightforward forms of art as *genre* and landscape painting which made few demands on the intellect. The Dutch outlook on art was uniquely

122 Hendrick Terbrugghen
St. Sebastian tended by St. Irene and the Maid, 1625
Allen Memorial Art Museum,
Oberlin College, Oberlin, Ohio

St. Sebastian's jack-knifed body contributes to the flaunting of the Italian convention of an elegant portrayal of the saint.

materialistic: whereas in Italy and elsewhere artists were anxious to establish their superiority over ordinary craftsmen, painters here turned out canvases as they would any other domestic furnishing. This production-line mentality explains why so many of the famous Dutch artists were so narrowly specialized: some concentrated on seascapes, others on architectural interiors, peasant and lowlife scenes, military *genre*, still-lifes, portraits and so on. Once an artist had developed a profitable line of painting, he was generally forced to keep to it if he wished to survive. In spite of the great demand for canvases, the Dutch artist found himself in an exceptionally competitive business in which even those with the most seemingly assured reputations could suddenly experience extreme financial hardship: at the height of his popularity, Frans Hals was being sued by his butcher, baker and shoemaker. Other leading Dutch artists had to take on other jobs to support themselves: Cuyp was a landowner, Jan Steen ran a tavern, and Hobbema supposedly abandoned painting altogether to become a wine gauger. Such a situation would have been unheard of in a country like Italy, where genius was regarded as being incompatible with such demeaning activities. The more pedestrian attitude of the Dutch might seem healthier to us now, but it had the unfortunate consequence at the time that painters of such magnitude as Vermeer could live lives of relative obscurity, regarded merely as competent practitioners of their trade.

Up to as late as the early 19th century, a visit to Italy was generally considered to be an essential part of any European artist's training. The Dutch took a very different attitude. Their painters generally did not need to travel there because their artistic vision was not dominated by any Italianate notions of the ideal and lacked, for instance, any dependence on the antique or on such conventional figureheads as Raphael. Like any generalization about art, however, this one needs a certain amount of qualification. The earliest artists associated with the United Provinces – such as Cornelis Van Haarlem – painted in fact in an Italianate style, and some of them even spent long periods in Italy. In addition there were a number of Dutch painters throughout the 17th century who continued to find their inspiration in this Mediterranean country. Many of them came from Utrecht, a town which was always predominantly Catholic and which was thus exceptional in being able to provide artists with religious commissions. Hendrick Terbrugghen, the most important of these Utrecht painters, lived in Rome for a reputed ten years before settling permanently in his native town in 1614. While in Italy, he had been strongly attracted to the art of Caravaggio, an artist who indeed exerted the strongest influence on Terbrugghen's compatriots who travelled south; the appeal of Caravaggio's art to the Dutch was perhaps inevitable, as it satisfied a love for realism which had always been a pronounced feature of the native school of painting. Terbrugghen's *St. Sebastian tended by St. Irene and the Maid* (pl. 122) was painted almost ten years after his return from Italy and shows a very Dutch and pedestrian interpretation of the Caravaggesque idiom; while Italian painters were invariably attracted to the morbidly erotic qualities inherent in this particular subject, Terbrugghen portrays two women with coarse Nordic features and bright red noses setting about the task as if plucking a pheasant for supper. A later generation of Dutch artists who were attracted to Italy were the Bamboccianti, a group of painters based in Rome who gathered around the colourful personality of Peter van de Laer

123 Frans Hals
Banquet of the Officers of the Guild of
St. George's, 1616
Frans Halsmuseum, Haarlem

Even in this apparently unposed
group Hals is anxious to give
everyone their fair share of
importance; some by obvious
prominence, others by vivacity of
expression.

('Bamboccio'), and who specialized in scenes of low-life. Among the
other Dutch painters lured by Italy, special mention must be made of
the group of landscapists who were inspired by Claude's idyllic scenes
of the Roman campagna; many of these artists continued to paint in
such vein long after their return to Holland, and there was evidently
quite a market for their works among those stay-at-home Dutch
burghers with a longing for sunnier climates. It should also be
mentioned that however ethereal these landscapes were in inspiration,
the figures who appear in them are not in classical but in contemporary
peasant garb, thus propagating the Dutch taste for realism in this most
unsuitable of genres.

The beginnings of a truly indigenous Dutch School of painting are
evident in the works of Frans Hals, who lived all his life in Haarlem.
The first of the large group portraits which were to establish his
reputation as one of the liveliest portraitists of his age was not painted
until 1616 (pl. 123). The group portrait, a typically Dutch genre and
one symptomatic of the democratic middle class society of 17th-
century Holland, presents exceptionally difficult problems to the
painter who wishes to avoid a stiff and formal composition. Hals's
achievement in the *Banquet of the Officers of the St. George's Guild* can be
likened to that of a school photograph in which the photographer has
departed from convention by making his subjects move around and
strike up engaging postures.

The result could easily come close to parody, and this is exactly
what happened in the work of many of the Dutch painters who tried to
follow Hals's example. Hals's portrait has, however, both genuine
spontaneity and, aided by the striking red banner flung across the
centre, great compositional unity. Hals was himself a member of this
company from 1612 to 1615, and his lively characterization of each
officer might partly stem from a personal knowledge of them. The
militia groups, of which this was one, were comprised of burghers
who came together to defend their towns in case of attack; Hals's very
cheerful representation of the St. George's Company was painted,
however, at a time of great peace and prosperity when the group's

more serious civic duties could give way to pleasant socializing.

Very little is known about Hals's life, but much of what is written about his character has been based on the extrovert quality of many of his portraits. Thus he is generally presented as a swashbuckling alcoholic; and there might be a certain degree of truth in this as one of the earliest references to Hals's conduct describes the artist as 'somewhat merry in life'. His last group portraits, however, one depicting the Regents and the other the Regentesses (pl. 124) of the hospital of Haarlem, seem to be by a very different artist, and are usually interpreted as a sign that Hals acquired a more profound understanding of human character in his old age. It would nonetheless have been odd if he had portrayed the hospital staff sitting down to a jolly dinner party; in addition, the mournful character of these works reflects the new fashion in Holland for dark and sombre clothes as opposed to the more colourful costumes worn by the members of the St. George's Company. In Hals's group portrait of the Regentesses one can admire the expressive handling of the paint and the powerful clenched fists which later might have inspired van Gogh in his *Potato Diggers*; but it would be rash to equate serious faces with more serious works of art. Rembrandt spent all his life painting people with unsmiling expressions, and yet in doing so, he was not necessarily a more profound portraitist than Hals.

The myths surrounding Rembrandt are perhaps greater than those associated with any other European painter. It was indeed Rembrandt who largely fostered the popular image of the artist of genius as someone who suffers extreme financial and emotional hardship and whose works meet with complete incomprehension from his contemporaries. This is in fact a very misleading picture of Rembrandt, an artist who from the very start was immensely successful and who

124 Frans Hals
The Women Governors of the Haarlem Almshouse for the Aged, 1664
Frans Hals Museum, Haarlem

To belong to a committee such as this was an honour, status being more important than charitable disposition.

125 Pieter Pietersz Lastman
Ulysses and Nausicaa, 1619
Alte Pinakothek, Munich

The shipwrecked and barely decent
Ulysses asks for help from the
Princess Nausicaa and her servants
who are washing clothes.

received important commissions right into old age. As a young man in
Leiden in the 1630s, it was predicted that he should become one of the
most important painters of all time. Having attracted during this
period the attention of the influential connoisseur Constantin
Huyghens, secretary to the Stadtholder Frederick Henry, he became
one of the few Dutch painters to receive commissions from the House
of Orange; moving to Amsterdam in 1640, he soon gathered around
him more pupils and followers than any of his contemporaries.

Rembrandt's principal teacher had been Pieter Lastman, one of the
leading Italianate painters in Holland and someone who specialized in
dramatic Biblical and mythological themes. One of Lastman's most
famous paintings was the *Ulysses and Nausicaa* (pl. 125) of 1619, a work
which showed again an interest both in Caravaggesque realism and in
the more heroic manner associated with the Bolognese Classicists.
Rembrandt inherited from his teacher a similar love of dramatic
subject-matter, but went much further than Lastman in his quest for a
realistic interpretation of it. *The Danae* of 1636 (pl. 126) was painted
right at the end of this Leiden period: the sumptuous flamboyance of
the setting contrasts with the extremely naturalistic and unclassical
portrayal of the artist's naked wife. The whole is brought together by
the powerful and mysterious treatment of light: although this is a
hallmark of all his paintings, it is here directly related to the work's
subject, which is taken from Ovid's *Metamorphoses* and concerns
Jupiter's seduction of Danae in the form of a shower of gold.
Rembrandt's replacement of the coins by a brilliant shaft of gold light

both rationalizes the story and gives it an added mystery. Rembrandt tried his hand at every category of painting, including portraits, *genre* scenes, and even landscapes; in each of these categories he displayed a remarkable originality. The *Night Watch* (pl. 127) is his largest and perhaps his most famous work. The title is in fact a misnomer and was given to it much later by those misled by the work's sombre tonality. The painting is actually set in daytime, and portrays the private militia company of Captain Frans Banning Cocq. Even Hals's lively transformations of the generally static *genre* of group portraits do not compare with Rembrandt's: the militia company is here shown on the point of marching out into the street, an event to which the artist has added idiosyncratic touches, such as the brilliantly illuminated girl running through the crowd in the background. Although it has often been said that this bizarre work aroused considerable hostility and lack of comprehension among Rembrandt's contemporaries, there is no evidence of this. On the contrary it seems that the members of the company who posed for it were very pleased with the artist as they handsomely rewarded him.

Rembrandt did suffer a severe financial setback and a significant drop in commissions during the 1650s, but as we have seen, this was a

126 Rembrandt van Rijn
The Danae, 1636
Hermitage, Leningrad

Rembrandt's staunch naturalism is also shown in the cupid, who is included not as a mythical figure but as the decorative bedhead.

127 Rembrandt van Rijn
The Company of Captain Frans Banning Cocq and Lieutenant Willem van Ruytenburg, known as *The Night Watch,* 1642
Rijksmuseum, Amsterdam

The figure of Captain Cocq at the centre of this glorious chaos is an allusion to Raphael's *School of Athens,* the apogee of classical order.

fate not exactly unknown to even the most successful Dutch artists. In Rembrandt's case it can be attributed to both a new fashion in Holland for works of a brighter and more careful finish, and also to the fact that the artist spent an increasing amount of his time painting solely for his personal pleasure with no market in mind. He painted himself and members of his family to an unprecedented degree, and even his biblical themes, often of the most obscure subject-matter, were generally painted not with the intention of being sold but as a self-indulgent exercise in story-telling. Rembrandt's last public commission, a scene from classical history depicting the conspiracy of Julius Civilis (pl. 128), was his only major work known to have been very controversial at the time. Originally intended to fill an arch at the end of a long corridor in Amsterdam Town Hall, it was soon removed and later cut down in size and sold as an easel painting. One can understand the hostility: such uncompromising brutality would have looked out of place in any civic environment.

None of Rembrandt's innumerable pupils could match their master in versatility, and virtually all specialized in one particular branch of painting. Gerard Dou, who practised essentially as a rather slick *genre* painter, was the most successful, and indeed came to surpass Rembrandt in popularity in the late 1650s and 1660s. Perhaps the most talented was Carel Fabritius, who brilliantly assimilated Rembrandt's style while making original contributions of his own. In his paintings

128 Rembrandt van Rijn
*The Conspiracy of Julius Civilis:
the Oath,* 1661
Nationalmuseum, Stockholm

In the conspiracy of the one-eyed
Batavian King Julius Civilis against
the Romans, the Dutch saw a symbol
of their struggle against Spanish
domination.

129 Rembrandt van Rijn ▷
Self-portrait as the Apostle Paul, 1661
Rijksmuseum, Amsterdam

The use of self-portraiture in fancy
dress is one way in which Rembrandt
can express his concern with religion
and humanity in general.

which he executed after his move to Delft in 1650, he developed a
luminous tonality and a pronounced interest in the atmospheric effects
of clear daylight which were profoundly to affect the work of his
major pupil, Jan Vermeer.

Vermeer, who ranks with Hals and Rembrandt as the most
outstanding Dutch painter of the 17th century, is the one who appears
to have received the least recognition in his time; the esteem in which
he is now held is largely due to his discovery in the mid–19th century
by a French art critic called Thoré-Bürger. Although he had a certain
reputation among the local community of painters in his home town of
Delft, Vermeer was quickly forgotten after his death; and his style of
painting was too personal and complex to be successfully imitated.
The *Woman Reading* (pl. 131) and the *View of Delft* (pl. 132) combine a
haunting stillness with a disconcertingly realistic luminosity and a
meticulous handling of paint. Very few works by Vermeer are known,
and those few might well represent most of his life's work. Each of his
canvases was apparently painted over a long period, a factor which
accounts for the high prices that they commanded at the time. In spite
of the costliness of his works, however, Vermeer's rate of production
was simply not good enough to insure a regular income, and much of
his life was spent in considerable poverty.

Vermeer's *Woman reading a Letter* is an example of *genre* painting at
its most refined. Something more, however, must be said about this
particular category of painting which, as we have seen, was one of the
most popular in 17th-century Holland. The term *genre* painting, for
which there is no English equivalent, is used to describe works that
portray scenes of contemporary life. The type and character of the
scene can of course vary enormously and, less obviously, its apparently straightforward appearance can hide deeper meanings. The first
great *genre* painter in 17th-century Holland was Adrian Brouwer.
Early biographies of this artist describe him as a dissolute character,

and stories abound concerning his hatred for social hypocrisy: at a wedding, for instance, to which he had been invited on account of having recently acquired a suit, he poured gravy all over his clothes saying that they too should join in the merrymaking as it was their presence and not his that had been originally requested. Brouwer spent much of his life in Flanders, and his paintings have their roots in the Flemish tradition of Bosch and Breugel. They portray humanity at its most primitive level, untainted by the veneer of social sophistication which the artist reputedly despised: *Tavern Interior* (pl. 133) shows extreme inebriation producing unconsciousness, vomiting, stupidity and also a possibility of violence (suggested by the unsheathed knife tucked underneath the fat man's belt). The purpose of works of this sort was obviously to amuse, but the people who appreciated them were by no means as unsophisticated as those whom the works depict. In fact there is evidence that Brouwer's paintings, just like those of Breugel, appealed to intellectual and discriminating tastes, and among

130 Carel Fabritius
The Goldfinch, 1654
Mauritshuis, The Hague

Rembrandt's most distinguished pupil, Fabritius, died when a powder magazine exploded in Delft in 1653 before fully realizing the potential shown in works such as this.

131 Johannes Vermeer
Woman Reading 1662–3
Rijksmuseum, Amsterdam

With almost scientific precision
Vermeer observes that there is not
enough light on some parts of the
face to detach it from the map
on the wall.

the artist's great admirers can be counted both Rubens and Rembrandt.

Brouwer's art obviously offers a few problems of interpretation. The same is true of those innumerable *genre* paintings of a later date (most notably by Vermeer, De Hooch, and Gabriel Metsu) which largely depict, sometimes in a sentimental manner and at other times in a spirit of matter-of-fact observation, the sober virtues of domestic life. Not so immediately apparent are the sexual innuendoes found in so many Dutch *genre* paintings which compensate for the almost complete absence of nudes in this country's art. In many cases these innuendoes have been played down by later owners of the pictures, who in the cause of decency have committed such acts as retitling a painting showing a soldier visiting a prostitute as '*The Gallant Officer*', and have even gone as far as to obliterate such telling details as a coin being held in a man's hand. At other times the erotic nature of the works appears veiled to us now because we are no longer aware of the sexual conventions of the time: the countless paintings of women reading letters, playing musical instruments, or being visited by doctors constituted the standard repertory of sexual *double-eutendre*, and would have been immediately understood by the Dutch public of the time. In addition, we fail to recognize today the contemporary proverbs and puns on which so many of the *genre* paintings are based. We might, for instance, mistake the great number of birds and bird cages which feature in the background of Steen's more lewd works as

132 Johannes Vermeer
View of Delft, 1658–61
Mauritshuis, The Hague

In spite of the bright tonality of the work, the foreground is in fact in shadow, and only the furthest houses on the right catch some sunshine.

delightfully naturalistic touches. In fact they probably refer to the Dutch word 'vliegen', which as well as meaning 'to fly', is also the slang equivalent of 'to fuck'.

Of all the Dutch *genre* painters Jan Steen is perhaps the one who has been the most misrepresented: not only do we now fail to recognize the wealth of literary allusions that feature in his works, but we also have reservations about an art which appears purely humorous in its intentions. And yet little attempt has been made to look into why exactly Steen's paintings are funny. One of the more remarkable aspects of his art is its variety, ranging from coarse drinking scenes in a style indebted to Brouwer, to outdoor scenes of gallantry which prefigure the works of Watteau. But perhaps his most interesting paintings are those which give a *genre* treatment to biblical and religious scenes. One of these is the *Sarah and Tobias* (pl. 134), a work of considerable complexity which combines both the light-hearted and the serious elements of Steen's art. The marriage forming the subject of this picture was not in itself a straight-forward one, owing to Sarah being possessed by a demon which had already killed off seven of her previous husbands on the wedding night. Steen brilliantly conveys the mixture of foreboding and rejoicing that must have accompanied the contract, by dividing the work into two distinct parts. Those engaged in the lively preparations for the wedding feast, on the right-hand side, are contrasted, on the other, both with the serious group preparing the

133 Adriaen Brouwer
Tavern Interior, 1624–5
Museum Boymans-Van Beuningen,
Rotterdam

Brouwer's paintings are invariably of
tavern scenes filled with drunken
activity; his own life was reputedly as
debauched as those of the people he
portrayed.

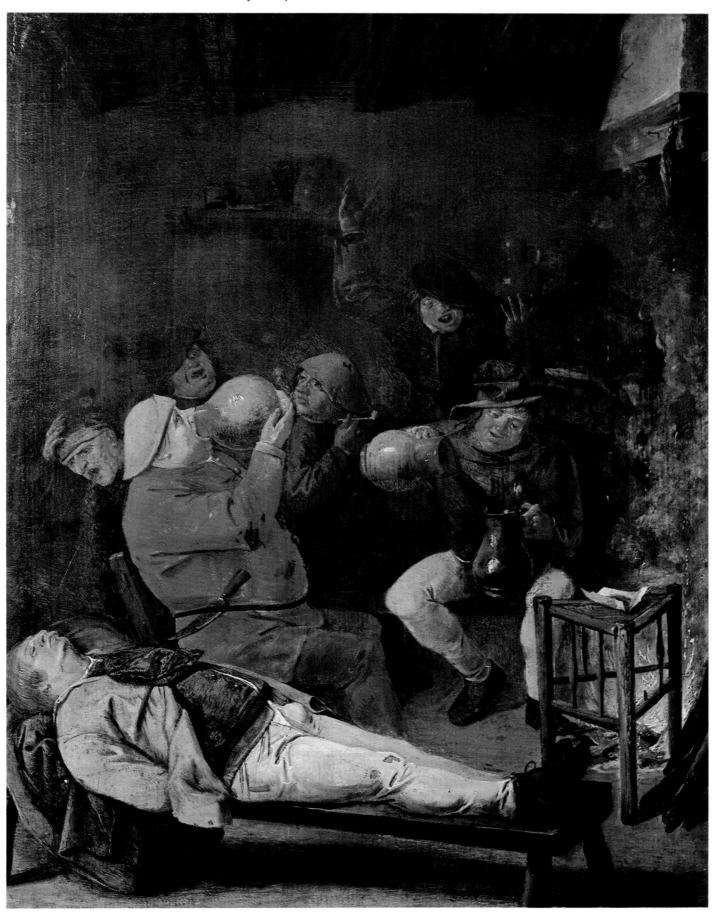

document and also with a rather sinister collection of figures in the background, one of whom draws a companion's attention to ominous signs in the sky. Bringing the two sides together is the figure of Tobias who stands right in the middle: his posture is farcical but his aspirations are lofty as he defiantly stares ahead to an uncertain future.

Steen's humour at its most sophisticated is not one which coarsely ridicules human beings but which rather points out the absurdly contradictory nature of their behaviour: ideals and pretentions are shown to be ridiculous in the context of reality. This is comedy in its highest form; and perhaps inevitably the paintings of Steen have often been compared with the plays of his French contemporary Molière. This comparison is in fact an appropriate one, as Molière's work enjoyed exceptional popularity in Holland, and Steen, himself a great enthusiast of the theatre, specifically illustrated a scene from one of his plays on at least one occasion. The greater sophistication of Dutch art as a whole in the late 17th century can in fact largely be attributed to the growing influence of France. *Genre* paintings of this period are not only more precious technically but also portray increasingly elegant settings. Eventually, just as France was to dominate the United Provinces politically, so too was Dutch society and culture to be subjugated to French tastes. Jan Steen was in many ways the greatest artist working in the United Provinces at the end of the century: he was exceptional both in responding to the more sophisticated atmosphere of the times and also in retaining an inherently Dutch love of realistic observation and healthy commonsense.

134 Jan Steen
Sarah and Tobias, 1667
Herzog Anton Ulrich Museum,
Braunschweig

In contrast to other Dutch genre painters, Steen has a much greater interest in telling stories in his work; this explains why he painted so many biblical subjects such as this.

135 Jacob Isaaksz. van Ruisdael
The Jewish Cemetery, c. 1660
Detroit Institute of Arts, Detroit

Beyond the tombs, dead tree and
ruins, all symbols of mortality, is a
rainbow signifying the divine pledge
of redemption.

As well as taking an unprecedented interest in contemporary
society, the Dutch painters devoted themselves to landscape to a
greater extent than any artists before them. Although one would have
thought that the Dutch landscape as a whole would be limited in its
appeal, the majority of Dutch landscapists concentrated on just one of
its aspects: thus there were dune painters, marine painters, river
painters. One artist whose work consistently transcends the pedestrian
is Jacob Ruisdael. Much of this painter's youth was spent wandering
around Germany, and memories of his early travels provided him with
inspiration for many of his later works such as the *Jewish Cemetery*
(pl. 135). Goethe wrote of this that 'even tombs in their ruined
condition point to the past beyond the past: they seem to be tombs of
themselves'. The essay in which this statement appeared was entitled
Ruisdael as a Poet; and indeed Goethe recognized that this artist did not
blindly portray nature as did his Dutch contemporaries, but rather
used it to evoke intense human emotions. Ruisdael's example was to
be of profound importance for the Romantic era.

Rococo Painting in Italy and France

Light, frivolous, decadent: these are the adjectives invariably used to describe the art and architecture of the period known as the Rococo. The word 'Rococo', like 'Baroque', was originally coined in a flippant manner, in this case to describe the shell-like forms typical of much ornamental art of the 18th century. Although the word 'Baroque' is no longer used as a term of abuse, 'Rococo' still carries with it such derogatory connotations of insubstantial charm that general surveys of painting invariably treat this style as if it were a pleasant but unimportant interlude between the major developments of art in the 17th century and those in the 19th. To defend the Rococo against such an attitude is by no means to dismiss the fact that it is a light and frivolous style, and that it came about initially as a reaction against the pompous classicism which had developed in Rome and France in the late 17th century: it is however to acknowledge that Italian and French painting of this period is also sufficiently varied to deny any rigid categorization. And more importantly, it is to emphasize the short-sightedness of accusing the art of the 18th century of being merely intended as light-hearted entertainment while refusing to accept that the now revered art of earlier periods such as the Renaissance was often equally unprofound in its intentions.

By the end of the 18th century, as we have seen, France came to enjoy a supremacy in the arts similar to that which Italy had enjoyed during the previous 200 years. However, Italian art was by no means a spent force; in fact in the 18th century it achieved an international significance greater than ever before, and Italian artists and architects were called to work in almost every European country including Russia.

In addition, the foreign tourist trade to Italy was stepped up in a dramatic manner, as it became almost obligatory for any gentleman of leisure to spend some time here; and when, towards the end of the century, changing European fashions and an increasingly insecure political and economic situation finally lessened its cultural importance, Italy lived on as a tourist centre, encouraging people, to this day, to visit it not out of any respect for its contemporary culture but instead to marvel at the artistic treasures of its past.

Venice, whose pre-eminence in the 17th century as an art market has already been noted, now came to be the most visited city in Europe. Writers on 18th-century Venice invariably characterize it as a city of pleasure, where gambling, evening visits to the theatre, the abduction of nuns and gliding on gondolas to a musical accompaniment were the order of the day. This romantic notion of Venice, although containing a certain element of truth, thoroughly detracts from a serious understanding of its art. The life of the Venetian painter was in fact an especially hard one, for in spite of the flourishing art market in the city, contemporary easel pictures were not greatly sought after unless they happened to be of local views that the tourist could take back home as souvenirs. The State, which had been a major source of patronage in

136 Giovanni Battista Piazzetta
Rebecca at the Well, c. 1740
Pinacoteca di Brera, Milan

Isaac's servant Eliazer offers Rebecca
costly jewellery when she is
gathering water at the well, offering
with it his master's hand in marriage.

the 16th century, was moreover too concerned with growing financial
burdens to devote much of its time to the commissioning of works of
art. The Church, in contrast, continued to offer painters a steady
stream of commissions, but, as with most other aspects of artistic
patronage in Venice at the time, it rewarded speed of execution more
than it did genius. Thus Piazzetta, the most outstanding Venetian
religious painter of the Rococo and someone whose works are the very
denial of insubstantiality, died in great poverty for the simple reason
that he could not paint fast: in the words of one contemporary he
sacrificed 'material gain in favour of quality in art'. The free and
spontaneous style of painting which was evolved by Piazzetta's
contemporaries, which to us now seems to embody the spirit of the
18th century and to be the expression of a joyful relaxed outlook on
life, can actually be interpreted to a large extent as the outcome of
extreme financial pressures.

The major commissions of 18th-century Venice were in the field of
large-scale decorative paintings, a field in which the Italians had always
been the acknowledged European masters. The artists who specialized
in this, however, worked for rich but increasingly reactionary patrons
and, in the second half of the century, they lived to see this type of
painting go rapidly out of fashion.

The greatest Venetian decorator of this period and indeed the last
Italian painter of genius to work on a grand scale was Giambattista
Tiepolo. Born in 1696, Tiepolo grew up at a time when the favoured
style of painting in Venice combined Caravaggesque realism with
strong echoes of Tintoretto. Already, however, there were isolated

painters (most notably, Sebastiano Ricci, Gian Antonio Pellegrini, and Jacopo Amigoni) who, inspired by the example of Luca Giordano, were evolving a more decorative and colourful style which looked back to Veronese. Although the innovations of these progressive figures were not easily accepted by the Venetian public, they singled out the direction in which Venetian painting would turn in its last great phase. By the late 1730s Tiepolo, who had actually begun his career painting in the then more popular style derived from Tintoretto, was likened by contemporary critics to Veronese, a comparison intended as the highest form of praise. The fact that this comparison was made is indication not only of changing tastes, but also of Venice's increasingly reverential attitude towards its artists of the past. For it is not as if Tiepolo was just copying elements from Veronese's style, but he was actually borrowing costumes and settings as well. Tiepolo's art in its maturity, although unparallelled in its dazzling splendour and technical virtuosity, reflected a city whose slowness in its response to change was matched by an ever more intense nostalgia for the great age of its history.

Tiepolo's most celebrated frescoes in Venice were in the huge

137 Sebastiano Ricci
Esther before Ahasverus, 1733–4
National Gallery, London

One of a series of religious paintings commissioned in Venice. The colouring and decorative style greatly influences 18th-century Venetian painting.

138 Giovanni Battista Tiepolo
Phaeton, 1731
Bowes Museum, Barnard Castle

A sketch for an early fresco cycle for a Milanese Palace shows Phaeton begging his father Apollo to lend him his chariot.

banqueting hall of the Palazzo Labia (pl. 139). The owners of this palace, the Labias, were rich businessmen of Catalan origin who had recently bought their way into the nobility. By employing the most acclaimed artist of the day, the Labias were clearly anxious to show off their extraordinary wealth and new found prestige. Their ostentatiousness was reflected in the actual subject matter of the frescoes: on one wall Tiepolo shows the Roman General Mark Anthony, who has come to Egypt with the specific intention of subjugating the Emperess Cleopatra, being swayed in his duty by the magnificent and provocative apparel which she has put on especially for him; on the other wall Cleopatra is shown dissolving a pearl in a glass of vinegar as part of a boast to Anthony that she would give him the most priceless banquet imaginable. Classical history painting of earlier generations was largely concerned with heroic scenes of war and was often of a very violent nature; the ancient world portrayed in Tiepolo's frescoes in the Palazzo Labia is merely one of sumptuous but shallow extravagance tempered by a strong degree of female interest.

It is but a short step from Tiepolo's blatant propaganda for his patrons in the Palazzo Labia frescoes to specific allusions to the nobility in his glorious apotheoses of the 1750s and 1760s. In 1751 Tiepolo was

139 Giovanni Battista Tiepolo
Anthony meeting Cleopatra (detail),
1745–50
Palazzo Labia, Venice

The Palazzo Labia was the most profusely and tastefully decorated palace of the Venetian 18th century; visited by virtually all the tourists to the city at the time, it later fell into disrepair, and was in a sadly abandoned state until recently restored by Italian Television.

140 Giovanni Battista Tiepolo
Apollo conducting Beatrice of Burgundy
to Barbarossa (sketch for a ceiling
fresco in the Kaisersaal, Residence,
Würzburg), 1750–51
Staatsgalerie, Stuttgart

The exuberance of this work's
composition was appropriate to the
architectural setting for which it was
intended: a dazzling rococo
framework of white and gold stucco.

called to Germany to fresco a room in the palace of Prince-Bishop Karl
Philipp von Greiffenklau at Würzburg: in the most elaborate Rococo
setting of gilt and white stucco (pl. 140), he portrayed scenes from the
life of an earlier member of the patron's family, the Emperor
Barbarossa, who was also shown on the ceiling being led by Apollo
into the heavens. The success of this decoration was such that Tiepolo
was asked to stay on in Würzburg to paint the ceiling of the staircase
(pl. 141); for this, the largest fresco of his career, he was made to show
a portrait of von Greiffenklau himself, suspended in mid-air and
surrounded by allegories of the world's four continents.

Greiffenklau's combination of exceptional wealth and an intensely
reactionary outlook on life was more extreme than in any of Tiepolo's
Venetian patrons. With the great social changes that were spreading
over Europe in the 18th century and that were to culminate in the
French Revolution, men like Greiffenklau and the large-scale decorations which they favoured would shortly, however, seem absurd.
There is certainly a very strong element of pathos in Tiepolo's final
years as a decorator, which he spent at the service of the most powerful
remaining bastion of traditional values in Europe – the court of Spain.
Even Tiepolo's apotheoses now seem somewhat lost in the context of
the massive, inhuman proportions of the Royal Palace in Madrid; and
in looking at these frescoes glorifying Spain one cannot help casting
one's mind forward in time to the satirical portraits of the Spanish
Royal family which Goya was to paint only 30 years later. Rubens'
glorifications of similar subjects, such as the life of Maria de'Medici,
succeed because the artist fervently believed in what he was representing; Tiepolo's succeed through the conviction of technique alone.

There is another side to Tiepolo's art – more intimate and openly
concerned with good and entertaining story-telling. This is revealed
especially in a series of frescoes for the Villa Valmarana near Vicenza;
in these Tiepolo portrayed lyrical interludes (scenes of love celebrated,

141 Giovanni Battista Tiepolo
*America, from Olympus with the
Quarters of the Earth* (detail), 1752–3
The Grand Staircase, Residence,
Würzburg

The success of the Kaisersaal at
Würzburg had prompted the patron
to commission Tiepolo to fresco the
ceiling of the staircase as well.

but above all of love frustrated) from the great epics of Homer, Virgil, Tasso and Ariosto. The overall decoration of the villa was probably enjoyed at the time in a similar way as is today a Hollywood tear-jerker or a sentimental novel. Tiepolo was aided in the Villa Valmarana and in its adjoining annexe (or *foresteria*), by his son Giandomenico. It is often said that the latter's frescoes in the *foresteria*, now in the Ca'Rezzonico, Venice (pl. 142), which forsake the world of myth-ology in favour of often amusing scenes derived from everyday life or from popular entertainments of the time, constitute a deliberate reaction against the grand manner of his father. This is actually far from being the case, for both father and son were simply adjusting their styles to meet the function of the building in which they were working: the Villa Valmarana was a modest country retreat, which afforded relaxation after the pressures of city life, and a convenient place to entertain guests.

One should also be wary of reading too much into the *genre* scenes of Pietro Longhi. Longhi's name is invariably coupled with that of the playwright Carlo Goldoni, whose writings were concerned with the portrayal of everyday life in Venice and occasionally contained slightly satirical observations on the nobility. The novelty and freshness of Goldoni's plays, which offered an alternative to the artificial and pompous costume drama of the time, made them especially appealing to the more free-thinking and enlightened circles in the city; but satire

142 Giandomenico Tiepolo
Pulcinella and the Rope Dancer (detail), 1791–3
Ca' Rezzonico, Venice

Troupes of the kind depicted here are exponents of a traditional Italian form of street entertainment called the *Commedia dell'Arte*.

143 Pietro Longhi
The Rhinoceros, 1751
Ca' Rezzonico, Venice

It is a measure of art's dependence
upon art rather than upon observed
nature that this rhinoceros
reproduces Dürer's engraving of two
centuries earlier.

was a dangerous business in the closed and defensive context of
Venice, and Goldoni was forced to move to Paris where the
atmosphere was more liberal and tolerant. Longhi's work, however,
had no satirical intentions and was painted solely for the pleasure of the
nobility, which enjoyed seeing depicted the leisurely and seemingly
untroubled world in which they moved; paintings like the *Rhinoceros*
(pl. 143) have an appealing but of necessity bland quality, and, like the
genre scenes of Tiepolo, they provide no hint of the biting social

144 Canaletto
The Stonemason's Yard c. 1730
National Gallery, London

The ruled precision of his
architecture does not prevent
Canaletto's views from possessing
atmosphere; dusty sunlight is here
magnificently conveyed.

commentary that characterizes the art of Longhi's English contemporary, William Hogarth.

One cannot leave 18th-century Venice without some mention of the innumerable view-paintings that catered for the extensive tourist trade. By far the most successful of the artists who specialized in this field was Antonio Canaletto, who, aided by the notorious English entrepreneur Joseph Smith ('The Merchant of Venice'), managed on occasion to command higher prices than Tiepolo. Francesco Guardi, who is compared with Canaletto, was in contrast little appreciated at the time and lived most of his life in very straitened circumstances; nor was he exclusively a view-painter, but rather accepted any commission that came his way, whether this was for an altarpiece, a portrait or a still-life. Guardi's works are today admired for their seemingly proto-romantic combination of free brush-strokes and sombre atmospheric effects; but perhaps these qualities were partly determined by the speed at which the artist had to work to make a living and by his lack of money to buy more durable colours. It was certainly an ironical reversal of fortune that whereas Tiepolo's art did not long survive the fall of Venice in 1797, Guardi's grew in popularity to such an extent that it is now praised in a way that would have seemed excessive to an 18th-century observer.

In 1720 the Venetian decorative painter Antonio Pellegrini paid a visit to Paris to execute a large apotheosis for the ceiling of the Banque Royale. Apart from the fact that the Bank itself shortly suffered a financial disaster, Pellegrini's fresco was heavily criticized at the time; for it represented a type of decoration that was antipathetic to

145 Francesco Guardi
Ascension Day on the Piazza S. Marco,
1775–6
Museu Calouste Gulbenkian, Lisbon

Napoleon described the Piazza San
Marco as the 'largest drawing-room
in Europe', alluding both to its
splendour on feast-days such as this,
and to the lively crowds of Venetians
and tourists who gathered here
normally.

contemporary French tastes, which had come to prefer the small-scale
and the openly light-hearted.

French taste had undergone a radical change since the hey-day of
Louis XIV and Charles le Brun. Towards the end of the 17th century
the once autocratic and unchallenged establishment of the Académie
Royale was split by dissension: on the one hand there were the more
reactionary artists, headed by Le Brun, who advocated the severe and
pedantically archaeological style of Poussin, and on the other there
were those, led by de Piles, who favoured the more colourful and
accessible art of Rubens. The latter, the *Rubénistes*, eventually won the
day. Symptomatic of the great changes in French culture and society at
the beginning of the 18th century is a painting by a leading artist of this
period, Antoine Watteau: this, the *Enseigne de Gersaint* (Paris, Louvre)
is a scene inside an art dealer's premises, and includes in the left hand
corner a man putting a portrait of Louis XIV into a packing case.

Watteau, who was born in 1684 at Valenciennes near the Flemish
border, moved to Paris in 1702 and was engaged for a while in the
lowest form of hack work, executing copies in a sort of picture factory
which paid very badly; he was not fully established as an artist until the
age of 28, when he was invited to join the Académie. The three major
sources of inspiration for his work were Rubens, the great Venetian
painters of the Renaissance and the theatre. His love for Rubens was
partly the result of his friendship with a decorative artist called
Audran, who at one time had a post as keeper of the Luxembourg
where the Flemish master's great cycle of paintings of the life of Maria
de'Medici was housed; never straying far from Paris, Watteau's
knowledge of Venetian painting was likewise gained from works
which he could have seen in his adopted city. Watteau evolved a new

category of painting, the *Fêtes Galantes*, in which fancifully dressed lovers are shown walking nonchalantly in landscapes that seem to be theatrical backdrops. The *Embarkation from Cythera* (pl. 146), of which there are two versions, is the most famous of these, and shows amorous couples reluctantly leaving the Island of Love. There was a wistful quality in Watteau's art, which writers since the 18th century have attributed to the artist's known mental and physical ill-health which led to his early death from tuberculosis at the age of 37.

The underlying melancholia in Watteau's fanciful paintings (the spirit of which is epitomized in the image of the sad clown in *Gilles* (pl. 147) somehow makes him more acceptable to present-day tastes. No such quality can be found in the work of Boucher, however, who specialized in luscious scenes of blatant pornography. Frivolous and undemanding, Boucher's art represented one extreme of the French Rococo; and the artist lived to see his works go out of fashion (a fate from which they have not recovered to this day) and be chastized by the backlash of morality.

The canvases of Greuze, a young contemporary of Boucher who eventually outstripped him in popularity, can be equally pornographic, yet their careful sentimentality had an increasingly greater appeal for the French public of the second half of the century; and several of the pictures, illustrating scenes from contemporary life, had a strong moralizing element that looked forward to the works of David. A more attractive foretaste of what was to come in the 19th century was provided by the simple *genre* scenes and still-lifes of Chardin, an artist who enjoyed at the time a very modest success in comparison to Boucher. Their source of inspiration is in Dutch art, but their advocacy of the virtues of humble domesticity finds also a parallel in the writings of contemporary thinkers such as Voltaire and

146 Antoine Watteau
The Embarkation for Cythera, 1718
Schloss Charlottenburg, Berlin

In his *Garden of Love*, from which this derives, Rubens repeatedly paints himself; the poignancy of this painting is that the artist is a non-participant.

147 Antoine Watteau
Gilles, c. 1718
Musée National du Louvre, Paris

The notion of a clown being a tragic
figure, which persisted until the time
of Charlie Chaplin, can be said to
have begun with this painting.

148 François Boucher
L'Odalisque 1744–5
Musée National du Louvre, Paris

Boucher, who was one of the most
prolific painters of the nude in the
18th century, shocked Reynolds by
telling him that he had never painted
directly from the model since his
youth.

Rousseau. The last great representative of the more frivolous side of
the French Rococo was Jean-Honoré Fragonard. The *Swing* (pl. 150),
showing a young girl offering a revealing glimpse of her legs to an
admirer, is more exhuberant in its composition than anything to be
found in Boucher; at other times, in Fragonard's art, such exhuberance
of composition is matched by an almost febrile intensity of colour and
a freedom in the handling of paint that makes even the works of Frans
Hals seem restrained. It is appropriate for a discussion of the French
Rococo to end with Fragonard just as it was appropriate that one on
the French Baroque should have ended with Le Brun: both these
painters stood for the two opposing elements in the French character,
the one for the light-hearted and spontaneous, the other for the rational
and severe. The qualities represented by Fragonard were challenged by
Louis David and the French Neo-classicists; but they were to be
revived at the end of the 19th century by Renoir and the Impressionists. The years immediately following the French revolution were
nonetheless hard times for artists of Fragonard's generation. Aged and
forgotten, Fragonard himself lived on until 1806 when, ironically
enough for this quintessentially Rococo painter, he dropped dead from
the shock of eating an ice-cream on a hot summer's day.

149 Jean Baptiste Siméon Chardin
The Kitchenmaid
National Gallery of Art, Washington
D.C. (Samuel H. Kress Collection)

Chardin's application of rough
pastel-like oil paint, for all its
sobriety, is as beguiling as the
exuberance of any of his
contemporaries.

150 Jean-Honoré Fragonard
The Swing, 1767
Wallace Collection, London

From his drawings of the Villa d'Este
at Tivoli Fragonard derived the
conception of a 'pleasure garden'
which served him for innumerable
paintings.

Neo-Classicism and Romanticism

During the years 1750 to 1850 art underwent fundamental changes. The period witnessed transformations so radical, complex and pregnant with future possibilities that one can speak for the first time of a decisive break with tradition, and the exploration of recognizably modern modes of expression. The vast and militant aesthetic literature of the time answered the need to describe, explain and often attack what was essentially different about contemporary art. 'Romantic' was the word most frequently applied to this quality and to the loose confederation of dissenting artists seeking to break with traditional values in art. Yet ironically the self-proclaimed standardbearers of orthodoxy, the Neo-classical faction, had not long before taken up the stance of a rebellious avant-garde, affirming their own vision of artistic regeneration. Their break with tradition was almost as radical as that of the Romantics, and in one respect defined the character of the later development, since Neo-classicism was the first self-conscious revolt against pictorial attitudes to justify itself with a reasoned ideology. As such, it set a pattern for modern art as a whole. The art politics of the time may encourage the idea that Neo-classicism and Romanticism were opposing camps in a battle of styles, but from our own viewpoint, the essential unity of the period becomes clear. The fact that the well-known Neo-classical painter J. L. David was claimed by the Romantics as the founder of modern French painting did not strike contemporaries as incongruous. Since the earlier revolution had defined the conditions upon which the later one was based, we can see the Classic-versus-Romantic debate did not centre on the issue of the break with tradition as such, but on the principles that should lie behind such a break.

The new attitude in the arts formed part of the general cultural transformation of Europe around this time. That crucial movement in the history of ideas known as the 'Enlightenment' initiated and developed patterns of thought which are essentially those of our own time. Taking as their guiding principle the idea that rationalism and an earnest spirit of enquiry would sweep away superstition and reveal the right way in which to live, educated gentlemen concentrated their intellectual energies upon every aspect of existence. Neither the mysteries of nature, nor the human heart, nor the accepted truths of conventional religion were exempt from the critique of reason. Men realized that a new era had dawned, and that one had every cause to be positive; yet they were also well aware that the legacy for the future was an equivocal one. The 'Enlightenment' released forces of change that ultimately transformed the structure of society through a series of technological and political upheavals; its progeny were the 'dark satanic mills' of the Industrial Revolution and the political revolutions in America and France that heralded the modern political world. Its ideas, taken to their logical conclusion, and sometimes beyond it, were to change irrevocably the structure of every man's experience.

'Paint like they spoke in Sparta.' Denis Diderot's challenge to the

151 Jean Baptiste Greuze
The Son punished, 1777
Musée National du Louvre, Paris

The dissolute son returns home too late to effect a reconciliation between himself and his father.

painters of France was spurred by the demands of late 18th-century intellectuals that painting should abandon the sensuous enchantments of the Rococo and regain its lost purity by adopting the austere ideals of antiquity. The *philosophes* wished to preside over a renewal of the arts based upon a return to first principles. They saw in the classical past an ideal which they urged artists to emulate in order to chasten their style and develop a clear-headed and morally improving art. In their view, the function of art was not to entertain but to teach, and the heroic deeds of antiquity were to be depicted not as an escape from reality, but as an *exemplum vertutis*, a guide to moral behaviour in the contemporary world. That the age should hark back to antiquity for its sustaining ideals reflects pervasive influence of the classical tradition in European culture. Yet this particular classical revival can be distinguished from its predecessors by its coherent and unique vision of the past, and its moral urgency. It presented a chaste, rational view of Antiquity from which the libidinous and irrational Gods had fled and where Man dominated the stage.

It was the archaeologist, historian and art critic, J. J. Winckelmann who most memorably voiced the ethical values that his generation saw embodied in antique art. The philosopher J. J. Rousseau had proposed that in the advanced stage of European civilization life was both more artificial and less virtuous than in societies closer to the 'state of nature'. Winckelmann identified Rousseau's ideal of the 'noble savage' with the more primitive eras of classical Greece and republican Rome,

152 Jacques-Louis David
The Oath of the Horatii, 1784
Musée National du Louvre, Paris

This painting was inspired by a play
by Corneille which David saw at the
Comedie Française; it does not,
however, illustrate a specific scene
from it.

seeing the art of the Antique and the literature of Homer, Hesiod and
Aeschylus as the expression of an exemplary state of natural virtue.
What made his vision so compelling to the 18th-century mind was the
fact that for him the Antique did not simply embody a critique of the
present fallen state of civilized Man, but could serve as the source of his
moral regeneration. By following the examples of an age closer to the
'state of nature', and so more virtuous, modern Man could once more
achieve the spiritual harmony that was his rightful heritage. 'For us the
only way to become great and if possible inimitable, is by the imitation
of the Ancients'.

Winckelmann believed that his ideas were realized in the art of the
German painter Anton Raphael Mengs, whose *Parnassus* in the Villa
Albani in Rome (1766–7) was a conscious attempt to give to the Neo-
classical programme an appropriate visual language. In fact, Mengs'
fusion of Renaissance and Baroque classicism with the Antique only
makes clear how difficult it was for the painters of his generation to
sever roots which were embedded in the prevailing Rococo style. The
work may have spoken to Winckelmann of the 'noble simplicity and
calm grandeur of the Ancients, but it had little of the moral backbone
that critics such as Diderot required of the new style. 'To make virtue
attractive, vice odious and ridicule forceful,' Diderot once wrote; 'that
is the aim of every honest man who takes up the pen, the brush or the
chisel.' On the question of style, however, Diderot was less dogmatic
than Winckelmann and it was the work of J. B. Greuze, largely devoid

153 Jacques-Louis David
The Death of Marat, 1793
Musées Royaux des Beaux Arts,
Brussels

This painting, with 'A Marat'
written above the artist's own name,
becomes a personal message of
homage from artist to hero.

of classical trappings, that he felt was closest to his concept of art. Greuze's achievement was to adapt the format of Dutch *genre* to the educative and moralizing purpose of historical painting. Works such as *The Son punished* (pl. 151) of 1777 show him chastening his Rococo instincts by following severe compositional principles derived from Poussin. Rather than becoming diffused amid voluptuous Rococo billows of paint, the moral message is spelt out with a maximum of formal clarity.

The break with the Rococo and the establishment of pre-conceived, rationally-defined principles according to which art should be produced gave Neo-classicism a willed quality alien to the instinctive processes of normal artistic creation. A painter of the most rigorously logical turn of mind was needed to forge the synthesis that its programme demanded. This painter emerged in the figure of Jacques-Louis David, whose ruling virtues were will and passion, and whose achievement was the outcome of a determination to push his talents further than his initial difficulties as a painter seemed to justify. As a student he had attempted suicide after failing, for the third time, to win the coveted Prix de Rome; yet through sheer doggedness he had pulled himself together, entered the competition again, won it at last and become one of the most brilliant and controversial young painters of his day. Though passionate, excitable, and instinctively drawn to the sumptuous, gestural manner of Rococo painting, David respected above all the primacy of the intellect; and it was the cerebral nature of Neo-classicism that first attracted him. It is a curious and surprising fact that when he arrived in Rome in 1775 he was certain that Antiquity could offer him nothing. A chance meeting while in Naples with the art theorist and archaeologist and disciple of Winckelmann, Quatremère de Quincy, changed the direction of his art; and it is revealing that the man who opened his eyes to the greatness of the

154 Jacques Louis David
The Consacration of the Emperor Napoleon I and the Coronation of the Empress Josephine, 1806–7
Musée National du Louvre, Paris

David employs Rubens *Crowning of Marie de' Medici* as a source for this composition, except that here Napoleon is not crowning his queen but himself.

155 Antoine-Jean Gros
The Battle of Eylau, 1808
Musée National du Louvre, Paris

The presence of Napoleon gives
strength to the dying man in the
foreground who gestures as if
towards Christ himself.

Antique was not a painter but an intellectual. De Quincy inspired in
the young artist a sense of urgent reformatory purpose, but an
appropriately 'purist' style had still to be evolved. His years in Rome
saw David alert to anything in the art of the past that might give his
own art definition, and the range of sources upon which he drew was
wide: Greek and Roman sculpture, Caravaggio, Baroque classicists
such as the Carracci, Poussin and even the Italian 'primitives'. His
Belisarius Receiving Alms painted in 1780–1 was a first step towards
pictorial reform. At this stage his style follows rather than leads,
however, for its consciously Poussinesque flavour owes much to the
achievement of a fellow student at the French Academy in Rome, J. F.
Peyron. David later said that 'Peyron showed me the way' and his
work certainly seems to have been focused and given direction by the
example of his rival. But within a short time, he had surpassed him,
producing in 1784 what was to be considered the canonical work of
Neo-classical reform, the *Oath of the Horatii* (pl. 152).

When it was put on public display, first in Rome and then at the
Salon in Paris, *The Oath of the Horatii* caused a sensation. The cream of
the social and intellectual worlds flocked to see it and many sensed that
here, at last, was a work that gave form to their concept of a regenerate
art. David concentrates with a stark clarity upon the essentials of the
narrative; nothing that might distract the spectator from its meaning is
allowed to obtrude. The scene is realized in sharp focus; it takes place
in a bare perspectival box lit by a raking light which strikes with its
keenest intensity upon the male protagonists; the figures are disposed
across the picture plane in profile so that the uniting gesture of the
oath-taking becomes almost diagrammatic; and the archaic pictorial
device of repetition gives the gesture a dynamic insistence symbolizing

stern resolve. The conditions of the State's commission had stipulated a rather different subject from the one David finally elected to paint: that of Horatius pardoned by the people of Rome on account of his exemplary service to the republic, after beeing sentenced to death for killing his own sister Camilla, whom he had found mourning the death of an enemy of Rome. For David this was morally too ambivalent to be an appropriate expression of Roman virtue, so he decided to illustrate a scene that is in fact only implied in the standard versions of the story: the point at which the Horatii swear to sacrifice their lives for their country. David thus applied the same principle of maximum clarity to his subject-matter as to his formal means.

The uncompromising quality of David's painting has led some critics to interpret it as a revolutionary call to arms. It must be remembered, however, that the work was painted (and accepted) as an official commission, and that its patriotic theme was perfectly atuned to *ancien régime* nationalism. Its revolution was a purely artistic one and,

156 Anne-Louis Girodet-Trioson
Ossian receiving the Generals of the Republic, 1801
Château, Malmaison

The most successful literary hoax of all time, the story of Ossian, was written by a 19th-century Scotsman, Macpherson, who claimed it to be a genuine Gaelic romance.

157 Pierre-Paul Prud'hon
The Rape of Psyche, 1808
Musée National du Louvre, Paris

The love affair of Cupid and Psyche
continued so long as the mortal
Psyche was content not to know the
identity of her divine lover Cupid.

moreover, one that was quite in keeping with the very progressive
artistic policy of Louis XVI's administration, which was that of
curbing Rococo extravagance and encouraging greater moral and
social purpose. *The Oath of the Horatii* was the outcome of that policy
and a summation of the intellectual aspirations that lay behind it.

After the outbreak of the French Revolution in 1789, David's art
underwent further transformations. He placed himself unequivocally
at the service of the Revolution, and this in itself was an innovation,
because although past régimes had been alive to the potential of art as
propaganda and had employed artists for specifically political ends, it
was virtually unprecedented for the artist on his own initiative to make
his work the expression of his personal political ideals. In the
revolutionary period all art became political and the classical theme
(whether through the conscious intention of the artist or not) became a
metaphor for the contemporary event; for in the rhetoric of the day,
the only parallel to the purity and vigour of the Revolution was to be
found in the history of the Roman Republic. David's *Brutus* of 1789
had originally been acquired by the Crown and yet, during the
revolutionary period, it became one of the icons of a cult of Brutus
who, as the most uncompromising hero of the Roman Republic,
played an important role in the propaganda of the new régime. By the
same token, the antique metaphor could be used as a means of dissent,
and in P. N. Guérin's *The Return of Marcus Sextus* of 1798–9, the

158 Jean Auguste Dominique Ingres
Bather of Valpincon, 1808
Musée National du Louvre, Paris

The softly-modelled pose depicted here was used in several other compositions by Ingres, including the *Turkish Bath*.

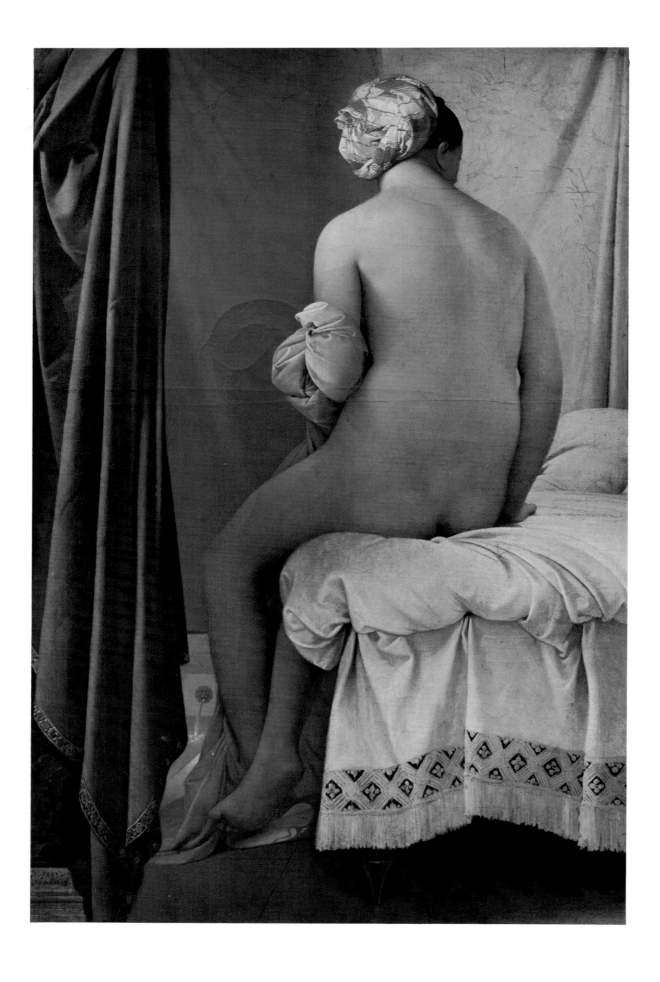

159 Jean Auguste Dominique Ingres
Mademoiselle Caroline Rivière, 1805
Musée National du Louvre, Paris

The model, her name alluded to by the river in the distance, is given a swan-like appearance.

experience of the *emigrés* who returned to France after the Revolution is parallelled in that of a Roman who has returned home from exile to find his wife dead and his daughter stricken with grief.

David became deeply involved with the most radical wing of the Revolution. He joined the Jacobin Club in 1790 and became a friend of both Robespierre and Danton; and as a Deputy for Paris at the National Convention, he was one of the signatories of the King's death warrant in 1793. During the Terror he sat on many committees, including the infamous Committee of Public Instruction, and only barely escaped with his life when a coup toppled Robespierre's régime. He organized revolutionary pageants such as the 'Festival of the Supreme Being' of 1794, and commemorated in paint the events and martyrs of the Revolution. Reality had taken on such an heroic quality that even classical metaphor appeared redundant. It was time to look the new age directly in the face, and David did so for the first time in his unfinished *Oath in the Tennis Court*. In this work, commissioned by the National Convention of 1790 to record the act that had sparked off the Revolution, David garbed the antique rhetoric of *The Oath of the Horatii* in frockcoats and wigs. In his commemoration of the revolutionary martyr J. P. Marat (pl. 153), he transfigured the sordid death of a rather dangerous man by reference to the iconography of Christian martyrdom. A Jacobin politician, Marat had been stabbed to death in his bath by the Royalist sympathizer Charlotte Corday on 13 July 1793. In David's hands these facts become the matter of a secular cult image with the resonance of a *Pietà*. Old religious values may have been pronounced dead, and religious art an anachronism, but the new era never ceased to measure itself up against the exemplary achievement of the past. David himself spoke of Marat in the same breath as

160 Théodore Géricault
The Raft of the Medusa, 1818–19
Musée National du Louvre, Paris

The French government was not unnaturally annoyed at this sensational piece of investigative journalism into the wreck of one of their ships.

161 Théodore Géricault
Lovers, 1815–16
Private Collection, Geneva

Cézanne, in his violent and brooding early period, was struck by this picture and freely copied it in a painting mysteriously entitled *A Naples Afternoon.*

the classical martyrs to Truth, Cato, Aristides and Socrates, and his death inspired one orator to intone: 'Oh heart of Jesus! Oh heart of Marat.' David's painting is a visual equivalent of exactly this kind of rhetorical hyperbole. And yet it is the image's stark realism that gives it its power. The knife lying bloody on the floor, the quill still in the hand, are means of emphasizing the shock of the murder, which has taken place literally a moment before. In 1802 Napoleon was crowned Emperor and David became his principal painter, celebrating yet another régime, now in a neo-Baroque style redolent of imperial pomp. This was no compromise, however, merely the pragmatic fulfillment of an ideal as dear to David as any specific political allegiance: that of placing his art at the service of the State.

It was Napoleonic patronage, however, that was to bring about the crucial break with Neo-classicism. Imperial propaganda (the glorification of Napoleon and of the military victories upon which his régime was founded) required that painting should forsake the Antique and find a new style appropriate to the recording of contemporary events. David himself modified his style without sacrificing its essential classicism. But in the hands of his pupils Antoine-Jean Gros and A. L. Girodet, Davidian objectivity and control dramatically gave way to a manner of painting designed to provoke the most irrational responses in the spectator. They created a propaganda weapon directed not at the intellect but at the emotions, dwelling above all on the exciting, the spectacular and the dangerous. Gros's *Battle of Eylau* of 1808 (pl. 155), for example, is not an objective account of that particular battle but an evocation of battle in general, revealing a fascination with violence, exaltation and the sight of men responding to their darkest instincts.

In the *Pest House at Jaffa* of 1804, Gros infuses Napoleon's figure with all the mystique of a saint, showing him touching a plague-stricken soldier as if exercising some supernatural power of healing. In the *Battle of Eylau* his hero is shown as the benign and noble Emperor, revered even by his defeated enemies and personally appalled by the bloodshed that his victory has entailed. Moved to compassion he intones: 'If all the Kings of the world could contemplate such a spectacle, they would be less avid for war and conflict.' Fine words, and excellent propaganda. On seeing the painting on show at the Salon, Napoleon immediately took the badge of the Légion d'Honneur from his own coat and pinned it on to Gros's, creating him a Baron on the spot. Though personally devoted to David and Davidian principles, Gros had unwittingly prepared the ground for Romanticism. As Alfred de Musset was later to declare, 'Look at Eylau ... and remember Géricault.' In later life, however, Gros became a pillar of classical orthodoxy and an active opponent of the subversive new movement. His own failure to create a classicism that presented any kind of challenging alternative to Romanticism finally led him to take his own life in 1835.

The restrictions upon the free play of the individual imagination that Neo-classical rationalism imposed were increasingly resented during the period of the Empire. The inevitable tension between subjective and objective attitudes to art had been anticipated by the champion of classicism in Britain, Sir Joshua Reynolds, when he made the

162 Eugène Delacroix
The Death of Sardanapalus, 1827
Musée National du Louvre, Paris

This depiction of sadistic brutality shows Delacroix's complete misunderstanding of the almost passive hero of the play by Byron from which this painting is derived.

163 Eugène Delacroix
Liberty leading the People, 1830
Musée National du Louvre, Paris

The allegorical figure of liberty
carries the French flag; Revolution is
the highest form of patriotism.

supremely anti-Romantic pronouncement that 'we need not be
mortified or discouraged at not being able to execute the conceptions
of a romantic imagination. Art has its boundaries, though imagination
has none.'

A conviction that it was the artist's right to extend these boundaries
and to strive to 'execute the conceptions of a romantic imagination' led
one of David's most brilliant pupils to break with his teacher and create
a complex and extravagant personal style that was the perfect vehicle
for his bizarre and irrational temperament. On leaving David's studio
and arriving in Rome in 1790, A. L. Girodet made an assertion that
embodies the essential idea of the Romantic movement: 'I no longer
wish to occupy myself with anything except my own ego.' Yet
Girodet's preoccupation was not the world of experience, or the
'mysterious way' of the human soul explored by other Romantic
masters, but the purely artistic problem of establishing his individuality in a world dominated by the achievement of David. The wilful
strangeness of his art was an extreme form of self-assertion. Taking it
on its own terms, the highest praise it can be accorded is that it in no
way resembles the art of his master. *Ossian Receiving the Generals of the
Republic* (pl. 156) of 1802 reaches such a pitch of fantasy that it might
have been painted deliberately to antagonize David. If so, it certainly
succeeded. 'Either Girodet is mad,' the older artist exclaimed on seeing
it, 'or I no longer know anything of the art of painting'.

164 Francisco José de Goya y Lucientes
The Third of May 1808, 1814
Museo del Prado, Madrid

Goya's painting *The Second of May* represents the Spanish insurrection against the invading French army. This sequel, *The Third of May*, shows the French recriminations.

A pronounced vein of fantasy runs through the art of the Empire. Gros's *Death of Sappho* of 1801, for example, is a near-visionary image of Orphic despair. But the most appealing of the artists to paint such highly-charged themes was P. J. Prud'hon, whose style was nourished by an alternative tradition of classicism to that of David, that of the subtle and erotic art of Correggio and Leonardo, and of modern masters such as Canova, who pursued lyrical ideals of grace and charm.

The desire to move beyond David motivates the early work of another of his pupils, J. A. D. Ingres. Later in life, when Romanticism actually threatened to submerge the values for which David stood, Ingres was to take on the role of guardian of classical orthodoxy. Yet in his youth, he displayed the characteristic traits of the rebellious avant-garde artist. Right at the beginning of the new century he wrote, 'Art could well do with reforming ... and I would like to be the revolutionary who does it.' At this time he was influenced by the most radical faction in David's studio, the group of 'Primitifs', whose extremist creed rejected the whole tradition of European painting and addressed itself to creating an art appropriate to the regenerate age by returning to a 'tabula rasa'. Their inspiration was ultimately political and their interest in the most primitive styles of the Antique, those of early Greek vase painting and Attic reliefs, was based upon the virgin sensibility such works were thought to convey. With Ingres, however, these sources become the raw material of an art sustained by purely formal concerns.

165 Francisco José de Goya y Lucientes

The Colossus, 1810–12
Museo del Prado, Madrid

A mistranslation from the official guide book to the Prado is irresistibly quotable: 'In his Black Period', it reads, 'Goya was at his most genial'!

'What is Romanticism?' The poet and critic Charles Baudelaire felt that this question still lacked a definitive answer as late as 1846. The meaning of the word had been discussed and analysed constantly since it was first used by the German critics August Wilhelm and Frederick Schlegel, around 1800, to denote those aspects of a work of art that were intrinsically modern. From the Schlegels onwards 'Romantic' became a badge which some artists wore to assert their individuality and which others, such as Constable and Delacroix, had pinned upon

them because no other seemed to fit. Perhaps the best way of defining the term is to examine just how these artists differed from the Neo-classicists. In classical theory, the artist's duty is to educate, ennoble and delight. His work has a clear social role since it must affirm established values; he mutes his personality in order to express his message with maximum clarity; inspiration is not denied, but it is controlled and directed by a calm and orderly mind.

The Romantic artist's duty is to himself alone; his work is an expression of feeling and personality, the illumination of personal ideals or a particular point of view. His art serves no social function since it is essentially the product of an independent vision; it may be immoral, or even subversive. The Romantic work of art is the product of a mind in turmoil, the outcome of fervent enthusiasm and imagination. There is no Romantic style; there are only Romantic artists, each of them pursuing an individual path into uncharted territory.

French Romantic painting reflects the sense of malaise and restless anxiety which characterized France after the fall of Napoleon and came to be known as the *Mal du Siècle*. The events of the Revolution and the Empire were such that those who had lived through them felt that a chasm separated them from the secure world of 'Enlightenment' values that had existed under the *Ancien Régime*. The old certainties that gave life unity and meaning had been left behind in France's forced march towards the modern world. The only certainties now were those of the individual's own experience; they alone had authenticity

166 William Hogarth
Mariage à la Mode: shortly after the Marriage, 1742–6
National Gallery, London

Hogarth is equalled only by Jan Steen in the variety of states of mind he can portray; in this case he brilliantly captures a general feeling of boredom.

167 Sir Joshua Reynolds
Nelly O'Brien, 1760–2
Wallace Collection, London

This portrait, depicting a close
personal friend of the artist, gives
ample proof of Gainsborough's view
of Reynolds as an artist of immense
variety and sensitivity.

168 Thomas Gainsborough
William Hallet and his Wife Elizabeth
Stephen (or *The Morning Walk*), 1785
National Gallery, London

One of the most sophisticated
examples of Gainsborough's
integration of figures and landscape,
both of which are bound by the same
restrained colour range.

and meaning, constituted some kind of reality and were the legitimate
raw material of art.

Théodore Géricault, one of the first Romantic French painters, had
private means and did not need to make a living from his work. Art for
him was a calling; he painted out of an internal necessity. His career
was fragmented with long intervals of lethargic depression, during
which he could paint nothing, followed by bursts of intense creative
activity. It was probably while undergoing a cure for some mental
illness that he painted a series of portraits of the insane, registering the
effects of that most disturbing of conditions with tenacious concentra-
tion; it was as if the artist needed to test himself, to see whether he
would be capable of expressing such bleak and confusing states of
mind and making them part of his art. He once said: 'If there is any
certainty on earth, it is our pain, only suffering is real.' Experience
compelled him to paint. He felt an urge to release and express inner
tensions through the creative act; and in centring his art upon himself,
by making his own fears, obsessions and enthusiasms his subject-
matter, he was introducing a new purpose into the visual arts. The
legacy of Romanticism has made this attitude commonplace and today
we take it for granted that the artist must above all express himself. In
Géricault's day, to do so was an act of defiance; by opting out of the
social framework in which classical art operated, the painter risked

169 Johann Heinrich Fuseli
Titania caressing the Head of Bottom,
1793–4
Kunsthaus, Zürich

Fuseli sees in Shakespeare's idyllic
and fanciful *Midsummer Night's Dream*
those elements which are grotesque
and fantasmagorical.

isolation, and also the possibility that his work would be misunderstood.

Géricault's *Raft of the Medusa* (pl. 160) of 1819 takes a topical disaster and transforms it into a simultaneously personal and universal statement on the human condition. The drifting life-raft had been a scene of all the degradations to which men will sink in order to survive; there had been mutiny and even cannibalism. But Géricault chose to depict the moment that was most poignant and full of suspense; when a rescue ship passes nearby, but fails to see the raft. The scene is one of false hope, asserting the futility of man's efforts and his insignificant position in a hostile and incomprehensible universe. The artist painted the picture in a state of almost manic excitement. He shaved his head, renounced the world, and locked himself away in his studio for some 18 months. To give the work authenticity, he collected a portfolio of information about the story, interviewed those who had been on the raft and even had a copy of it made by the ship's carpenter. This documentary approach was given special point by Géricault's obsessive dwelling on morbid detail. In order fully to understand what it had been like on the raft, he visited hospitals and mortuaries, observing and painting the dead and dying, and surrounded himself in his studio with a macabre collection of severed heads and limbs from victims of the guillotine. It is as if, to create the tension

170 Johann Heinrich Fuseli
The Nightmare, 1871
The Detroit Institut of Art, Detroit

Both the horse, a symbol of strength and passion, and the vulnerable position of the girl, make this a nightmare about rape.

171 William Blake
Newton, 1795
Tate Gallery, London

The figure recalls Blake's rendering
of God creating the world, except
that here Newton is banished to the
bottom of the sea.

necessary for the effort this vast canvas demanded, Géricault had to
feel the presence of Death at his elbow as he worked.

The art of Eugène Delacroix is the culminating achievement of
French Romantic painting. His exploration of the wilder reaches of
European literature, his celebration of violence and energy in both
animals and man, his fascination for the exotic and the decadent, and
his nostalgia for the medieval past gave the Romantic imagination its
ultimate definition. Yet Delacroix himself was too independent,
intelligent, and self-absorbed to consider himself part of a new
movement. He firmly believed in tradition and tried to keep out of art
politics; and when someone committed the *faux pas* of calling him a
Romantic, he wryly replied that he was a 'pure Classicist'. There is
certainly a sense of ultimate control – a classical virtue – in even his
most febrile works. But his art is essentially Romantic, above all
because it is focused upon the life of the ego. Delacroix himself stated
on another occasion: 'If by Romantic they mean the free manifestation
of my personal impressions, my efforts to get away from the types
eternally copied in the schools and my dislike of academic recipes, then
I admit that not only am I a Romantic, but I have been one since I was
fifteen.' Delacroix deliberately cultivated the individuality of his art,
extending its range by means of an increasingly expressive use of
colour and a free handling of paint. His work is the outcome of a state
of creative fervour. In his *Death of Sardanapalus* (pl. 162) of 1826, in its
unfettered violence and sensuality and its subversion of all the moral
qualities that the Neo-classical attitude deemed necessary to the work

of art, is probably the most important work of the artist's career. It is certainly the most definitively Romantic. Sardanapalus, whose empire has fallen, orders the destruction of all the possessions that have given him pleasure in life, including his concubines and his fine horses, and lounges impassively on the crown of the funeral pyre, watching the killings like a bored spectator at an entertainment.

Spanish painting of the late 18th and early 19th centuries is dominated by one isolated genius, Francisco de Goya. His artistic position is summarized in the inscription on one of his prints; 'The sleep of reason brings forth monsters.' Goya was a man of the 'Enlightenment' made Romantic by the sheer enormity of what he saw around him. His art is a despairing commentary upon the sway of destructive and irrational forces over mankind. It presents a world in which there are no certain values; the only truth is personal experience. Even during the Napoleonic invasion of Spain, the artist stood apart. Yet he recorded the atrocities committed in a brutal and unflinching series of engravings called *The Disasters of War* and in such paintings as *The Third of May 1808* (pl. 164).

Lord Byron wrote in a letter to Goethe of 1824 that in England there was no conflict between Romanticism and Classicism. At the beginning of the era with which this chapter is concerned, British art contained both nascent Romantic attitudes and tendencies that have recognizable affinities with continental Classicism. Romantic art in Britain hardly ever involved a collective act of renunciation, a conscious break with tradition, and was never associated with an avant-garde. There was no self-conscious movement, only individual achievements. The story of painting in Britain between 1750 and 1850

172 Joseph Mallord William Turner
Rain, Steam and Speed: the Great Western Railway, c. 1844
National Gallery, London

In the painting, as in the title, Turner combines the incomprehensible forces of nature with those of nascent technology.

173 John Constable
Study for 'The Leaping Horse', 1825
Victoria and Albert Museum,
London

Constable painted full-sized sketches
for all his important compositions;
their experimental freshness often
appeals to us more directly than the
final works.

is one of swift change and innovation. Indeed, the complexity of 18th-
century British art, its empirical and pragmatic character, make it the
most varied and advanced in Europe. In the wide range of its subjects
and styles, in its involvement with the bizarre, the apocalyptic and the
irrational, and in its stress on originality and the individual achievement, it anticipates French Romanticism by decades.

British art in this period was subject to very different conditions
from those that existed in France. The character of French art was
largely controlled by State patronage and the art policies of the
Academy; Classicism being the official canon. In Britain, State
patronage was fragmentary and followed no concerted policy, and
important commissions tended to be given to foreign artists. The only
flourishing *genre* was portraiture: and throughout the 18th century,
working as a portraitist was the only way a British painter could be
sure of making a reasonable living. The most pugnacious and
indomitable campaigner against this situation in the early 18th century
was William Hogarth. Frustrated by the lack of support for historical,
allegorical, mythological and religious paintings, Hogarth invented a
new *genre*, the 'modern moral subject'. This cross between Dutch *genre*
and British subject-painting dealt with contemporary issues, developing plots and characters through a sequence of striking images that
demonstrate not only the imaginative skill but also the high moral
intentions of the artist. The modern moral subjects were not painted
for specific patrons but for reproduction in the form of engravings; and
so the artist was at liberty to handle themes that were both popular and
appealing to his own rather cruel imagination. Hogarth had no
successors in the new *genre*, but his desire for a native school of painters
tackling serious subjects came to be a reality; and such works as his

Satan, Sin and Death, a theme from Milton, pointed the way for such late artists as James Barry and William Blake.

It is with Sir Joshua Reynolds that the British school comes of age. Reynolds saw painting as an intellectual profession which in Britain was not accorded the status it deserved. Since portraiture was still the only *genre* that the British patron was willing to entrust to native artists, Reynolds took the logical step of painting portraits that had the erudite and allusive quality of subject painting. A picture such as *Lady Sarah Bunbury Sacrificing to the Graces* of 1765 may seem an uncomfortable compromise, showing a buxom and very English-looking lady observing solemn rights in a classical Arcadia, but it was an original and pragmatic solution to the problem of educating taste toward the acceptance of native British painting.

The strain of individualism in British art is epitomized by Reynolds' brilliant rival, Thomas Gainsborough. Instead of searching after an elevated style that would proclaim the artist's seriousness of purpose, Gainsborough offered the public an art without pretension, which was frankly intended to delight and, in the virtuoso dazzle of its brushwork, to amaze. A born painter and in his own words 'a wild goose at best', Gainsborough's lyrical art is a throw-back to the heyday of the

174 Philip Otto Runge
The Hülsenbeck Children, 1805–6
Kunsthalle, Hamburg

The artist's concern to present children with no adult pretensions reflects his desire for an unsophisticated style.

175 Caspar David Friedrich
Man and Woman gazing at the Moon,
1824
Stiftung Staatliche Museen,
Nationalgalerie, Berlin/West

The object of contemplation in
Friedrich's work is deliberately kept
at a distance. It was because of this
that his *Crucifixion* was refused by the
church for which it was intended.

Rococo; yet at the same time his painting is innovatory in that its
charm and its mood of dreamy fantasy were for Gainsborough a form
of self-expression. *The Morning Walk* (pl. 168) is more than just an
engaging depiction of a newly-married couple in the countryside;
Gainsborough's subtle observation of the expression on his sitters'
faces suggests that he may have had some interest in the discussion of
states of mind which fascinated his contemporaries. But unlike Fuseli
or Barry, he did not extend his explorations to the darker side of
human nature, preferring to concentrate on the sunnier, more appealing aspects.

Perhaps inevitably, the major focal point of Neo-classicism was
Rome. In the 1770s, the artistic community in the city included the
Anglo-Swiss J. H. Fuseli, the French J. L. David, the Scandinavian N.
Abildgaard and the British painters, Romney, Barry, the brothers John
and Alexander Runciman and Gavin Hamilton. The British circle
played an important role in the definition of the Neo-classical style;
and yet, taking a lead from Fuseli, they created works which
anticipated Romanticism in both style and subject matter. Fuseli later
settled permanently in London, where his eminent if rather eccentric
example gave encouragement to other artists to explore psycho-
logically adventurous subjects. His most influential work was the
famous *Nightmare* (pl. 170), which shows a woman in the throes of a
sinister erotic dream.

'I am under the direction of messengers from heaven, daily and nightly.' Thus spoke Fuseli's friend, the poet, painter and visionary William Blake. In Blake's view, an artist was a prophet whose calling was to make manifest the realms of the spirit. He invented his own mythology, which related both to unchanging spiritual truths and to the political events of his turbulent age. His idea of the world was essentially Christian, but with radical transformations. Most notably he saw the Creation as an evil act in that it bound man's spirit by the laws of physical nature. In the *Newton* (pl. 171) of 1795, the great physicist is seen as one whose materialist philosophy will never allow him to understand the mysteries of the absolute. 'He who sees the infinite in all things sees God,' Blake once appended to this image. 'He who sees the ratio only sees himself.' As in all Blake's work, the figure of Newton is realized in the sharp focus that Blake felt to be appropriate to his visions: 'A spirit and vision are not vaporous but organized and minutely articulated beyond all that mortal and perishable nature can produce.'

One of the particular achievements of British Romanticism, as opposed to French, was the exploration of landscape as a means of self-expression. J. M. W. Turner was acutely conscious of the transience of human life. He was a fatalist who believed that all Man's efforts were doomed to disaster since they were subject to forces beyond his control. The title of the long, rambling and at times completely opaque poems he wrote to accompany a number of his works is *The Fallacies of Hope*. The first of these paintings was the typically spectacular and dramatic *Hannibal crossing the Alps*. As well as treating

176 Caspar David Friedrich
Moon rising over the Sea, 1822
Stiftung Staatliche Museen,
Nationalgalerie, Berlin/East

The presence of the heads in the golden light of the dawn produces the impression that this very light is the emanation of their thought.

177 Franz Pforr
Entry of the Emperor Rudolf of Habsburg into Basle in the Year 1273, 1808–10
Städelsches Kunstinstitut, Frankfurt am Main

The Nazarenes introduced a type of subject matter which was to be immensely popular in the 19th century: the grand reconstruction of Medieval history.

such historical subjects, Turner developed a type of landscape that was largely his own invention, in which scenes of everyday life are depicted on a monumental scale and made to express similarly elevated ideas. *Rain, Steam and Speed: the Great Western Railway* (pl. 172), for example, reflects a fascination with a protean reality, which is an essential aspect of the Romantic vision. In fact, the picture is based on direct experience: the artist held his head out of the window of the London to Exeter express for 9 minutes during a rainstorm.

The same desire for authenticity motivated John Constable, though with a wholly different result. Our way of seeing the English countryside today is so conditioned by Constable's vision that it is difficult for us to appreciate how radical his art was in the context of his own age. He was an avant-garde artist and his decision to centre his art upon the candid portrayal of the English landscape and trust his own experience rather than conform to time-honoured formulae was a very bold step. It was by no means the outcome of näivety; Constable was a very highly self-aware artist and his motives were far more ambitious and concentrated than they may at first sight appear. In 1802, at the outset of his career, he left London to return to his childhood home in the Stour valley in Suffolk, declaring that 'there is room enough for a natural painture', and setting out through relentless sketching to register the most fugitive effect of light and atmosphere. The fruits of his labour were transmuted into art in his series of large canvases of the 1820s recording scenes on the Stour, called 'six-footers' by the artist himself; the *Hay Wain* is the most famous of these. Constable was only successful in painting landscapes with personal association, and memory and nostalgia play an important role in his work. For all its proto-realist concern with fact, his art is ultimately romantic in that it is a response to the needs of his inner life.

'We must romanticize the world. In this way we will rediscover its original meaning ... When I confer a higher meaning upon the commonplace, a secret aspect upon the ordinary, the dignity of the unknown upon what is familiar, or an appearance of infinity upon the finite, I romanticize it.' These words of the poet Novalis convey the mystical side of German Romanticism: its obsession with speculative metaphysics and arcane knowledge, its view of nature as the signature of the divine and its conception of art as a medium of revelation. August Wilhelm Schlegel's description of beauty as 'the symbolical representation of the Infinite' could almost have been coined as its motto. The art of Philip Otto Runge, in its attempt to embrace the totality of experience and create a personal cosmogony which could serve as a substitute for religion, has much in common with Blake. Yet whereas that artist invented a mythology in which the physical world was seen as a barrier between man and spiritual reality, Runge saw in nature an intimation of the divine. His most ambitious work, the *Times of Day* cycle, employs a combination of landscape and symbolic figures to express abstract ideas concerning Man's position in the divine scheme. The artist once said: 'We must become as children again if we wish to achieve the best'; and in a number of his works, including the *Hülsenbeck Children* of 1805–6 (pl. 174), he expresses a typically romantic fascination with the child as the unspoilt guardian of nature's secret energies.

Caspar David Friedrich sought to express a sense of divinity in nature through landscape alone, without the elaborate symbolic language of Runge. This is not to imply that his paintings are literal transcriptions of given places; his work is rather a synthesis of landscape details, sometimes recorded over extended periods of time and derived from various localities. His finished pictures are the result of a meditative, even visionary process. He once advocated in a letter to a fellow artist: 'Close your physical eye so that you may first see your picture with the spiritual eye. Then bring to the light of day that which you have seen in the darkness, so that it may react upon others from the outside inwards.' His are landscapes of the interior; to the Romantic generation, the secrets of the universe lay in the individual heart, as well as beyond. Friedrich's pantheism is strongly marked by his Protestant background. He called nature 'Christ's Bible' and frequently invested natural phenomena with specifically Christian symbolism. The waxing moon in the *Man and Woman gazing at the Moon* (pl. 175) of 1819, for example, is a symbol of Christ, and the stony path a symbol of His Life. Friedrich once said: 'God is everywhere, even in a grain of sand.' But God's presence is indicated most insistently by light; and it is to the source of light that his human protagonists turn in their communion with the divinity.

The key theme of German Romanticism, the idea of art as a form of religion and of the work of art as a form of worship, were defined by Wilhelm Wackenroder in his book *Outpourings from the Heart of an Art-loving Monk* of 1797. In his assertion that each artist should find his own way of expressing himself rather than emulating the vision of others, and in his advocacy of medieval art, Wackenroder gave a decisive stimulus to the many artists who resented Classicism as a symbol of French cultural domination. Their call for artistic regenera-

178 Johann Friedrich Overbeck
The Triumph of Religion in the Arts,
c. 1831–40
Städelsches Kunstinstitut, Frankfurt
am Main

Overbeck recalls Raphael's fresco of
the *Disputa* in the Vatican Stanze,
except that here the arts have usurped
the role played by the Church in
Raphael's work.

tion took the form of a return to Christian values and pre-Renaissance
styles of painting. Wackenroder cited these as the highest expressions
of the spirit, but it was Frederick Schlegel who championed the cause
with the most fanatical zeal. For him, a medieval work of art was 'a
hieroglyph, a symbol of the divine, and that is what every worthwhile
painting must be.' Inspired by Wackenroder and Schlegel, a group of
young artists at the Vienna academy seceded from the art establishment and formed in 1809 the 'Brotherhood of St. Luke', an extreme
sect that closed its ranks against the world in order to evolve an art
purified by a return to the example of the medieval past. The
Brotherhood moved to Rome, worked in a disused monastery, grew
their hair long and wore archaic robes, which later won them the
nickname of The Nazarenes. The two main luminaries of the
movement were Franz Pforr and Friedrich Overbeck, its 'leader' and
its 'priest'; and most notable among the lesser members was Schnorr
von Carolsfeld. Pforr died young in 1812 and with his passing the

experiment lost its momentum; the remaining Nazarenes went on to dominate official art in mid 19th-century Germany.

The radical nature of the Romantic break with the past can only be understood if seen as a reaction to, and an elaboration of, the equally radical break with tradition already achieved by Neo-classicism. The rigorous logic with which the purpose of art was defined by Neo-classicism established an artificially rigid demarcation upon the limits of creativity which young artists, perhaps inevitably, came to resent. In its earlier reforming phase, Neo-classicism was fired by an enthusiasm that commanded respect. The idealism of an art serving the highest principles had been perfectly in tune with the ideological temper of the time. But conditions changed and those qualities essential to the classical experience were made irrelevant by a new, more complicated and ambiguous reality. Revolution, war and the general tide of men's thought made it clear that old certainties were no longer tenable.

179 Julius Schnorr von Carolsfeld
The Fall from the Rocks, 1833
Collection Georg Schäfer,
Schweinfurt

The fall from the rock is not a literal escape from a jealous father but rather a symbolic, dream-like representation of the experience of surrendering to love.

Realism and Impressionism

Gustave Courbet referred to his painting of *A Burial at Ornans*, (pl. 180) now in the Louvre, as 'the burial of Romanticism'. Historical perspective has borne out his assertion. The *Burial* does indeed seem to have inaugurated a new phase in art; one sees in it the first major manifestation of an attitude which is anti-Romantic – and equally anti-Classical – and which persists among avant-garde painters, including the Impressionists, until the mid-1880s. To define the period with which this chapter is concerned more precisely, one can take the date of the *Burial*, 1849, as a point of departure, and 1886, the year of the last Impressionist exhibition, as a convenient closing date.

From a political point of view, the most important country in Europe during this time was Great Britain. The liveliest artistic centre, however, was undoubtedly Paris; this had been the case since the mid-18th century, and would continue to be so right up until the Second World War. Here, within living memory, great events had taken place; and they had inspired great art. One thinks of how the work of David was bound up with the careers of his successive heroes, Robespierre and Napoleon. For better or worse, however, political life in France after Napoleon's departure was a distinctly unglorious affair; and the key moments were fiascos: an inconsequential 'revolution by accident' in 1848, and a humiliating war with Prussia in 1870. Artists certainly continued to involve themselves in politics, to a greater or lesser extent, and this is sometimes reflected in their work. But the tone is seldom propagandist, or even topical, and the views expressed or implied are wide-ranging; within the Impressionist group, for example, Pissarro was an anarchist and Renoir a staunch reactionary. More to the point is what such apparently disparate artists had in common; and this lay not in the conclusions they drew about the world, but in their way of looking at it in the first place.

Like many developments in the history of painting, Realism grew partly out of a dissatisfaction among young artists with what the older generation had done, and a determination somehow to do the opposite. To painters like Courbet in France and the Pre-Raphaelites in England, the differences between Romantic and Classical attitudes suddenly seemed a mere distraction from the important issue, for, judged by the criterion of Truth, they were equally damnable. Classical idealization and the Romantic notion that art should be personal and objective came to be regarded as shameful and outworn excuses to tell lies in paint. What was needed was a return to Nature, a way of showing things not as they would look in an ideal world, not as they appear to some self-obsessed individual's imagination, but as they really are. Everything that the artist had previously interposed between the spectator and the subject of the work of art must be removed; his job should be to record, not to comment; in short, it was time to do away with the whole idea of style. This aim was in fact an impossibility; a painting is a translation of three dimensions into two, and as with literary translation, two very different versions can be equally faithful to the original. Thus the Realist attitude could foster dissimilar, even apparently antithetical ways of painting from the meticulous delineation of details practised by the Pre-Raphaelites to the rapid, notational technique of the Impressionists.

Since the Renaissance, painters and critics had put a premium on the suppression of incidentals. Figures by Raphael and Michelangelo do not have warts, or any other idiosyncratic, identifying marks, unless the theme or the story demands it; and all the everyday 'irrelevant' distractions that surround events in the real world are omitted, leaving only what is essential. For the Realist, there is no such thing as irrelevance. Having accepted his subject, his duty is to go to it humbly and unselectively, inventing nothing. This is why portraiture takes on a special importance. Portraiture had traditionally been regarded as one of the lowest forms of art, precisely because it dealt in the given and the particular rather than the general. Now it becomes the basis of everything. Millais's *Ophelia* (pl. 181) is not an ideal of female beauty but an un-stereotyped portrait of a given young lady. Her setting is also a portrait – that of a stretch of riverbank at Ewell, a few miles south of London, as it appeared in the summer of 1851. Similarly, the Parisian places of entertainment in Renoir's paintings are populated with likenesses of his relatives and friends; and Courbet's *A Burial at Ornans* is a portrait of an actual event. *The Studio of the Painter* (pl. 182), the other great monument of Courbet's career, is more complex, but just as dependent on portraiture. The artist described the work as a 'real allegory'. As such, it is a bringing down to earth of one of the most elevated branches of painting. Traditional allegories use idealized figures to personify ideas; Courbet uses himself, his friends, his patrons and specific individuals he has observed.

There is an obvious parallel to this factual kind of painting in the concurrent rise of experimental science. As early as the 1830s John Constable had said that 'painting is a science, and should be pursued as an inquiry into the laws of nature'; in this, as in certain aspects of his art, he showed himself as precursor of the Realist movement. The idea that one's understanding of the world could be increased by patient and exhaustive observation, without *a priori* theories or beliefs, was certainly shared by Gustave Flaubert, author of Realist novels. 'The

180 Gustave Courbet
A Burial at Ornans, 1849–50
Musée National du Louvre, Paris

Courbet shows 50 of the villagers of Ornans gathered in the cemetery where his grandfather was to be buried.

181 Sir John Everett Millais
Ophelia, 1851–2
Tate Gallery, London

Events from Shakespeare's plays
figured frequently in the works of the
Pre-Raphaelites; here the theme is
derived from Gertrude's speech in
Hamlet.

time for Beauty is over', he wrote; 'the more art develops, the more scientific it will be'. In the precise documentation of the visible world, science's most exciting new tool was, of course, photography. Some painters regarded photography as a rival, but for the most part (and certainly among the greatest painters) it was seen as a challenge, an aid, or even an inspiration. The uncomposed look of photographs and the way figures and objects are cut by the edge of the image, were effects that were widely employed to give a slice-of-life quality to paintings.

The scientific attitude was applicable to all kinds of painting. In the case of historical scenes, for example, there was a new insistence: on getting the details right and avoiding anachronisms; making the spectator literally an eye-witness of the event, rather than spelling out its significance in terms of clear, theatrical gestures. But the most characteristic expression of Realism, as far as subject-matter is concerned, was the portrayal of contemporary life. The demand for 'modernity' received its most eloquent expression in Charles Baudelaire's article, *The Painter of Modern Life*, written in 1859–60. 'Modernity', he wrote, 'is the transient, the fleeting, the contingent; it is one half of art, the other being the eternal and immovable. There was a form of modernity for every painter of the past; the majority of the fine portraits that remain to us from former times are clothed in the dress of their own day. They are perfectly harmonious works because the dress, the hairstyle, and even the gesture, the expression and the smile (each age has its carriage, its expression and its smile) form a whole, full of vitality. You have no right to despise this transitory fleeting element, the metamorphoses of which are so frequent, nor to dispense with it.'

Mention has already been made of the English landscapist John

182 Gustave Courbet
The Studio of the Painter, 1855
Musée National du Louvre, Paris
(see pl. 2)

Constable, whose fact-recording, scientific attitude was in spirit proto-Realist. More immediately influential upon the development of Realism, however, was the work of a group of French landscapists known as the Barbizon School. Landscape painting in France had been dominated since the 17th century by the classical ideal of harmony in nature epitomized by the work of Claude. The artists of the Barbizon School, who came together in the 1840s and were named after the village they colonized in the forest of Fontainebleau, espoused an alternative, Northern tradition, stemming from the Dutch contemporaries of Claude and, indeed, including Constable. Their aim was to shun idealization in favour of observation, to put the emphasis on capturing the actual forms and colours of the forest, the play of light and weather effects, rather than making a beautiful scene that never existed, and never could exist, out of a stock of favourite elements. The most gifted member of the Barbizon School was Théodore Rousseau; his companions included Charles-François Daubigny and Narcisse-Virgile Diaz.

The formation of groups of artists like the Barbizon School is characteristic of the period with which this chapter is concerned. Romanticism had been essentially anti-social: it is symptomatic that Delacroix was famous for his aloof 'dandyism', and Turner, England's most important Romantic painter, became surly in company and often extremely rude. Many Realist painters maintained a similarly intransigent stance towards society at large; in fact, living the Bohemian life and baiting the bourgeoisie became standard behaviour for young artists. But to develop an intensely personal vision was not their aim; on the contrary, they welcomed the cross-fertilization of ideas, the camaraderie and the mutual assistance that close contact with other artists engendered. The Barbizon School, the Pre-Raphaelites and the Impressionists are probably the best-known examples of this phenomenon, but many others could be cited.

Barbizon was the home from 1849 to 1870 of Jean-François Millet. Though becoming closely associated with the Barbizon School, he remained independent from it in that he was primarily a figure-painter rather than a landscapist. The dominant theme of his work is agricultural labour. Though by no means a peasant himself (as he was once believed to be), Millet came from a fairly simple country background, and had handled peasant *genre* subjects, amongst others, during the early years of his career in Paris. In Barbizon, he developed an approach to this particular branch of painting that had the innovatory directness of Rousseau's approach to landscape. Peasants had traditionally been presented either as mere picturesque elements in a landscape, or as cartoon characters with amusing habits, flirting in forest glades or pissing against tavern walls. Millet shows them engaged in their more habitual activity of working; and, what is more, brings out the paradoxical effects their labour has upon them, brutalizing and ennobling at the same time.

Most of the Barbizon artists were Naturalists: they dealt in facts about the visible world. But Millet has a greater claim to be called a Realist in the fullest sense, because Realism transcends Naturalism in concerning itself characteristically with the harder kind of facts – those, in short, that may be unpalatable but must be faced. Facts about the rural working classes are a case in point, for the exhibition-going, picture-buying public was almost exclusively middle-class and Parisian; and the revolution of 1848 had shown (if little else) that labour was going to be a major issue, even a force to be reckoned with, in the

183 Théodore Rousseau
Willow Trees, 1856
Musée d'Art et d'Histoire, Geneva

The Barbizon artists had the technical freedom of the Impressionists but not their feeling for light and space; their paintings are sketches within a small compass.

political life of the future. Whereas Britain was already heavily industrialized, the backbone of the European economy was still the peasant. Accordingly, the peasant is a recurrent theme in Realist art, not only with Millet, Courbet and other painters in France, but also with lesser-known figures elsewhere, such as Wilhelm Leibl in Germany.

Courbet's particular contribution to the development of the peasant theme was to abrogate the convention whereby the treatment of 'low life' was confined to paintings on a small scale, while the grand subject, be it allegorical, mythological, scriptural or historical, was generally grand in size as well. The very wording of the title of *A Burial at Ornans*, with its indefinite article, is significant; for this is not an event of great moment like the funeral of Phocion painted by Poussin or the entombment of Christ painted by Raphael, Caravaggio and innumerable others; it is the burial of a nobody – in fact Courbet's grandfather – whose name was not even important enough to be worth mentioning. And yet the picture is huge. It is over three metres tall and the figures are roughly life-size. This is why it was regarded as a public outrage when exhibited in Paris in 1850; it was an affront to the established order of things, a parody, a monument to an occasion that distinguished itself only by its triviality. More disturbing still was its lack of any Christian, or even moral, dimension; all that happens when a man dies, it seemed to say, is that he is buried.

The scandalized reaction to the *Burial* was curiously paralleled in that to John Everett Millais's *Christ in the Carpenter's Shop* (now in the Tate Gallery in London) in the same year. Here the Holy Family was for the

184 Jean François Millet
The Gleaners, 1857
Musée National du Louvre, Paris

This portrayal of peasants working is saved from sentimentality by the austerity of its formal conception.

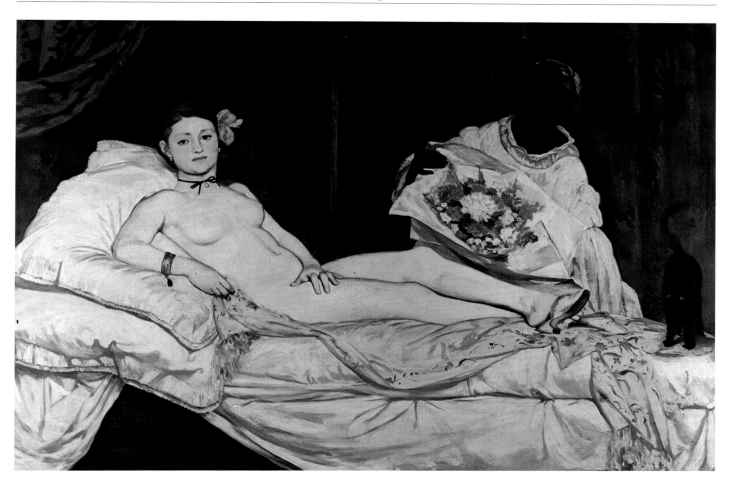

185 Edouard Manet
Olympia, 1863
Musée National du Louvre, Paris

Courbet said of this painting, when it was exhibited in 1863, that Manet 'paints figures like the faces on playing cards'.

first time portrayed, plausibly enough, as working-class and not especially good-looking; as people with dirty finger nails rather than perfect heavenly beings. The Pre-Raphaelite Brotherhood, of which Millais was a founder-member, was committed to reviving qualities that its adherents associated (rightly or wrongly) with art before Raphael. In their view, the painters of the early Renaissance had approached nature humbly and meticulously, and the idealization practised by Raphael and most painters since the Renaissance was a Fall from Grace. The sharp-focus naturalism they developed was essentially an expression of the same Realist spirit that animated avant-garde painting on the Continent; and they too soon began to treat scenes from modern life as well as more traditional subjects.

The urban counterpart to the peasant, as a favourite Realist figure, was the prostitute. This fact of city life provided both Courbet and the Pre-Raphaelites with subjects for major pictures in the 1850s, but its *locus classicus* in painting was reached in Edouard Manet's *Olympia* (pl. 185) of 1863. Baudelaire advocated the idea of the modern nude, and countered critical reactions against the *Olympia* some years before it was even painted, when he wrote in *The Painter of Modern Life*: 'If an artist . . . were commissioned to paint a courtesan of today, and, for this purpose, were to get inspiration (to use the hallowed term) from a courtesan by Titian or Raphael, the odds are that his work would be fraudulent, ambiguous, and difficult to understand.' Taking inspiration from such sensual masterpieces as Titian's Venuses was exactly what a painter of the nude was expected to do. Manet did the opposite; or at least, he took traditional elements and made of them something entirely modern. Titian's nudes are passive, often slumbering, realizations of male erotic fantasies. Olympia is pert and active; she scrutinizes the spectator (her client) rather than *vice versa*; she appears to have a mind as well as a body. When Baudelaire complained that the modern courtesan would be 'difficult to understand' when cast in a conventional mould, it was this specifically modern psychological content that he was calling for. *Olympia* would remind men neither of revered paintings of the past nor of their fantasies; but it might remind them of real encounters with living women.

The masterpiece of the Pre-Raphaelite painter Ford Madox Brown is called simply *Work*. This, another favourite Realist theme, was, surprisingly, an innovatory one; for work had never before been considered a worthy subject for painters to tackle. It is certainly not a subject likely to appeal to those who regard art as an escape from all that is unpleasant in the world; but then again, that attitude is basically opposed to Realism itself. Though ostensibly an everyday scene of navvies digging up a road, Brown's picture is in fact replete with symbolism; it is a tract in paint on the virtues of honest toil. This is characteristic of the explicitly moral stance often adopted by British Realists. More obviously attractive to 20th-century taste is the deadpan approach of Edgar Degas, whose art is all about work, and over-work,

186 Edgar Degas
Two Laundresses, 1884
Musée National du Louvre, Paris

The figures in this work seem unaware of the spectator who views them, in Degas' own words, 'as if through a key-hole'.

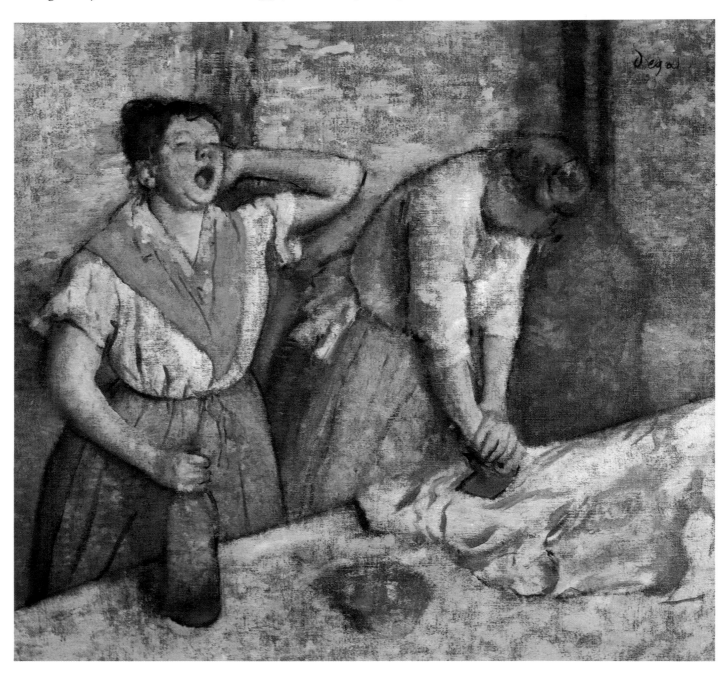

187 Frédéric Bazille
The Toilet, 1870
Musée Fabre, Montpellier

The nude recalls a figure of Danae by Correggio and contrasts with the Renoir-like figure on the right. The unresolved movement of the latter suggests an interest in photography.

in Paris. Even the ballet scenes for which Degas is bestknown today emphasize the laborious side to the dancers' lives, showing them often in a state of near-exhaustion after long hours of exercising and rehearsing. Indeed, there could hardly have been a more suitable field of investigation for the Realist than the ballet, beneath the glamorous facade of which he could reveal a harsher truth. Degas looks at ballet-dancers, jockeys, laundresses and shop-girls with the eye of a photographer and the understanding of a sociologist, recognizing momentary gestures that speak volumes more about the lives they lead than any literary symbolism, and recording them in the most detached, apparently artless manner possible.

Manet (born 1832) and Degas (born 1834) were middle-generation Realists; that is, they were younger than Millet (born 1814) and Courbet (born 1819) and older than the group of painters labelled

188 Camille Pissarro
Landscape near Pontoise, 1874
Nationalmuseum, Stockholm

The firmness of structure and
assertion of texture here show that
Pissarro was working side by side
with Cézanne at this date.

189 Alfred Sisley
The Flood at Port-Marly, 1876
Musée des Beaux Arts, Rouen

The Impressionists did not minutely copy a scene, they reproduced the experience of seeing it; thus only the word Nicolas is legible.

'Impressionists', who were almost all born in or around 1840. The most important members of this group were Claude Monet, Pierre-Auguste Renoir, Camille Pissarro, Frédéric Bazille (who died young) and Alfred Sisley. Impressionism developed gradually over a number of years in the late 1860s and early 1870s and the period of High Impressionism is generally considered to be from 1874, the date of the group's first joint exhibition, to 1886, the date of its last. Manet and Degas were closely associated with the group, and their work of the 1870s and '80s shows an Impressionist influence; but there were basic differences of emphasis in their views on art. Manet and Degas were interested above all in social facts; naturalism – objectivity in the depiction of people and things – was for them a means to an end.

The Impressionists inherited their concern with chronicling modern life and tackling new subjects; their early work was especially indebted to Manet, and the way they avoided idyllic countryside in their landscapes in favour of scenes in the Paris suburbs shows the same perverse spirit as both older men in their choice of subject-matter. The Impressionists felt, however, there was still a great deal to be said about what people and things really looked like, quite independently of sociological or psychological observations. In short, the truth they wanted to get at was an optical rather than a human one.

The Impressionists believed in the innocent eye; that is, the notion

191 Claude Monet ▷
Women in the Garden, 1867
Musée National du Louvre, Paris

Monet attempted to gain official
recognition by painting a large figure
composition. The three women to
the left are all portraits of his mistress
Camille.

190 Claude Monet
Impression: Sunrise, 1872
Musée Marmottan, Paris

Both the time of day and choice of
motif aid Monet in disregarding
detail and concentrating on effects of
atmosphere and light.

that a scene could, and should, be recorded wholly impersonally, as if
the artist were unaware of the structure of what he is looking at. Manet
said that he wished that he had been born blind and suddenly regained
his sight, because this would have enabled him to paint solely what he
saw, as opposed to what he knew to be there, to capture precisely the
momentary disposition of coloured lights playing on his retina. To
illustrate this idea, one might take the way in which snow had always
been depicted in art as the pure white that every one knows it to be. In
fact, of course, snow is coloured by whatever light falls on it; if the sky
above is blue, so is the snow, and the Impressionist will paint it as
such. Similarly, because of an effect known as the 'negative after-
image', objects are coloured by their surroundings. A white dot on a
red background appears tinged with red's 'complementary', or colouristic opposite, green. (The main complementaries are red and
green, orange and blue, and yellow and violet.) By the same process,
the shadows in a piece of red drapery are not merely a deeper shade of
red, they are greenish; and again, in order to be true to his optical
experience, the Impressionist paints them as such.

Before the Impressionists, landscapes were normally painted from
start to finish in the studio, on the basis of preparatory sketches made
in front of the motif. The few artists who did actually paint outdoors,
such as Constable and the Barbizon School, were effectively sketching
in an alternative medium to chalk or pencil, since the works they
considered finished and exhibitable were invariably done as studio

192 Pierre Auguste Renoir
La Baigneuse au Griffon, 1870
São Paolo, Museu de Arte Moderna

Renoir, more than any other
Impressionist, respected the art of the
past. This slightly staged nude pays
tribute to Rubens and the *Medici
Venus.*

productions. The Pre-Raphaelites painted backgrounds for important
pictures outdoors, but the figures were always added in the studio,
often with rather artificial-looking results. The Impressionists, by
contrast, made painting *en plein air* a positive article of faith. How
better to capture one's experience directly than by altogether abolish-
ing the intermediary sketch? Or, to put it another way, the Impressionists, to the dismay of their more conservative colleagues,
regarded the 'sketch' made outdoors as a work of art complete in itself.
Working directly from the motif went hand in hand with working
quickly, in order to register light and weather effects before they
changed beyond recognition and thus negated the whole point of being
outdoors at all. For the Impressionists saw nature as being in a constant
state of flux; to be fully naturalistic, therefore, was to record a fleeting

impression; and hence their name. The typical Impressionist picture was painted in a very short time, and – intentionally – it shows. The brush work is clearly visible, suggesting rapid dabbing, stroking and flecking movements, freshness and spontaneity.

Certain motifs lend themselves to treatment in the Impressionist idiom better than others, and the most sympathetic of all is water. Broken brushwork is well suited to conveying movement on the surface of lakes, rivers and the sea. But more important is the way in which solid objects are reduced, when reflected in choppy water, to a confusion of colours difficult to interpret in terms of structure. For this reason, choosing to paint water is a simple aid to painting without preconceptions; it is a way of putting oneself in the position of the man born blind who has regained his sight and perceives neither space nor three-dimensional form, only colour. Water features in innumerable Impressionist paintings, among them some of the key works of the movement: the pictures Monet and Renoir painted in the summer of 1869 at a bathing-place on the Seine called La Grenouillère were in many ways the first fully Impressionist pictures; Monet's *Impression: Sunrise* (pl. 190) was the work that prompted a critic, in a spirit of derision, to give the group the name by which it has been known ever since; and Alfred Sisley's greatest paintings were inspired by the floods at Port-Marly in 1876.

The Impressionists were fascinated by any form-dissolving, and transient effect, including some never before thought worth painting.

193 Philip Wilson Steer
Boulogne Sands, 1892
Tate Gallery, London

Steer inserts into his Impressionist examination of dazzling sunshine something of the world of Lewis Carroll.

When one of Monet's scenes of fog was criticized for the unsuitability of its subject, he characteristically determined to find an even foggier one for his next picture, finally hitting upon a view inside the steam and smoke filled Paris railway station of Saint-Lazare. What attracted the Impressionists to snow, another favourite motif, was exactly the quality of reflectivity that has already been described. The snowy scene was a branch of landscape-painting where, to use a scientific analogy of which the Impressionists would have approved, there was plenty of scope for research and experimentation. And in summer the play of brilliant sunshine on beaches provided material for equally challenging case studies. With interior subjects, there was a distinct preference for places of popular entertainment, with their multifarious lights and reflections. Renoir's *La Loge*, a scene in a theatre, is a particularly beautiful example, with its observation of colours reflected in the white parts of the couple's clothes. Renoir believed that a picture should be a celebration of sensual pleasure, both in the manner of painting and the subject, and he made many studies of parties and dances at places such as the famous *Moulin de la Galette* in Montmatre, taking a delight in capturing complex mixtures of natural and artificial illumination.

The Impressionists were the most original artists in Europe in the 1870s, but they were hardly recognized as such at the time; in fact, if they were publicly known at all, it was as a distinctly unrespectable clutch of free-thinkers, whose major claim to fame was that their work was universally held up to ridicule whenever it was exhibited. It is not surprising, therefore, that Impressionism was little disseminated outside France, at least until critical reactions to it softened in the following decade. In England, it was pioneered by Philip Wilson Steer, Walter Sickert and other painters associated with the New English Art

194 George Hendrik Breitner
Bridge over the Singel at the Paleisstraat in Amsterdam, 1893–8
Rijksmuseum, Amsterdam

This Dutch Impressionist took to Holland Degas' conception of the eye as camera. His sombre realism earned him the name 'The Zola of Amsterdam'.

195 Max Liebermann
The Man with Parrots, 1902
Museum Folkwang, Essen

The two red parrots conversing
provide an ironic commentary on the
social activity portrayed in the
background.

Club. Influenced by both Monet and Renoir, Steer's greatest works are
the shimmering beach scenes with girls playing that he painted in the
late 1880s and early 1890s. At the same time in Amsterdam, Georg-
Hendrick Breitner was developing a Dutch Impressionist idiom
characterized by earthier colours inherited from the Barbizon-in-
fluenced 'Hague School', within which he had been trained; and a
similar path – from Millet to Monet – was followed in the 1890s by the
German painter Max Liebermann.

By the time Impressionism was catching on abroad, the original
members of the Impressionist group were beginning, each in his own
way, to question the whole basis of the movement. The creation of an
impression of a given scene at a given instant, with a real feeling of
outdoor light and atmosphere, had initially seemed a valid aim in itself.
But once this had been mastered, one faced the problem of sheer
repetitiveness. The solution was to sacrifice the principle of maximum
naturalism in the interest of other qualities. The colours in Monet's
canvases became increasingly vibrant, to the point of implausibility,
even as the heightened retinal experiences of a blind man suddenly

cured; Renoir became more of a figure-painter than a landscapist, pursuing his tendency to explicit hedonism; in his later work, his particular *joie de vivre* finds its embodiment in an obsessive study of the female nude; and Pissarro fell heavily under the influence of Georges Seurat, one of the young painters of the 1880s who similarly addressed themselves to finding ways out of the Impressionist *impasse* and whose work is discussed in the next chapter. The fact that Impressionism was superseded as the avant-garde movement in French art did not, however, mean that pictures of quality ceased to be painted in an Impressionist idiom. Pierre Bonnard and Edouard Vuillard carried the tradition into the 20th century, showing some awareness of Post-Impressionist ideas but, more insistently, reaffirming the movement's first principles. Theirs is a Post-Impressionist Impressionism.

The position of Realism and Impressionism in the history of painting is a paradoxical one; each movement was simultaneously a beginning and an end. Realism's importance lies largely in the realm of

196 Pierre Bonnard
Nude in Lamplight, c. 1912
H. R. Hahnloser Collection, Berne

Bonnard adopts Degas' 'key-hole' view of nudes, but the model is his wife and the attitude tender and intimate.

197 Edouard Vuillard
The Public Garden, 1894
Musée National d'Art Moderne, Paris

Vuillard's art is more concerned with
decorative effects than with realistic
representation.

subject-matter. After *A Burial at Ornans*, artists saw that anything,
whether in the human world or in nature, could be the basis for a work
of art; nothing was beneath their attention; indeed, it was their duty to
face those facts of life that artists had previously shunned. But almost
as soon as this great liberation had taken place, there was a shift of
emphasis whereby the artist's choice of subject came to be regarded as
less important than his manner of treating it. Beginning with
Impressionism and continuing in an increasingly blatant form through
Post-Impressionism, Fauvism and Cubism, the motif became a mere
peg on which to hang a style. The ultimate expression of this attitude
was, of course, the development of Abstract Art.

The greatest legacy of Impressionism was the liberation of colour.
As will be shown in the next chapter, even those artists who regarded
their work in some ways as a reaction against the Impressionists,
acknowledged that their freshness and boldness of colour represented a
breakthrough without which their own experiments would not have
been possible. Impressionism was literally the last word in naturalism,
the culmination of a process of approximating art to actual visual
experience that had begun in the Renaissance. After this point had been
reached, however, artists began to develop a radically different
conception of what a painting should be, and one that had more in
common with pre-Renaissance and 'primitive' art. It was time, they
felt, to acknowledge the fact that a picture is a surface decorated with
colours and lines; and that disguising this surface as a piece of the real,
three-dimensional world is neither essential nor even desirable, since
the artist's job is not primarily to represent, but to create.

Symbolism and
Post-Impressionism

This chapter is concerned primarily with painting from the mid 1880s, a time when advanced artists were becoming disenchanted with Impressionism, to the watershed year of 1905, in which the first Fauve paintings were produced and the first steps taken towards Cubism. The period is dominated by the four great Post-Impressionists, Seurat, van Gogh, Gauguin and Cézanne. Before discussing their work, however, it is essential to consider an aspect of artistic life in the second half of the 19th century that has not yet been mentioned, both because it has an important bearing on Post-Impressionist painting, and for its own sake. This is what was often called 'Idealism' in its own day, but is now generally known as Symbolism.

Symbolism was an alternative, both to the vapid, conservative kind of painting that was popular with the public but is now largely ignored, and to the Realist-Impressionist tradition which is the subject of the previous chapter. It matured first in French art of the 1860s, particularly in the work of Pierre Puvis de Chavannes and Gustave Moreau; but it was an international phenomenon, developing independently in England, Germany, Switzerland and the Low Countries around the same time. Symbolism is one of those movements in art that are easier to define by examples than by principles. It can be said, however, that the basic requirement of a Symbolist painting is that it should represent an idea or thought rather than merely something observed in the real world. The concept is an anti-Realist one. Courbet asserted that painting was a concrete art, in which there was no place for the abstract; the Symbolists, by contrast, believed that finding an appropriate physical clothing for the spiritual was art's only legitimate concern. The Realists made a point of taking subjects from everyday life. The typical Symbolist work of art has nothing at all to do with the modern world. It has timelessness rather than immediacy; its title is probably some abstract noun, like Hope or Charity, Spring or Summer, Sleep or Death, because it is concerned with some general truth, not a particular fact. The spectator meditates upon this truth, often encouraged by elements of mystery and ambiguity in the work, and absorbs it into his own experience if he chooses.

Artists concerned with timeless values have traditionally looked for inspiration to classical art and literature, and Puvis de Chavannes espoused the French classical tradition in painting stretching back to Poussin via David. Like his predecessors, he was indebted to Greek and Roman sculpture, and emphasized drawing as opposed to colour. Yet his work is in certain respects completely opposite to theirs. The paintings of Poussin and David are distinctly masculine in character, with male heroes playing the leading roles and the severest virtues on display. Puvis takes up the more feminine conception of classicism that informs certain works by Ingres; he stresses the female nude; his figures are passive and static; their importance lies not in what they do, but in what they are. The serene ideal of beauty, the clear draughtsmanship and the boldness of composition favoured by Puvis, along

198 Pierre Puvis de Chavannes
Hope, c. 1871
Musée National du Louvre, Paris

This figure of *Hope* shows how
insipid Symbolism can be when not
accompanied by artistic conviction.

with the fact that his themes never go out of date, made him
particularly qualified for monumental decorative painting; examples of
his work in this public idiom can be seen at the museums in Marseilles,
Lyons and Rouen and at the Panthéon in Paris. In spite of receiving a
profusion of such official commissions, however, Puvis never became
an establishment figure. He was an 'artist's artist' and exerted a
powerful influence on younger painters, such as Seurat and Gauguin.

If Puvis is the Ingres of Symbolism, then Gustave Moreau is its
Delacroix, for he adapted Romanticism as Puvis adapted Classicism,
using its richness of colour and brushwork, but replacing vigour and
dynamism with dreaminess and immobility. Moreau took his subjects
from disparate sources, including classical mythology, the Bible and
ancient history. What he was always looking for was the archetype: a
character or situation that embodies some constant of Man's spiritual
life. His works are deliberately vague, both in subject and in style, and
their ambiguity stimulates the spectator's imagination, encouraging
him to make his own poetic connections as he daydreams before them.
Almost invariably, they relate in some way to sex or art, and
frequently to both. His treatment of the mythological theme of the
nymph Galatea (pl. 199) lovingly spied upon by the monstrous
Cyclops is a case in point. The element of sexual encounter is obvious,

199 Gustave Moreau
Galatea, 1880–1
R. Lebel Collection, Paris

The infatuation of the one-eyed
Cyclops Polyphemus for Galatea
eventually leads to his destroying her
lover, Acis.

but beyond that, Moreau undoubtedly intends to provoke some more general reflection on deformity (the Cyclops) as against perfection (Galatea), and hence on the flawed physical world as against the world of spiritual realities – art being the only bridge between the two.

Moreau's *Galatea* made a strong impression on the younger artist Odilon Redon, who took up the same theme in one of his own works, making the ugliness of the Cyclops and the sense of the two figures inhabiting different worlds far more explicit. Puvis (born 1824) and Moreau (born 1826) were close contemporaries, both evolving personal styles relatively late in life, in the 1860s; Redon was of a different generation, that of the Impressionists, and like the Impressionists, he came to artistic maturity in the 1870s. His attitude towards his naturalistically-minded contemporaries, however, was one of deep antipathy. In fact, he deliberately worked in monochromatic media (mainly charcoal drawing and lithography) in direct reaction against their insistence on the over-riding importance of colour; only late in his career, in the 1890s, did he begin to work in pastel and oil. Whereas the Impressionists attempted to capture the experience of the eye, Redon was interested in that of the imagination at its furthest remove from reality. The essentially descriptive attitude that lay behind Realism and Impressionism found literary expression in naturalistic naturalistic novels such as those of Emile Zola; Redon's work is the visual equivalent to a certain kind of highly metaphorical poetry, and

200 Odilon Redon
The Cyclops, 1898–1900
Rijksmuseum Kröller-Müller,
Otterlo

Redon concentrates on Polyphemus'
deformity, making him a creature of
personal fantasy, and arousing the
primordial fear of being watched.

in particular to that of the American writer Edgar Allan Poe.

Symbolism in Britain developed in the 1860s in the work of Dante Gabriele Rossetti and Edward Burne-Jones. Their work has been called post-Pre-Raphaelite. It represents both a return to the idealization that the Pre-Raphaelites had despised and a reaction against the story-telling in paint that characterized not only Pre-Raphaelitism but British painting as a whole. The 'Aesthetic Movement', of which Burne-Jones and Rossetti were the leading lights, stood for the idea that narrative was unimportant; what counted was content. Like the French painters already discussed, their work has close affinities with poetry. Rossetti was himself a poet and, moreover, identified himself strongly with Dante. Subjects connected with Dante's love for Beatrice recur throughout his work, reflecting his own obsession with the idea of the beautiful woman as an embodiment of spiritual perfection. Rossetti uses much flower symbolism, which is a characteristically British feature; his avoidance of facial expression is typical of Symbolist painting as a whole. The characters in Burne-Jones's work also wear masks of impassivity that set them apart from the common run of humanity. They are generally mythological or

201 Dante Gabriel Rossetti
La Ghirlandata, 1873
Guildhall Art Gallery, London

Rossetti's wistful-looking females are responsible for what has come to be known as the 'Pre-Raphaelite' look.

202 Edward Burne-Jones
Atlas turned to Stone, 1876–88
Southampton Art Gallery,
Southampton

Anyone who looked on Medusa's
head was turned to stone.
Perseus managed to avoid the fate to
which Atlas has succumbed.

legendary figures presented with a minimum of circumstantial distraction from their archetypal significance.

The best-known work of Arnold Böcklin, a Swiss Symbolist of the same generation as Puvis and Moreau in France and Rossetti and Burne-Jones in England, is *The Island of the Dead* (pl. 203). His treatment of the theme of death, the most important one an artist can attempt, provides a telling contrast with each of the characteristic approaches taken by painters of the Neo-classical, Romantic and Realist movements and clarifies how Symbolism stands apart from those movements. The Neo-classical view is that death is a test of virtue, to be faced stoically, and even welcomed if there is a moral issue at stake; this is the implication, for example, of David's *Death of Socrates.* The kind of death extolled in Romantic art tends to be more spectacular, and meaningful only as an assertion of individual will; the hero of Delacroix's *Death of Sardanapalus* commands the slaughter of all his household as a prelude to his own death, but looks on with indifference, lost in introspection. For the Realist, there is nothing to death beyond the mere fact of ceasing to live and being buried, as in Courbet's *A Burial at Ornans.* The Symbolist does not take up such a bold stance. Böcklin has no specific message about death to convey in his work; he merely evokes the solemnity and the mystery associated with it and leaves the rest to the spectator's imagination. *The Island of the Dead,* to quote the artist's own sub-title, is 'a picture to dream on'.

203 Arnold Böcklin
The Island of the Dead, 1880
Kunstmuseum, Basle

Although his earlier sketches reveal a
freshness of execution, Böcklin's final
paintings are generally overstated and
sentimentalized.

In the mid-1880s, young artists brought up on Impressionism, and
indeed the Impressionists themselves, grew dissatisfied with the
movement's commitment to the transient and began to explore ways
of investing their work with timeless, spiritual qualities. This aim
clearly coincides with that of the Symbolists; and at least two of the
major painters with whom the rest of this chapter is concerned, Seurat
and Gauguin, were deeply indebted to Puvis. Gauguin in fact had a
reproduction of *Hope* pinned to the wall of his hut in Tahiti, and called
his Tahitian paintings 'coloured Puvis'. But there was a fundamental
difference between him and Puvis, as between the Post-Impressionists
and the Symbolists in general; for Gauguin, Seurat, van Gogh and
Cézanne conveyed ideas and feelings not by means of symbols, but by
the purely artistic means of colour, line and brushwork. This is what
links the Post-Impressionists together; but it is important to remember
that they were in no way the kind of coherent group that the
Impressionists were. Post-Impressionism, as a term, is more like
Realism and Symbolism in that it embraces artists who developed
quite independently of one another; and it is a measure of the disparate
nature of what it describes that the term (which was invented as late as
1910) is a negative one, implying only the surpassing of a previous
movement.

The first artist to evolve a mature Post-Impressionist style was
Georges Seurat, in the years 1885–6. His work demonstrates immediately how important the Impressionists' liberation of colour was for
the younger generation. Seurat invented 'Pointillisme', a technique of
building up an image with innumerable coloured dots. He acknowl-

edged the Impressionists' observations on, for example, colour in shadows; but whereas they showed shadows in red drapery as a greenish red, Seurat simply interspersed the red dots that indicate the drapery's 'local colour' with pure green ones. Similarly, to show that coloured light is reflecting from a surface, he makes no overall modification but mixes in dots of whatever colour the light is. The value of Pointillisme is twofold: the contrast of juxtaposed colours makes for a shimmering intensity well suited to evoking sunlight; and, more importantly, the overall quality of the painting's texture lends the image coherence and stability. The dot, moreover, does not have the same connotation of movement as the characteristically rapid-looking Impressionist brushstroke. Pointillisme was exactly the right technique for realizing Seurat's feeling that art should be somehow more monumental than that of the Impressionists, and what better demonstration of this than to take one of their favourite motifs, that of people at leisure by the river Seine, and make of it something as static and durable as the pyramids? This is exactly the challenge Seurat met in his huge painting of *A Sunday Afternoon on the Île de la Grande Jatte*.

But the *Île de la Grande Jatte* picture (pl. 204) is more than just an Impressionist scene translated into another idiom. It is an exercise in harmonious composition, with simple, predominantly rectilinear lines and formal rhymes, such as that of the parasol in the upper right corner with the sail of the yacht in the upper left, which fuse the elements all the more completely together. Seurat was very conscious of the associations of lines and colours: horizontals and cool colours with repose, verticals and warm colours with strength and energy, and so on. He even drew up an elaborate code of visual formulae guaranteed to inspire corresponding emotions in the spectator. He held form to be

204 Georges Seurat
A Sunday Afternoon on the Île de La Grande Jatte, 1884–6
The Art Institute of Chicago, Helen Birch Bartlett Memorial Collection

The monkey, traditionally a symbol of lust, seems incongruous in this dispassionate scene of the Bourgeoisie.

more important than subject-matter: it is not what the artist paints that counts, but how he paints it. This went together with an emphasis on design, respecting the flatness of the canvas at the expense of creating an illusion of the third dimension. Seurat even seems to poke fun at the traditional concept of a painting as a kind of window through which we are made to believe we see into space. In *Les Poseuses*, for example, he playfully introduces spatial ambiguity in the representation of the corner of the room; and the bourgeois couple on the right of the *Île de la Grande Jatte* (which happens to be hanging on the wall) still tend to 'read' as parallel to the picture surface, even though the picture-within-the-picture is at an angle.

Seurat's career as a mature artist lasted only five or six years (he died in 1891) but he was enormously influential. He became the acknowledged head of a whole school of young French painters who continued to follow up the implications of his work long after his death. His most gifted follower was Paul Signac, whose portrait of the writer Félix Fénéon flirts with the complete abstraction that might be seen as the logical conclusion of his ideas. The picture's full title exploits the analogy between abstract form and music: *Against the Enamel of a Background Rhythmic with Beats and Angles, Tones and Colours, Portrait of M. Félix Fénéon in 1890* (pl. 206). Outside his native country, Seurat's influence was felt most strongly in Italy, where his style was adapted to standard Symbolist themes by artists such as Giovanni Segantini. In the hands of Alessandro Morbelli and Giuseppe Pellizza da Volpedo, it

205 Paul Signac
Sailing-boats in the Harbour of St-Tropez, 1893
Von der Heydt-Museum, Wuppertal

Signac, who lived for much of his later life at St. Tropez, was much less concerned with serene stillness than was his mentor, Seurat.

206 Paul Signac
*Against the Enamel of a Background
Rhythmic with Beasts and Angels, Tones
and Colours, Portrait of Félix Fénéon,*
1890
Joshua Logan Collection, New York

Félix Fénéon, an influential art critic,
was a friend of Signac and a tireless
exponent of Divisionist art theories.

was also used with a neo-Realist kind of subject-matter in the cause of
Socialism. Painters like Segantini, Morbelli and Pellizza have suffered
unfair neglect as a result of the French bias of most accounts of late
19th-century art, and have only recently begun to be accorded
something like the attention they deserve.

The greatest artist to come under Seurat's influence was Vincent van
Gogh, a Dutchman who lived in France. Initially working in a rather
gloomy style derived from Millet and then adopting an Impressionist
technique, van Gogh came finally into contact with Seurat's ideas in
1886–7. What affected him most deeply was the technique of
juxtaposing strong colours, often complementaries, to achieve a
boldness and intensity not possible with more gradual transitions. The
fact that he never adopted the dot as his unit of brushwork, however,
points to an important difference between van Gogh and Seurat. The
very graphic, often thickly impasted brushwork with which van Gogh
is associated is so clearly the result of vigorous movement on the part
of the artist that the spectator cannot but be aware of his presence in the
work. The dot carries nothing like the same implication of physical
involvement. It suited Seurat because his art is totally impersonal; the
bold brushstroke suited van Gogh because he regarded painting
essentially as a means of self-expression.

Certain favourite motifs of van Gogh link him to the Symbolist
movement. The sun was particularly significant for him, since he
identified it imaginatively with the idea of divine beneficence; and by

207 Giovanni Segantini
Amor at the Fountain of Life, 1896
Civica Galleria d'Arte Moderna,
Milan

The interest in Divisionism is here
used to portray the theme of love, a
subject showing Segantini's kinship
with the Symbolists.

the same token, sunflowers took on anthropomorphic associations,
representing Man (or possibly just van Gogh) as weather-beaten but
always struggling to keep his face turned towards the divinity. Van
Gogh's imagery is complex and fascinating, but the most innovatory
aspect of his work lies in his use of heightened colour and strongly
directional brushwork to express his emotional response to what he
paints. He records the scenes and people before him not as he sees
them, but as he feels them. Thus a sunset becomes a drama of greens
and blues against yellows, radiating lines against concentric; a self-
portrait becomes a strident orange set against blues, staccato brush-
strokes against lines that swirl and eddy. Like Seurat, van Gogh died
young (in 1890) but his impact upon the history of painting was
resounding. Everyone knows about his life: how he cut off his ear (in
fact he probably only cut off a very small part of it); how he suffered
fits of insanity and committed suicide; and this has given rise to a
tendency to read his work entirely in terms of mental instability. To do
so is seriously to underestimate him. By making paint his vehicle of
expression – as opposed to what paint could represent – he opened up
possibilities that his predecessors had never even dreamt of.

The third major figure of Post-Impressionism was van Gogh's
friend Paul Gauguin. Like Seurat and van Gogh, Gauguin was trained,
so to speak, in the Impressionist school, having become friendly with
Pissarro and built up a collection of Impressionist canvases as well as
adopting the idiom in his own work. But he found his personal style
only after moving well away from the metropolitan and suburban
environment on which Impressionism fed, to Pont-Aven in Brittany.
For Gauguin's particular reaction against Impressionism rested on the
idea that naturalism was an over-sophistication and what was needed

208 Vincent van Gogh
Self-portrait, 1890
Musée National du Louvre, Paris

The self–portraits of van Gogh are too often interpreted in terms of revealing insights into the artist's tormented psyche; more prosaically they can be seen to reflect van Gogh's self-consciousness about his ugly features.

was a return to simplicity. The best way to achieve this, he felt, was to adopt, or at least observe, a simple life-style. 'I love Brittany,' he wrote in a letter of 1888; 'I find there the savage, the primitive. When my clogs ring out on the granite soil, I hear the dull, muted, powerful tone that I seek in my painting.' Pursuing this idea even further afield, Gauguin lived for most of the 1890s in Tahiti.

Much of Gauguin's subject-matter relates to the lives and beliefs of the Breton and Tahitian peoples. In them he found the same unchanging, primeval quality that Puvis found in the classical world, as Gauguin himself recognized when he said; 'Puvis is a Greek; I am a savage.' But his art stands apart from Symbolism in that its meaning is conveyed by form and colour as much as by subject-matter. His anti-naturalistic attitude is well illustrated in the advice he gave one day to his young follower Paul Sérusier. 'How do you see that tree?' he asked; 'It's green? Then choose the most beautiful green on your palette. And this shadow? It's more like blue? Do not be afraid to paint it with the purest blue possible.' Unlike van Gogh, Gauguin seldom painted outdoors, executing most of his pictures purely from his imagination, and at times his colour becomes wholly fictitious; a field, for example, may be shown as red to suggest a state of burning awareness in a character or characters depicted. This is matched by a tendency to simplify forms, using only a minimum of modelling, so that they seem to hover somewhere between two and three dimensions. He called his distinctive way of building up a picture with flatly-coloured, interlock-

209 Vincent van Gogh
Sunrise at Saint-Rémy, 1889
Private Collection

Once committed to St. Rémy mental asylum it was with difficulty that van Gogh obtained permission to paint; this expresses his joy at being able to work again from nature.

210 Paul Gauguin
Vision after the Sermon, 1888
National Gallery of Scotland,
Edinburgh

Gauguin offered this painting to a
local church in Brittany but, not
surprisingly, it was refused.

ing shapes 'cloisonnisme' (a 'cloison', in French, is a dividing line, as between sections, usually of a single colour, in a piece of 'cloisonné' enamel).

The *Vision after the Sermon* (pl. 210) is the first masterpiece of Gauguin's mature style. Coming from church, some Breton women in folk dress see a vision of the Old Testament story of Jacob wrestling with the Angel. Everything is strongly outlined in the cloisonnist manner, and the slanting tree effects an almost diagrammatic compartmentalization of the picture into areas signifying the real world (below and to the left) and the visionary one (above and to the right). There is little sense of space. The field has none of the perspectival hints that most artists rely upon to give an illusion of recession; and its colour is non-representational. The cow in the upper left corner is a crucial element, indicating what has stimulated the vision, for the two wrestling figures distinctly resemble a four-legged animal, with the angel's wings reminiscent of horns. In this respect, the *Vision after the Sermon* is a picture about art, or rather, Gauguin's view of art. Painting borrows forms from the real world in a highly selective manner, and by simplifying and abstracting them opens up their associational possibilities; a state of 'seeing things' is induced in the spectator, just as it was induced in the Breton women by the sermon, in which a cow can quite easily become Jacob and the Angel.

Of all the Post-Impressionists, Gauguin best exemplifies the tendency that has already been described, to 'flatten' three-dimensional elements and bring them into parallel with the picture surface, so that the spectator used to reading pictures in terms of space is brought up short, and reminded that what he is looking at is in fact planar. Hence the slightly pejorative label of 'decorative' which is often applied to Gauguin and surface-conscious painters like him; their works have a non-illusionistic quality reminiscent of the abstract designs on curtains, carpets and wallpapers. More to the point is their relationship with non-European art. Gauguin learnt a great deal from the bold, flat design of Japanese prints, which were becoming widely known and collected in this period. His enthusiasm for them was shared, among others, by van Gogh, whose liking for the South of France, where he spent the last years of his life, was in part determined by his feeling that the place had a simplified, 'Japanese' look. Gauguin also admired Breton sculpture which, similarly, stood outside the naturalistic tradition in which he had been brought up; and the most pervasive influence on his later work came from the sculptures of the Buddhist temple of Borobudur in Java.

With Seurat and van Gogh dead and Gauguin in Tahiti, the Parisian avant-garde of the 1890s lacked leadership. As a result, the decade was one of consolidation rather than innovation, during which Post-Impressionist ideas were more fully explored and more widely disseminated. The immediate disciples of Gauguin, led by Sérusier and calling themselves the 'Nabis' (or 'Prophets'), pursued his experiments in pictorial symbolism into more overtly religious channels. Equally religious but more international in character was the group who exhibited at the Salon de la Rose + Croix, which was set up by the arch-Roman Catholic writer Joséphin Péladan to show works of art as antipathetic as possible to Realism; the kinds of subjects called for were 'first the Catholic Ideal and Mysticism, then Legend, Myth, Allegory, the Dream [and] the Paraphrase of great poetry.' Among the artists

211 Paul Gauguin
Loss of Virginity, 1890–1
Chrysler Museum, Norfolk

Gauguin referred to himself as 'half-savage'; wild animals in his work, such as this fox, are perhaps intended as self-representation.

212 Paul Sérusier
Melancholy, c. 1890
Private Collection

Van Gogh's view that one should be
able to express meaning by landscape
alone is endorsed by this painting, in
which the allegoricalfigure seems
unnecessary.

associated with the Salon de la Rose + Croix were two of the most
important painters working in the Low Countries at this time: the
Belgian Fernand Khnopff, an interesting figure influenced by both
French and English art, and the Dutchman Jan Toorop. Toorop also
showed his work at the exhibitions of 'Les XX', an avant-garde group
in Brussels. Including decorative as well as fine art, these exhibitions
were the cradle of Art Nouveau. Toorop's work is obviously tied in
with the Art Nouveau movement in architecture and design, and
demonstrates in the extreme the decorative tendency of Post-Impressionism which has already been mentioned. Another associate of
Les XX was James Ensor, whose obsession with grotesque masks
reflects his disgust with the human dissimulation and hypocrisy he saw
around him. In his work flatness itself becomes expressive, enhancing
the idea that the characters depicted are mere cardboard cut-outs of
human beings.

The 1890s saw the Post-Impressionist idea that form can be as telling
as what it actually describes applied to standard Symbolist themes. The
use of abstract nouns as titles, which had passed out of fashion among
avant-garde painters in the 1870s and '80s, came back in the work of
Sérusier and others in France, Khnopff and others in the Low
Countries, Segantini in Italy and also painters working in Berlin, most
notably the Norwegian-born Edvard Munch. The girl in Munch's

213 Fernand Khnopff
The Sphinx, 1896
Musées Royaux des Beaux Arts,
Brussels

In the preface of the catalogue to the
second exhibition at the Salon of the
Rose + Croix, Khnopff was
proclaimed for this and other
paintings 'a wonderful and immortal
master'.

214 Jan Toorop
The Three Brides, 1893
Rijksmuseum Kröller-Müller,
Otterlo

Toorop recalls his childhood days in
Java; the figures derive from the
experience of seeing shadow puppet
theatres on the island.

215 James Sidney Ensor
The Entry of Christ into Brussels, 1888
Koninklijk Museum voor Schone
Kunsten, Antwerp

Most of Ensor's life was spent in the
Flemish town of Ostend; his macabre
paintings clearly have their roots in
the art of Flemish predecessors such
as Bosch and Bruegel.

Puberty (pl. 216) is the personification of an idea, just like the girl in
Puvis' *Hope* and the one in Gauguin's *Loss of Virginity*. What links the
Munch more closely to the Gauguin than the Puvis is not just their
obvious thematic relationship; it is the use of colour and form for their
associational, as opposed to merely descriptive, value. The dark shape
behind the girl is her shadow, but it is also, like the fox in the Gauguin,
a phallic symbol. A friend of Munch's visited his studio when he was
at work on *Puberty*. 'On the edge of the bed a naked girl was sitting,'
he later wrote. 'She did not look like a saint, yet there was something
innocent, coy and shy in her manner; it was just these qualities that had
prompted Munch to paint her, and as she sat there in the dazzling light
of the brilliant spring sunshine, the shadow cast by her body played as
though fatefully above her.'

It is one aspect of the complexity of art in the period 1886–1905 that
its major protagonists were of such disparate ages, from Seurat who
was only 28 years old in 1886, through van Gogh at 33 and Gauguin at
38, to Paul Cézanne, who was already 47. Moreover, it was the oldest
of them, Cézanne, who went on longest and had the most far-reaching
influence on 20th-century painting. Indeed, just as we understand van
Gogh and Gauguin to some extent through the later artists they
influenced, especially the Fauves, so we understand Cézanne – even
more so – through Cubism, the epoch-making style which was
evolved out of his work of the 1890s by Picasso and Braque, and which
will be discussed more fully in the following chapter. What the Cubists
found in Cézanne was a balance between representation and surface-
consciousness carried to such a degree of subtlety that the work
seemed to be about the very nature of painting itself.

Cézanne was of the same generation as the Impressionists, and his
first mature style was an Impressionist one, reached with the aid and
advice of his close friend Pissarro. (Pissarro was somewhat older than
the other Impressionists; he always took an avuncular attitude towards
younger painters and was on intimate terms with all four of the major
Post-Impressionists.) Typically, as soon as Cézanne had mastered

216 Edvard Munch
Puberty, 1893
Nasjonalgalleriet, Oslo

The almost human shadow which
threatens to envelop the girl seems to
embody all the anxiety which
accompanies sexuality.

Impressionism, he began to feel that there was more to art than merely
catching nature unawares. In his own words, he wanted to make of it
'something solid and durable like the art of the museums'. One of the
artists whose work he was thinking of as 'the art of the museums' was
undoubtedly Poussin, and he once spoke of his own work as
'revivifying Poussin in front of nature' – that is, reconciling naturalism
with the sense of harmony and structure that Poussin's pictures convey
with such clarity. This certainly did not mean painting Poussinesque
subjects (idyllic landscapes full of classical buildings, or people with
perfect features enacting heroic events) in a naturalistic manner. It
meant painting standard Realist – Impressionist subjects in such a way
as to create a Poussinesque feeling; harmony and structure would be
conveyed by pictorial means, by brushwork, form and colour.

Brushwork was as vital to Cézanne as it was to van Gogh, though
for a very different reason. Cézanne's brushwork is not expressive (nor
is his art as a whole) but it performs two important functions. Its
direction often suggests contour; and, generally consisting of dabs of a
similar size, it imparts the kind of unity to a picture that key imparts to
a piece of music. The idea of unity is further enhanced by the way
conventions of perspective are breached in order to relate what is

represented to the picture plane. In the *Card Players* (pl. 217), for example, the shoulder of the man on the left is seen from above, whereas his head is seen from the side; it is as if the shoulder were on the way to becoming a plane at right angles to the spectator's line of vision, thereby denying the impression that the man's head is any further away than his arm. Similarly, Cézanne sacrifices continuous modelling by tonal transition to the juxtaposition of dabs of strong colour, so that the brush-strokes tend to float forward from what they represent and become marks on a flat surface – which, of course, is what they are. Cézanne is probably the most 'difficult' of all pre-20th-century artists. As his own laconic and often impenetrable comments on his work suggest, the problems for which he was seeking solutions are not easily couched in everyday language. It is clear, however, that he was concerned in some way with finding a mode of painting that suggested the three-dimensional world without disguising its own two-dimensionality.

Post-Impressionism, then, was a break with the Renaissance concept of a painting as a window on nature. This development has been attributed to the threat to naturalistic painting posed by photography. The rise of photography in the 19th century certainly had a bearing on art; it took over the market for run-of-the-mill, small-scale portraits, for example. However, at the higher levels of artistic activity, it was a

217 Paul Cézanne
The Card Players, 1885–90
Musée National du Louvre, Paris

A subject which had traditionally been an excuse to show a cheat at work is here a metaphor for human isolation.

minor factor. The new concept of a painting as a surface on which the artist may make whatever marks he sees fit, was in fact the culmination of a spirit of independence and self-consciousness that had been growing among artists at least since the late 18th century. Working relatively seldom on commission, and contemptuous of the idea of saleability, the avant-garde painter had come to regard himself as something more like a scientist or a philosopher than the glorified craftsman he had been in earlier periods. It was only a matter of time before he realized that to live up to the new complexity of his situation, he must expand the very vocabulary of painting. This was the achievement of Post-Impressionism. It offered the 20th century immeasurable new possibilities; and, of course, it created correspondingly intricate new problems.

218 Paul Cézanne
Montagne Sainte-Victoire, 1904–6
Kunstmuseum, Basle

The mountain of Sainte-Victoire became a recurrent theme in Cézanne's later works and came to epitomize for him the countryside near his home town of Aix.

Modern Painting

In reading a general account of 20th-century painting, one can easily be misled into thinking that more has happened over the last 80 years than in any previous period in the history of art. 'Isms' – Fauvism, Cubism, Futurism, Expressionism, Surrealism etc. – seem to follow on in rapid succession, and soon become, as one critic recently put it, 'wasms'. In fact the time has not yet come for us to attempt a truly objective assessment of modern painting; artistic movements which to us now seem so important might well be almost forgotten in the future, so that someone writing, say, 200 years from now will be able to single out much more general patterns of artistic development. But, as with all periods, whatever generalizations emerge from the study of 20th-century painting, one must never lose sight of the fact that artistic evolution is not a logical process, and that the history of art is concerned essentially with individuals rather than with collective movements. The stress on an artist's individuality, a legacy of the romatic era, has in fact become so emphasized in this century that the artist has found himself in an increasingly isolated position. The growth of the various 'isms' is in a sense a negative outcome of this situation, a reflection of an artist's ever greater need to be associated with a specific group of people at a time when his work serves no apparent social function or appeals to no particular type of patron. Each of these 'isms' or groups has claimed to have made a significant contribution to the history of art, and to have introduced a manner of representation which constitutes a major advance on that of their predecessors. It is only for the sake of finding some degree of coherence in what to us now seems a hopelessly complex period that one has to respect their claims.

The most exciting and original years in the history of 20th-century art might well turn out to be those between 1905 and 1925. While it is always dangerous to relate history of art to social and political developments, there is undeniably some connection between the emotionally fraught years before, during and after the First World War, and the intense artistic experimentation which took place during this period, which both questioned the fundamental purpose of art and on occasion even challenged its very existence.

For the first part of this century, Paris retained its pre-eminence as the leading art centre of Europe, and to fail to come here at some stage in one's career implied cutting oneself off from the main currents of the European avant-garde. Yet a knowledge of Parisian artistic movements was disseminated both widely and rapidly by a number of highly influential retrospective exhibitions held elsewhere, the most important being the Sonnerbund in Cologne of 1907, the two Post-Impressionist exhibitions of 1910 and 1913 in London, and the Armory Show of 1913 in New York. The only art centres seriously to rival France in the first 30 years of the century were to be found in Germany – in such places as Dresden, Berlin, Munich and Weimar; Expressionism and Dada were essentially German phenomena and the principles of Abstract Art were first taught and discussed in a relatively systematic manner by the innovatory German group, the Bauhaus. With the rise of Hitler and Nazism, many artists from Germany and elsewhere took refuge in London, and virtually all came to live within a short distance of each other in Hampstead. For once London acquired a truly international importance as an art centre, although at the outbreak of the Second World War, the artistic community here was dispersed, some artists moving on to the small Cornish fishing village of St. Ives, and others emigrating to the United States. After the war St. Ives lived on incongruously as a major European centre of Abstract Art, rivalled only by Paris; but neither of these places could compare with New York which had rapidly risen to prominence during the 1940s and indeed was to give birth to most of the major artistic movements of the last 25 years.

Broadly speaking one can characterize 20th-century painting in terms of art which is cerebral in inspiration, and employs taut images to express often complex philosophical ideas, and art which is much more obviously spontaneous, whether displaying sensuous pleasure in the handling of paint, or conveying intensely personal emotional states. Of course, one cannot be too hard and fast in one's distinctions, and some of the greatest painters of this century cannot properly be contained within either category. One such painter is Henri Matisse.

Born in 1869, Matisse was a late starter as an artist, and it was not

219 Henri Matisse
Harmony in Red, 1908
The Hermitage, Leningrad

One of the rare examples of a 20th-century painting designed for a specific location: the dining-room of Matisse's Russian patron.

220 Pablo Picasso
Les Demoiselles d'Avignon, 1907
Museum of Modern Art,
Lillie P. Bliss Bequest, New York

Picasso had this canvas relined before
he began to paint, obviously aware
that this work was to make him the
leader of the avant-garde.

until he was 35 that he was first publicly recognized as a startling
innovator. As a pupil of Gustave Moreau in Paris in the early 1890s, he
was scarcely aware of the work either of the Impressionists or of the
Post-Impressionists: the revelation first came to him on a visit in 1897
to the Breton Island of Belle-Isle, where lived a rich Australian painter
and collector, John Russell, who had an extensive collection of works
by artists such as Monet and van Gogh. Although the art of these
painters helped Matisse to make more vivid his hitherto relatively
subdued colour range, it was the work of the Neo-Impressionists that
was to be fundamental in determining his early style.

   Matisse once wrote that his only ambition was to create art 'devoid
of any troubling subject-matter . . . as relaxing as a comfortable
armchair'. This statement is compounded in his paintings, which have
an idyllic, untroubled and to us now a very accessible quality. Yet,
however undemanding and even spontaneous they appear to be, they
are in fact the product of a rigorous intellectual discipline. It is no
coincidence that Matisse was one of the most prolific and articulate
writers on art of this century. His adoption of a Neo-Impressionist
style at the beginning of the century was in itself an indication of his
very structured and controlled approach to colour and pictoral
composition. When, aided by a younger painter, André Derain, he
later intensified his use of colour and adopted a much freer and more
radical handling of paint, he still subjugated expressive effect to a
harmonious arrangement of the picture surface. In 1905, a critic coined
the word 'fauve' (or 'wild beast') to describe the group of artists
headed by Matisse and Derain; but no word could have been less
appropriate. Matisse's most important and original work of his early
maturity, the *Joie de Vivre* of 1905–6, has in fact all the refinement

associated with classical evocations of arcadia, and is characterized by a linear and compositional elegance. Describing this painting's colours – which have finally been liberated from any descriptive function – Matisse said that 'they sing together, like a chord of music.' This musical analogy provides a key for the understanding of Matisse's art. The *Harmony in Red* (pl. 219) is precisely what its title implies – an exercise in modulating shapes and colours in accordance with a dominant red. Although a few lines serve to indicate perspectival recession, Matisse has essentially accepted the fact that a picture is a self-sufficient two-dimensional object which can be appreciated outside of any descriptive or literary context.

Matisse's position as the most radical artist of the first decade of the century was challenged by a painter of a completely different temperament – Pablo Picasso. In contrast to Matisse, Picasso was an infant prodigy who, in his own words, could draw 'like Raphael' by

221 Pablo Picasso
Still Life with Wicker Chair, 1912
Private Collection

This, the first cubist collage, uses the letters JOU, both referring to the French word for newspaper 'Journal', and also suggesting that the work is a 'jou-jou', a game.

222 Georges Braque ▷
Woman in an Armchair, 1911
Private Collection

Braque breaks up forms, and out of the fragments builds a complex scaffolding. Breasts, and the arm of the chair, are inserted to regain reality.

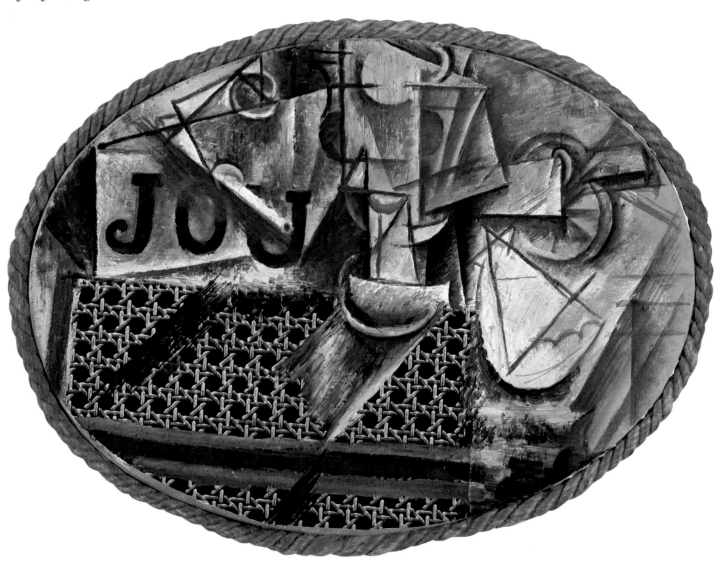

the age of 10. Much of his subsequent career, as he himself confessed, constituted an attempt to shake off this precocious sophistication and to achieve a genuinely child-like gaucheness. But Picasso's achievement cannot quite so easily be defined, for it was more wide-ranging than that of any other modern artist. Both as a painter and as a sculptor, Picasso was an innovator throughout most of his life, and his work, influencing many of the major movements of modern art, not only offered a radically new approach to the representation of the human figure, but also paved the way for complete abstraction.

In his earliest and most conventional works, depicting beggars, impoverished gypsies, and circus performers, Picasso displays a quality which is entirely lacking in Matisse's art: intense feeling. Even in his most intricate and complex paintings, Picasso is much more of an expressive painter than Matisse in that he always appears to be as interested in conveying emotional states as he is in creating carefully conceived formal structures. His combination of extraordinary

223 Umberto Boccioni
Forces of a Street, 1911
Niedersächsisches Landesmuseum, Hanover

The cubist fragmentation of the object is here used to express violence and movement rather than the sober explanation of form.

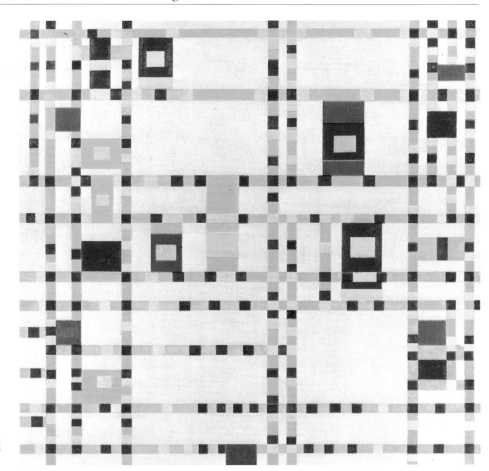

224 Piet Mondrian
Broadway Boogie-Woogie, 1942–3
Museum of Modern Art, New York

The rhythmic beat of Jazz served to inspire this painting and imbues it with a pulsating intensity at variance with the artist's earlier, more classical works.

energy, and depth of emotion might partly be held responsible for the carelessness of much of his work, but it also led to paintings such as the *Guernica* of 1936, which comments on the virtues of peace in a committed manner reminiscent of Rubens.

It must be remembered that the artist who most influenced Picasso in the early development of Cubism, Cézanne, was also someone who expressed a very passionate nature through ever more formal means. Cézanne's famous comment that he wanted to 'treat nature in accordance with the cylinder, sphere, and cone', provided a point of departure for Picasso's Cubist period; but Picasso was also interested in Cézanne's clumsy yet expressive stylization of the figure. Whereas Cézanne's distortions of the human form were partly determined, however, by real failings in draughtsmanship and by an extreme shyness which prevented the artist from copying directly from the model, Picasso's were a conscious imitation of primitive art. Whether Picasso was already aware of negro carvings when he began his *Demoiselles d'Avignon* (pl. 220) of 1907, or whether he derived inspiration entirely from Iberian sculpture of the 10th century, has been a subject of endless debate. What can be said, however, is that this painting represents a radical break from tradition and achieves a genuine primitiveness. The *Demoiselles* was not publicly shown at this time, and was only seen by a very small circle of Picasso's friends and acquaintances: their reactions were unanimously hostile, and the canvas was rolled up and was not to be seen again for the next 30 years. The inability of these people to take such a revolutionary work seriously was an understandable reaction; moreover, the work, frightening and intense though it is, was probably also conceived in a slightly humorous vein. In fact its title, given to it at a much later stage, came about partly as a result of a ribald suggestion that the

225 Wassily Kandinsky
Painting with Houses, 1909
Stedelijk Museum, Amsterdam

The spiritual roots of Kandinsky's
abstraction are admirably shown in
this transformation of a banal
German town into a fairy land.

Avignon grandmother of the poet Max Jacob had posed for one of the
figures.

The *Demoiselles d'Avignon* was the culmination of a series of
experiments with the primitive representation of the human figure that
Picasso had been engaged on since 1907. His work immediately
following the *Demoiselles* took a very different direction, and aimed at
a greater refinement of his formal means of expression. In Picasso's
period of so-called analytical or hermetic Cubism (roughly from 1910
to 1912) during which he worked very closely with the French painter
Georges Braque, he attempted to analyze conventional subject-matter
such as portraits and still-lifes in terms of a network of geometrical
planes. Picasso's dissolution of the picture surface was never as
extreme as was that of Braque who moreover was more interested in
the representation of objects than of human beings, but both artists,
however difficult it may sometimes be to interpret their analytical
Cubist paintings, were never completely able to depart from the motif.
In fact when analytical Cubism threatened to turn into pure abstraction, Picasso and Braque responded by adopting (for the first time
ever in the history of art) collage techniques and incorporating realistic
elements, such as actual chair-caning (pl. 221) and newspaper cuttings,
into their work. Shortly afterwards the two artists moved apart.
Braque devoted the rest of his life to ever more delicate and painterly
still-lifes. Picasso meanwhile, after a period of so-called Synthetic
Cubism in which figurative elements became much more strongly
pronounced and the patterns bolder and more colourful, reacted at the

beginning of the 1920s against any form of geometric stylization and reverted, albeit briefly, to a conventional and classical figurative style; always a restless artist, however, his career from the mid 1920s onwards mirrored the confused and inconsistent development of 20th-century art as a whole.

The influence of Cubism was exceptionally wide-ranging. Some artists, such as the English group, the Vorticists, and the Italian group, the Futurists, made use of Cubist methods to express the dynamic rhythms of the machine age. Others, such as Léger and the Purists, rationalized these methods, and turned Cubism, which had begun in a spirit of passionate experimentation, into an academic exercise in the rendering of objects and people alike. And then there were those artists such as the Orphists, the Suprematists and the Constructivists who fully exploited the abstract qualities inherent in Cubism.

The danger of creating an art which was entirely abstract – and a danger which both Picasso and Braque were fully aware of – was that painting could acquire a purely decorative function. To overcome this, abstraction was made to encompass profound philosophical ideas; and

226 Ernst Ludwig Kirchner
Nude, 1908–9
F. Burda Collection, Offenburg

According to the Expressionists the painting of nudes in a landscape was not an emulation of the art of the past, but a futile attempt to escape from the anxiety of urban life.

227 Marcel Duchamp
L.H.O.O.Q. (or: *Mona Lisa with Moustache*), 1919
Private Collection, New York

Another Surrealist, Salvador Dali played a rather more cumbersome joke with the Mona Lisa, by adding both a moustache and his own features.

it is significant that the leading abstract painters have had strong mystical leanings. Piet Mondrian was one of the first and most radical of these painters. Beginning his career as a straightforward landscapist, he gradually eliminated naturalistic detail in his work so as to create an increasingly simplified and abstract representation of nature. By 1916, however, his art had reached a point where it could seemingly go no further. It was then that he encountered a former Catholic priest turned Theosophist, M.H.J. Schoenmaeken, who was propounding a neo-platonic system which he called Primitive Mysticism, or Plastic mathematics. This system, which Schoenmaeken claimed would enable its initiates 'to penetrate, by contemplation, the hidden construction of reality', consisted essentially in the resolution of tensions between verticals and horizontals which in turn stood for contrasting elements such as active and passive, male and female, space and time and so on. Although Mondrian thoroughly embraced this system, the uncompromisingly severe grid-like structures which were encouraged by it were by no means lacking all connection with the visible world. In fact Mondrian's reduction of the picture surface to a few squares and rectangles, with sometimes only the slightest suggestion of colour, is very expressive of the flat and monotonous countryside of Holland; and when Mondrian moved to New York in 1940, he was able to evolve a more bustling and vivid manner in response to the exciting atmosphere of that city.

In spite of his last works painted in New York, Mondrian's approach to abstraction can never be described as exuberant in the same way as can that of Kandinsky, which had its origins not in Cubism, but in German Expressionism. The process by which Kandinsky arrived at a complete dissolution of the motif is hinted at in a description of an experience he had while looking at the *Painting with Houses* (pl. 225) of 1909: 'I was returning from sketching, deep in thought, when opening the studio door, I was suddenly confronted with a picture of indescribable incandescent loveliness. Bewildered, I stopped, staring at it. The painting lacked all subject, depicted no recognizable object and was entirely comprised of bright patches of colour. Finally I approached closer, and only then recognized it for what it really was – my own painting standing on its side on the easel... one thing became clear to me – that objectiveness, the depiction of objects, needed no place in my paintings and was indeed harmful to them'.

Kandinsky's justification of abstraction was expounded at great length, and in an emotional rather than rational fashion, in his *Über das Geistiege in Der Kunst* ('Concerning the Spiritual in Art'). The extraordinary freedom of line and colour in Kandinsky's work expresses a sense of ecstatic liberation and a discovery of an alternative reality. Later in life, when he was invited to join the Bauhaus, the teaching institution which offered a haven for abstract artists, he rationalized the forms of his art and developed a more scientific and less intuitive approach to colour; but although his paintings lost much of their almost visionary spontaneity, they still retained an energy and restlessness that stood out in marked contrast to the control of Mondrian's art.

Although they found their formal origins in Expressionism, Kandinsky's works, as indeed those of all the artists discussed so far in the chapter, lacked a quality that was fundamental to Expressionist painting: an interest in conveying psychological realism. The term,

L.H.O.O.Q.

228 René Magritte
The Human Condition I, 1933
Private Collection

There is deliberately no connection
whatsoever between this witty visual
joke and the grandiose title.

Expressionism, often loosely used to describe art of anguished intensity, can be more accurately identified with the German groups of artists, 'Die Brücke' and 'Der Blaue Reiter'.

All these Expressionists were much more generally 'Fauve' than were either Matisse or Derain – in that they made use of primary colours, not just for decorative effect, but to express extremes of violence, sexuality and fear. Humanity was invariably shown at its most bestial, whether indulging in the evil pleasures of city life, or responding to primitive urges in the countryside. Members of the Brücke spent in fact much of the summer months running about naked in the woods near Dresden. Kirchner's *Nude* of 1908–9 (pl. 226), one of the innumerable records of these outings, differs completely in spirit from the nude idylls of a Matisse. The boater which the protagonist wears emphasises her modernity, and increases our awareness of her nakedness. The work is both intensely erotic, and yet full of morbid undertones: the woman appears to kick her legs in a way which suggests both ecstatic pleasure and writhing hysteria.

The rendering of psychological states, which is a pronounced feature of Expressionism, became the principal objective of the Surrealists, who instead of being concerned with how emotions manifested themselves in scenes from everyday life, were interested in probing beneath the visible world in an attempt to evoke the workings of the mind itself. Surrealism grew out of another movement called Dada, which originated in Zurich during the First World War. The latter's leading theorist, the Roumanian poet Tristan Tzara, insisted that Dada was not a technique or style but was rather 'a state of mind'. The meaningless term Dada suggests the idiotic babble of a child; and indeed much of the Dadaists' extremely childish activities – such as organizing events at which 'negro' music would be improvised on drums and gongs, and quite unrelated texts recited in as many languages, all at the same time – were self-conscious attempts to capture infantile illogicality, which they considered to be more telling of the human psyche than adult reason.

By rejecting the traditional values associated with logic, the Dadaists inevitably began to attack the notion of Art. In this respect special mention must be made of Marcel Duchamp, who exhibited such objects as snow shovels and inverted urinals in order to question our reasons for considering what is worthy to be included in a museum and what is not. The *Mona Lisa with Moustache* (pl. 227), with the inscription L.H.O.O.Q. which read aloud sounds like 'elle a le chaud au cul' ('she's got a hot arse'), makes fun of a revered painting which had come to be regarded as the supreme expresion of western civilization.

Duchamp and other Dadaists such as Max Ernst, later joined the Surrealist movement, which was based in Paris and was led by the poet and writer André Breton. This movement, committed both to Marxism and Siegmund Freud, replaced the anarchic activities of the Dadaists with a serious and systematic approach to the problems of representing the subconscious. In spite of the clearly defined aims of Surrealism, each of the major artists associated with it evolved entirely idiosyncratic styles. Magritte, who was perhaps the most literary in inspiration, interpreted the sub-conscious in terms of realistically painted enigmatic images; the *Human Condition* (pl. 228), for instance, in which a landscape on a canvas is made indistinguishable from the real landscape in the background, comments on our perception of

229 Max Ernst
Les hommes n'en sauront rien (Men will know nothing of this), 1923
Tate Gallery, London

On the back Ernst inscribes an arcane description, even less illuminating than the title, containing such remarks as 'the sun is split into two the better to revolve'.

230 Peter Blake
Bo Diddley, 1963
Museum Ludwig, Cologne

Blake here uses the devices of Pop Art
to very different effect; instead of
commenting on the false glamour of
contemporary society, he
nostalgically portrays a cult figure of
his childhood.

reality. The imagination of Salvador Dali, in contrast, has its roots in
the grotesque fantasies of Bosch and Breugel and carries the Spanish
love of gruesomely realistic details to its most sensational conclusion.
The essentially abstract works of artists such as Yves Tanguy and
André Masson evoke those areas of the sub-conscious that do not lend
themselves so readily to analysis; the works of these artists were often
quite simply dictated by mental impulse. A Surrealist who combined
recognizable images within an invariably abstract framework was Max
Ernst. His *'Les Hommes n'en sauront rien'* ('Men will know nothing of
this') (pl. 229) in which a vagina is turned into a Shiva-like deity,
emphasises the sexual origin of so many of our dreams and anxieties.

   Most of the major movements in art since 1940 have not only
originated in the United States but also could be said to have
contributed relatively little to what had been achieved in those rich and

complex years between 1905 and 1925. The question as to which direction painting will now turn, is of course problematical. Since Picasso and Braque incorporated three-dimensional objects into their works, distinctions between the various arts have become increasingly blurred, and from the time of Duchamp, people have been questioning the purpose of art itself. Nonetheless, if any trend can be seen to be emerging at the present moment, it is ironically one of regression to more traditional values of art: there is evidence that figurative painting is once more becoming fashionable, and that moreover Europe is regaining something of her previous ascendancy in this field. In fact, Britain is at the head of this figurative revival and British painters such as Peter Blake (pl. 230), Ronald Kitaj, Lucien Freud and above all David Hockney (pl. 231) have achieved a much wider popularity than have most of the leading abstract or experimental artists of this century. The problem remains – and it is one which has been fundamental to the whole history of painting – as to how to revert to tradition while creating an art which is truly original.

231 David Hockney
Two Boys in a Pool, 1965
Private collection, London

David Hockney, one of the greatest living draughtsmen, believes fervently in a revival of figurative art.

List of Plates

40 Martin Schongauer
The Madonna of the Rose Garden, 1473
Oil on panel, 200 × 115 cm

41 Nuño Gonçalves
The Veneration of Saint Vincent (central panel of the São Vicente Altarpiece), 1465–7
Oil on panel, 207 × 129 cm

42 Jean Fouquet
Mary and the Child surrounded by Angels (right wing of the Melun Diptych), c. 1450
Oil on panel, 91 × 81 cm

43 Giovanni Bellini
The Doge Leonardo Loredan, c. 1501
Oil on panel, 61.5 × 45 cm

44 Gentile Bellini
Procession on the Piazza San Marco, 1496
Oil on canvas, 367 × 745 cm

45 Andrea Mantegna
Balustrade with Women and Putti, 1472–4
Ceiling fresco, diameter 270 cm

46 Andrea Mantegna
Mars and Venus, c. 1497
Oil on canvas, 160 × 192 cm

47 Andrea Mantegna
The Dead Christ, c. 1480
Tempera on canvas, 68 × 81 cm

48 Giovanni Bellini
The Transfiguration, c. 1487
Oil on panel, 115 × 151.5 cm

49 Vittore Carpaccio
Two Courtesans, c. 1495
Oil on panel, 94 × 64 cm

50 Giorgione
The Tempest, 1507–8
Oil on canvas, 82 × 73 cm

51 Giorgione
Sleeping Venus, c. 1508
Oil on canvas, 108 × 175 cm

52 Titian
Crowning with Thorns, 1570–6
Oil on canvas, 280 × 182 cm

53 Titian
Pope Paul III, surrounded by his Nephews (Cardinal Alessandro Farnese and Count Ottavio Farnese), 1546
Oil on canvas, 200 × 173 cm

54 Titian
Venus of Urbino, 1538
Oil on canvas, 119.5 × 165 cm

55 Titian
Bacchanal of the Andrians, 1516–18
Oil on canvas, 175 × 193 cm

56 Titian
Danae, 1553–4
Oil on canvas, 128 × 178 cm

57 Jacopo Tintoretto
The Removal of the Body of St. Mark, 1562–6
Oil on canvas, 398 × 315 cm

58 Paolo Veronese
Banquet in the House of Levi, 1573
Oil on canvas, 550 × 1280 cm

59 Correggio
St. John on Patmos, 1520–1
Dome fresco, diameter 966 × 888 cm

60 Lorenzo Lotto
Portrait of Andrea Odoni, 1527
Oil on canvas, 101.5 × 114 cm

61 Andrea del Verrocchio/Leonardo da Vinci
The Baptism of Christ, 1470–80
Tempera on panel, 177 × 151 cm

62 Leonardo da Vinci
The Last Supper, 1495–7
Mixture of oil and tempera on plaster, 460 × 880 cm

63 Leonardo da Vinci
Lady with an Ermine (Cecilia Gallerani), c. 1484
Oil on panel, 54 × 40 cm

64 Leonardo da Vinci
Mona Lisa, 1503–5
Oil on panel, 77 × 53 cm

65 Pietro Perugino
Delivery of the Keys to St. Peter, 1481
Fresco, 335 × 550 cm

66 Raphael
Marriage of the Virgin, 1504
Oil on panel, 170 × 118 cm

67 Raphael
The Liberation of Saint Peter, 1512–14
Fresco, base 660 cm

68 Raphael
The Sistine Madonna, 1513–16
Oil on canvas, 265 × 196 cm

69 Michelangelo Buonarroti
General view of the Sistine Chapel ceiling
Fresco

70 Michelangelo Buonarroti
The Last Judgment, 1536–41
Fresco, 1375 × 1220 cm

71 Andrea del Sarto
The Madonna of the Harpies, 1517
Oil on panel, 207 × 178 cm

72 Rosso Fiorentino
Moses defending the Daughters of Jethro, c. 1523
Oil on canvas, 160 × 117 cm

73 Jacopo Pontormo
Lamentation over the Dead Christ, 1525–8
Oil on panel, 313 × 192 cm

74 Parmigianino
The Madonna with the Long Neck, c. 1534
Oil on panel, 216 × 132 cm

75 Angelo Bronzino
The Princess Isabella de'Medici, 1542
Tempera on panel, 63 × 48 cm

76 Giulio Romano
The Bath of Amor and Psyche (detail), 1527–31
Fresco

77 Giulio Romano
The Fall of the Giants, 1532–6
Fresco, detail

78 Jacopo Zucchi
Amor and Psyche, 1589
Oil on canvas, 173 × 130 cm

79 Matthias Grünewald
Christ on the Cross (central panel of the Isenheim Altarpiece), 1512–16
Oil on panel, 269 × 307 cm

80 Matthias Grünewald
The Resurrection of Christ (right wing of the Isenheim Altarpiece, first opening), 1512–16
Oil on panel, 265 × 141 cm

81 Albrecht Dürer
Self-portrait, 1500
Oil on panel, 67 × 49 cm

82 Albrecht Dürer
The Four Apostles, 1526
Oil on panel, 215 × 76 cm each panel

83 Hans Holbein the Younger
Madonna of the Burgomaster of Basle, Jakob Meyer zum Hasen, 1526–8
Oil on panel, 147 × 102 cm

84 Lucas Cranach the Elder
The Nymph of the Spring, c. 1537
Oil on panel, 48.5 × 74 cm

85 Albrecht Altdorfer
Victory of Alexander the Great over Darius, King of the Persians, at the Battle of Issus, 1529
Oil on panel, 158 × 120 cm

86 Hieronymus Bosch
The Garden of Earthly Delights (central panel), 1503–4
Oil on panel, 220 × 195 cm

87 Pieter Bruegel the Elder
Hunters in the Snow, 1565
Tempera on panel, 117 × 162 cm

88 Pieter Bruegel the Elder
The Peasants' Dance, c. 1568
Oil on panel, 114 × 164 cm

89 Giuseppe Arcimboldo
The Fire, 1566
Oil on panel, 66.5 × 51 cm

90 Bartholomeus Spranger
Hercules and Omphale, 1575–80
Oil on copper, 24 × 19 cm

91 El Greco
The Burial of Count Orgaz, 1586
Oil on canvas, 487 × 360 cm

92 Caravaggio
Victorious Amor, 1596–8
Oil on canvas, 154 × 110 cm

93 Caravaggio
The Calling of St. Matthew,
1599–1600
Oil on canvas, 328 × 348 cm

94 Annibale Carracci
Triumph of Bacchus and Ariadne,
1597–1604
Ceiling fresco

95 Domenichino
The Last Communion of St. Jerome, 1614
Oil on canvas, 419 × 256 cm

96 Nicolas Poussin
The Martyrdom of St. Erasmus, 1628
Oil on canvas, 320 × 186 cm

97 Nicolas Poussin
Autumn, 1660–4
Oil on canvas, 118 × 160 cm

98 Claude Lorraine
Ulysses restores Chryseis to her Father,
1644
Oil on canvas, 119 × 150 cm

99 Pietro da Cortona
Allegory of Peace (detail), 1633–9
Ceiling fresco

100 Giovanni Battista Gaulli
The Worship of the Name of Jesus
(detail), 1676–9
Ceiling fresco

101 Andrea Pozzo
Triumph of St. Ignatius (detail),
1691–4
Ceiling fresco

102 Guercino
The Incredulity of St. Thomas, c. 1621
Oil on canvas, 115.5 × 142.5 cm

103 Bartolomeo Schedoni
The Three Marys at the Tomb, 1614
Oil on canvas, 200 × 281 cm

104 Jusepe de Ribera
Boy with a club-foot, 1652
Oil on canvas, 164 × 92 cm

105 Luca Giordano
The fall of the rebel Angels, 1666
Oil on canvas, 419 × 282 cm

106 Simon Vouet
Psyche looking at the Sleeping Amor, 1626
Oil on canvas, 112 × 165 cm

107 Georges de La Tour
The Card Players, 1619–20
Oil on canvas, 106 × 146 cm

108 Philippe de Champaigne
Ex Voto, 1662
Oil on canvas, 165 × 229 cm

109 Charles Le Brun
Chancellor Séguier, c. 1660
Oil on canvas, 295 × 357 cm

110 Peter Paul Rubens
The Descent from the Cross (triptych),
1612–14
Oil on panel, central panel
420 × 310 cm; wings 420 × 149.5 cm
each

111 Peter Paul Rubens
Madonna with Saints, 1638–40
Oil on panel, 211 × 195 cm

112 Peter Paul Rubens
*Double portrait (Rubens and Isabella
Brandt in the Honeysuckle Bower)*,
c. 1609
Oil on canvas (mounted on wood),
178 × 136 cm

113 Peter Paul Rubens
Het pelske (portrait of Hélène
Fourment), *c.* 1638
Oil on panel, 176 × 83 cm

114 Peter Paul Rubens
The Rainbow, c. 1636
Oil on panel, 92 × 122 cm

115 Anthony van Dyck
Portrait of Charles I, King of England,
1635–8
Oil on canvas, 272 × 212 cm

116 Diego Velázquez
Las Meninas (The Ladies-in-Waiting),
1656
Oil on canvas, 318 × 276 cm

117 Diego Velázquez,
'*The Topers*', 1628–9
Oil on canvas, 165 × 225 cm

118 Diego Velázquez
*The Rokeby Venus (The Toilet of
Venus)*, 1649–50
Oil on canvas, 122.5 × 177 cm

119 Diego Velázquez
The Spinners (Arachne and Minerva)
c. 1659
Oil on canvas, 220 × 289 cm

120 Francisco de Zurbarán
The Holy House of Nazareth, c. 1630
Oil on canvas, 165 × 230 cm

121 Bartolomé Esteban Murillo
Madonna and Child, 1650–60
Oil on canvas, 155 × 105 cm

122 Hendrick Terbrugghen
*St. Sebastian tended by St. Irene and the
Maid*, 1625
Oil on canvas, 150 × 121 cm

123 Frans Hals
*Banquet of the Officers of the Guild of St.
George*, 1616
Oil on canvas, 175 × 324 cm

124 Frans Hals
*The Women Governors of the Haarlem
Almshouse for the Aged*, 1664
Oil on canvas, 170.5 × 249.5 cm

125 Pieter Pietersz. Lastman
Ulysses and Nausicaa, 1619
Oil on panel, 92 × 117.3 cm

126 Rembrandt van Rijn
Danae, 1636
Oil on canvas, 186 × 201 cm

127 Rembrandt van Rijn
*The Company of Captain Frans Banning
Cocq and Lieutenant Willem van
Ruytenburg*, known as *The Nightwatch*,
1642
Oil on canvas, 363 × 437 cm

128 Rembrandt van Rijn
*The Conspiracy of Julius Civilis: The
Oath*, 1661
Oil on canvas, 196 × 309 cm

129 Rembrandt van Rijn
Self-portrait as the Apostle Paul, 1661
Oil on canvas, 91 × 77 cm

130 Carel Fabritius
The Goldfinch, 1654
Oil on panel, 33.6 × 22.5 cm

131 Johannes Vermeer
Woman Reading, 1662–3
Oil on canvas, 46.5 × 39 cm

132 Johannes Vermeer
View of Delft, 1658–61
Oil on canvas, 98.5 × 117.5 cm

133 Adriaen Brouwer
Tavern Interior, 1624–5
Oil on panel, 34.8 × 26 cm

134 Jan Steen
Sarah and Tobias, 1667
Oil on canvas, 131 × 172 cm

135 Jacob Isaaksz. van Ruisdael
The Jewish Cemetery, c. 1660
Oil on canvas, 135 × 172.5 cm

136 Giovanni Battista Piazzetta
Rebecca at the Well, c. 1740
Oil on canvas, 102 × 137 cm

137 Sebastiano Ricci
Esther before Ashasverus, 1733–4
Oil on canvas, 47 × 33 cm

138 Giovanni Battista Tiepolo
Phaeton, 1731
Oil on canvas, 95 × 70 cm

139 Giovanni Battista Tiepolo
Anthony meeting Cleopatra (detail),
1745–50
Fresco

140 Giovanni Battista Tiepolo
*Apollo conducting Beatrice of Burgundy to
Barbarossa* (sketch for a ceiling fresco
Kaisersaal Residence, Würzburg),
1750–1
Oil on canvas, 65.3 × 106.5 cm

141 Giovanni Battista Tiepolo
*America, from Olympus with the Quarters
of the Earth* (detail), 1752–3
Ceiling fresco

142 Giovanni Domenico Tiepolo
Pulcinella and the Rope Dancer (detail),
1791–3
Fresco

143 Pietro Longhi
The Rhinoceros, 1751
Oil on canvas, 62 × 50 cm

144 Canaletto
*The Stonemason's Yard with S. Maria
della Carità in Venice, c.* 1730
Oil on canvas, 124 × 163 cm

145 Francesco Guardi
Ascension Day on the Piazza S. Marco,
1775–6
Oil on canvas, 61 × 91 cm

146 Antoine Watteau
The Embarkation for Cythera, 1718
Oil on canvas, 128 × 193 cm

147 Antoine Watteau
Gilles, c. 1718
Oil on canvas, 184 × 149 cm

148 François Boucher
L'Odalisque, 1744–5
Oil on canvas, 51 × 64 cm

149 Jean Baptiste Siméon Chardin
The Kitchenmaid
Oil on canvas, 46 × 37.5 cm

150 Jean-Honoré Fragonard
The Swing, 1767
Oil on canvas, 81 × 65 cm

151 Jean Baptiste Greuze
The Son Punished, 1777
Oil on canvas, 130 × 162 cm

152 Jacques-Louis David
The Oath of the Horatii, 1784
Oil on canvas, 330 × 427 cm

153 Jacques-Louis David
The Death of Marat, 1793
Oil on canvas, 165 × 128 cm

154 Jacques-Louis David
*The Consecration of the Emperor
Napoleon I and the Coronation of the
Empress Josephine*, 1806–7
Oil on canvas, 621 × 979 cm

155 Antoine-Jean Gros
The Battlefield of Eylau, 1808
Oil on canvas, 533 × 800 cm

156 Anne-Louis Girodet-Trioson
*Ossian receiving the Generals of the
Republic*, 1801
Oil on canvas, 192 × 182 cm

157 Pierre-Paul Prud'hon
The Rape of Psyche, 1808
Oil on canvas, 195 × 157 cm

158 Jean Auguste Dominique Ingres
Bather of Valpinçon, 1808
Oil on canvas, 146 × 97.5 cm

159 Jean Auguste Dominique Ingres
Mademoiselle Caroline Rivière, 1805
Oil on canvas, 100 × 70 cm

160 Théodore Géricault
The Raft of the Meduse, 1818–19
Oil on canvas, 419 × 761 cm

161 Théodore Géricault
Lovers, 1815–16
Oil on canvas, 24 × 32.5 cm

162 Eugène Delacroix
The Death of Sardanapalus, 1827
Oil on canvas, 395 × 495 cm

163 Eugène Delacroix
Liberty leading the People, 1830
Oil on canvas, 260 × 235 cm

**164 Francisco José de Goya
y Lucientes**
The Third of May 1808, 1814
Oil on canvas, 266 × 345 cm

**165 Francisco José de Goya
y Lucientes**

The Colossus, 1810–12
Oil on canvas, 116 × 105 cm

166 William Hogarth
*Mariage à la Mode: shortly after the
Marriage*, 1742–6
Oil on canvas, 70 × 91 cm

167 Sir Joshua Reynolds
Nelly O'Brien, 1760–2
Oil on canvas, 126.5 × 100 cm

168 Thomas Gainsborough
*William Hallett and his Wife Elizabeth
Stephen* (or *The Morning Walk*), 1785
Oil on canvas, 236 × 178 cm

169 Johann Heinrich Fuseli
Titania caressing the Head of Bottom,
1793–4
Oil on canvas, 169 × 135 cm

170 Johann Heinrich Fuseli
The Nightmare, 1781
Oil on canvas, 101 × 127 cm

171 William Blake
Newton, 1795
Colour print, finished in watercolour,
46 × 60 cm

172 Joseph Mallord William Turner
*Rain, Steam and Speed: the Great Western
Railway, c.* 1844
Oil on canvas, 91.5 × 122 cm

173 John Constable
Study for The Leaping Horse, 1825
Oil on canvas, 136 × 180 cm

174 Philipp Otto Runge
The Hülsenbeck Children, 1805–6
Oil on canvas, 131 × 141 cm

175 Caspar David Friedrich
Man and Woman gazing at the Moon,
1824
Oil on canvas, 34 × 44 cm

176 Caspar David Friedrich
Moon rising over the Sea, 1822
Oil on canvas, 55 × 71 cm

177 Franz Pforr
*Entry of the Emperor Rudolf of Habsburg
into Basle in the Year 1273*, 1808–10
Oil on canvas, 90.5 × 119 cm

178 Johann Friedrich Overbeck
*The Triumph of Religion in the Arts,
c.* 1831–40
Oil on canvas, 392 × 392 cm

179 Julius Schnorr von Carolsfeld
The Fall from the Rocks, 1833
Oil on panel, 74 × 44 cm

180 Gustave Courbet
A Burial at Ornans, 1849–50
Oil on canvas, 315 × 668 cm

181 Sir John Everett Millais
Ophelia, 1851–2
Oil on canvas, 76 × 112 cm

182 Gustave Courbet
The Studio of the Painter, 1855
Oil on canvas, 361 × 598 cm

183 Théodore Rousseau
Willow Trees, 1856
Oil on canvas, 24 × 32 cm

184 Jean François Millet
The Gleaners, 1857
Oil on canvas, 83.5 × 111 cm

185 Edouard Manet
Olympia, 1863
Oil on canvas, 130.5 × 190 cm

186 Edgar Degas
Two Laundresses, 1884
Oil on canvas, 76 × 81.5 cm

187 Frédéric Bazille
The Toilet, 1870
Oil on canvas, 132 × 127 cm

188 Camille Pissarro
Landscape near Pontoise, 1874
Oil on canvas, 65 × 51 cm

189 Alfred Sisley
The Flood at Port-Marly, 1876
Oil on canvas, 50 × 61 cm

190 Claude Monet
Impression: Sunrise, 1872
Oil on canvas, 48 × 63 cm

191 Claude Monet
Women in the Garden, 1867
Oil on canvas, 255 × 205 cm

192 Pierre Auguste Renoir
La Baigneuse au Griffon, 1870
Oil on canvas, 184 × 115 cm

193 Philip Wilson Steer
Boulogne Sands, 1892
Oil on canvas, 60 × 76.5 cm

194 George Hendrik Breitner
Bridge over the Singel at the Paleisstraat in Amsterdam, 1893–8
Oil on canvas, 100 × 152 cm

195 Max Liebermann
The Man with Parrots, 1902
Oil on canvas, 109.5 × 72 cm

196 Pierre Bonnard
Nude in Lamplight, c. 1912
Oil on canvas, 75 × 75 cm

197 Edouard Vuillard
The Public Garden, 1894
Watercolour on canvas, three panels:
h. 213 cm, w. 73 cm, 153 cm, 81 cm

198 Pierre Puvis de Chavannes
Hope, c. 1871
Oil on canvas, 70 × 82 cm

199 Gustave Moreau
Galatea, 1880–1
Oil on panel, 85 × 67 cm

200 Odilon Redon
The Cyclops, 1898–1900
Oil on panel, 64 × 51 cm

201 Dante Gabriel Rossetti
La Ghirlandata, 1873
Oil on canvas, 115 × 87 cm

202 Edward Burne-Jones
Atlas turned to Stone, 1876–88
Tempera on canvas, 152.5 × 190 cm

203 Arnold Böcklin
The Island of the Dead, 1880
Tempera on canvas, 111 × 155 cm

204 Georges Seurat
A Sunday Afternoon on the Île de La Grand Jatte, 1884–6
Oil on canvas, 206 × 306 cm

205 Paul Signac
Sailing-boats in the Harbour of St-Tropez, 1893
Oil on canvas, 56 × 46.5 cm

206 Paul Signac
Against the Enamel of a background with Beasts and Angels, Tones and Colours, portrait of Félix Fénéon, 1890
Oil on canvas, 74 × 95 cm

207 Giovanni Segantini
Amor at the Fountain of Life, 1896
Oil on canvas, 75 × 100 cm

208 Vincent van Gogh
Self-portrait, 1890
Oil on canvas, 65 × 54.5 cm

209 Vincent van Gogh
Sunrise at Saint-Rémy, 1889
Oil on canvas, 71 × 80.5 cm

210 Paul Gauguin
Vision after the Sermon, 1888
Oil on canvas, 73 × 92 cm

211 Paul Gauguin
Loss of Virginity, 1890–1
Oil on canvas, 90 × 130 cm

212 Paul Sérusier
Melancholy, c. 1890
Oil on canvas, 73 × 60 cm

213 Fernand Khnopff
The Sphinx, 1896
Oil on canvas, 50.5 × 150 cm

214 Jan Toorop
The Three Brides, 1893
Pencil, black and coloured crayon on brown paper, 78 × 98 cm

215 James Sidney Ensor
The Entry of Christ into Brussels, 1888
Oil on canvas, 258 × 431 cm

216 Edvard Munch
Puberty, 1893
Oil on canvas, 150 × 110 cm

217 Paul Cézanne
The Card Players, 1885–90
Oil on canvas, 47.5 × 57 cm

218 Paul Cézanne
Montagne Sainte-Victoire, 1904–6
Oil on canvas, 60 × 72 cm

219 Henri Matisse
Harmony in Red, 1908
Oil on canvas, 180 × 220 cm

220 Pablo Picasso
Les Demoiselles d'Avignon, 1907
Oil on canvas, 244 × 233 cm

221 Pablo Picasso
Still Life with Wicker Chair, 1912
Oil and oilcloth on canvas, 27 × 35 cm

222 Georges Braque
Woman in an Armchair, 1911
Oil on canvas, 130 × 81 cm

223 Umberto Boccioni
Forces of a Street, 1911
Oil on canvas, 100 × 100.5 cm

224 Piet Mondrian
Broadway Boogie-Woogie, 1942–3
Oil on canvas, 127 × 127 cm

225 Wassily Kandinsky
Painting with Houses, 1909
Oil on canvas, 98 × 133 cm

226 Ernst Ludwig Kirchner
Nude, 1908–9
Oil on cardboard, 68 × 72 cm

227 Marcel Duchamp
L.H.O.O.Q. (or: *Mona Lisa with Moustache*), 1919
Reproduction with pencil additions
18.5 × 12.5 cm

228 René Magritte
The Human Condition I, 1933
Oil on canvas, 100 × 81 cm

229 Max Ernst
Les hommes n'en sauront rien (Men will know nothing of this), 1923
Oil on canvas, 80.5 × 64 cm

230 Peter Blake, 1932–
Bo Diddley, 1963
Acrylic on hardboard, 78.5 × 124 cm

231 David Hockney, 1937–
Two Boys in a Pool, 1965
Acrylic on canvas, 60 × 60 cm

Index of Painters